# Entertaining
# THE COSTCO WAY™

*Jean-Yves Mocquet's*
*Gewürztraminer Parfait*
*Page 94*

# *Entertaining*
# THE COSTCO WAY™

## A cookbook and practical guide
## to the art of entertaining

*Pat Volchok*
*Editorial Director*

*With a foreword by*
*Tom Douglas*

*Issaquah, Washington*

| | |
|---|---|
| *Publisher:* | Dave Fuller |
| *Editorial Director:* | Pat Volchok |
| *Art Director:* | Doris Winters |
| *Copy Editors:* | Judy Gouldthorpe |
| | Shana McNally |
| *Graphic Designers:* | Bill Carlson |
| | Brenda Tradii |
| *Business Manager:* | Jane Klein-Shucklin |
| *Advertising Manager:* | Steve Trump |
| *Production Manager:* | Pam Sather |
| *Food Stylists:* | Amy Muzyka-McGuire |
| | June Schuck |
| *Production Assistants:* | Brenda Link |
| | Antolin Matsuda |
| | Chris Rusnak |
| *Color Technician:* | MaryAnne Robbers |
| *Indexer:* | Nan Badgett |

FIRST EDITION

Photography by Iridio Photography, Seattle
Color by PressReady Imaging, Seattle
Printed and bound in China by Dai Nippon


ISBN 0-9722164-1-3
Library of Congress Control Number: 2002111067
5  4  3  2  1

# Contents

# To Our Valued Members:

We are delighted to present our very first cookbook, *Entertaining the Costco Way*. A collection of recipes and creative ideas from celebrity chefs, Costco members, employees and suppliers, the book is geared to year-round party-giving and entertaining with all the products you will find at Costco.

As you might expect, *Entertaining the Costco Way* has a heavy emphasis on quality and value—whether it is in what you buy or what you serve. Just as in our warehouses, you'll find all the basics here—meat, potatoes and some great salmon. And there's always an unexpected treasure to be discovered on the next page—like the recipe for sweet potato jalapeño soup with lime cream from one of our Arizona members.

In fact, a number of our members contributed to the cookbook, sharing some of their favorite recipes. These include clever ideas for using Costco stand-bys to create fast, easy, delicious meals. The chicken flautas on page 221, for example, use our famous rotisserie chicken, and the salmon fillets on page 203 are coated with pesto sauce from our deli section.

Our suppliers, of course, played a big role in making this book a reality. These are the same vendors who work so closely with our Costco buyers to constantly improve the quality and value of the food products we sell, and they have come up with some intriguing new ways to prepare their own specialties.

*Entertaining the Costco Way* is more than a cookbook. You'll find tips and ideas that will turn every meal into a special occasion, from making piñatas to picking the right wines for the season.

We are proud of the reputation Costco has earned as an innovator in food retailing, and we hope you will enjoy these gourmet suggestions throughout the year. Whether you're preparing a simple family dinner or getting ready for a grand affair, you can make it great the Costco way!

*Bon appétit!*

Jim Sinegal

President & C.E.O.
Costco Wholesale Corporation

# Foreword

Entertaining is not only my business but also my hobby. Even though we serve 10,000 people a week at our restaurants, I still enjoy dreaming up the perfect meal for friends and family at home. I came by this attitude early. Every meal at my folks' house was a party. That is, if you consider cooking for a minimum of 10, three times a day, a party. When relatives, neighbors and "special friends" were added in, the family table was often extended to accommodate 20. (You can see that my folks are naturals for big-volume shopping the Costco warehouse way.)

My mom and grandmas are all good cooks. Despite my own reputation as a "fancy" restaurant chef, my heart has always belonged to home cooking. While working on my cookbook, *Tom Douglas' Seattle Kitchen*, I often called up my mom to ask her to dig out recipes from her food-stained, yellowing card file.

A family favorite was her famous blue crab dip. Crab of any sort was a "special occasion" treat in our house. The "taste memory" of sweet blue crab meat, chopped hard-boiled eggs and her Thousand Island dressing, zesty with cherry peppers, makes me want to call up my clan and invite them over for a family feast. That's why I love a book like *Entertaining the Costco Way*, where Costco's food suppliers and people's moms, dads, nieces, nephews, cousins and best friends share their favorite recipes—the recipes people really treasure and cook for themselves at home. The fact that each of these recipes includes an item or two you can find at Costco is an added treat.

The truth is, when my wife, Jackie, and I stroll through Costco, each with our own shopping cart, we rarely have a meal plan for that night's dinner. Instead we roam the aisles looking for whatever's in season, like spring strawberries, summer peppers or fresh-crop fall apples. Typical Costco commodities like Penn Cove mussels, Angus beef and big bags of ruby-red grapefruit are always tempting. Finally, there are the "can't pass it up" super bargains like fat tiger prawns or beautifully trimmed racks of lamb.

Then, out of the blue, real inspiration strikes—enormous packages of baby back ribs calling out to me. They say, "Why don't you grab a couple bottles of wine, call some friends, fire up the grill and have a party?" Of course I oblige this moment of fate, this tryst with an inanimate object, and fill out my basket with fragrant tomatoes, sweet corn and plump cabbages for slaw. With *Entertaining the Costco Way*, you'll find yourself dreaming, plotting and filling up your basket for your own feast with friends and family.

*Tom Douglas*

Seattle restaurateur and author

# *About This Book*

Over the years, many members and friends of Costco have suggested that we publish a cookbook featuring some of the fabulous products we sell in our warehouses. We've agreed with them that it was a good idea, but our focus on Job One—finding, selecting and offering the best products at the best possible prices—has always taken precedence over getting into the publishing business. During the past year, however, we realized we could combine Job One and our desire to produce a cookbook for our members. How? By asking our vendors to join us in bringing this book to you through their contribution of recipes and funding.

We asked each of our vendors to provide a recipe or two, along with some entertainment tips, that would show off their product(s) to the greatest advantage—not just something from one of their box tops, but something new, exciting or unusually tasty. Their response was enthusiastic, and we hope you will agree with us that the recipes presented here fit that bill. Please note that each recipe contributed by a vendor has been identified with that vendor's corporate name or product branding. In some cases, the branded product may not be sold in your part of the country and you should substitute a similar product.

In addition to asking our vendors for recipes, we used our magazine, *The Costco Connection*, to ask our members for their favorite recipes using Costco products. We received more than 1,800 recipes in a few weeks' time. These were sorted into food categories and then 160 were selected for testing by a panel of Costco members who had the enviable but demanding task of narrowing the selections to the 48 recipes that received the "Tested and Approved" stamp you will find throughout the book.

Finally, we asked a few celebrity chefs to add some further spice to the brew. Once we had all of the recipes in hand, we spent weeks in the photo studio cooking and photographing these culinary delights. We hope you will find the resulting book informative, useful and fun.

THE EDITORS

### NOTE ON BRANDS

Many of the recipes published in this book were submitted by companies that hold copyrights to the recipes and/or trademark applications/registrations on the brands listed in the recipes. Each of the companies represented in this book asserts its ownership to the trademarks, application/registrations and copyrights it holds on its company name, brands or recipes. Trademark, application/registration and copyright symbols have been eliminated from the titles and text of the recipes by the publisher for design purposes only.

# Autumn Harvest

# THE GATHERING SEASON

# Autumn Reflections

There's no need to debate the fact that autumn is a glorious time of year. It's a time when the world seems to slow down and speed up simultaneously. Leaves carpet the ground in shades of burnished orange and gold, apples decorate bare limbs in vivid orbs of red and green, pumpkins puff out to their finest, market stalls groan with the weight of harvested fare, spiders cover the world in lace, and candles flicker in the windows once more.

As we welcome the season, there's an urge to gather, whether it's at football games, pumpkin patches or the family dinner table.

Our Autumn Harvest menus reflect this desire to come together and celebrate the goodness and bounty of life. Meals in this section include a Harvest Dinner cornucopia, a Family Night filled with comfort food, and two surprisingly easy party creations, the Drop-In Open House and Tailgate Party. We end with the theatrics of Halloween and the fellowship of Thanksgiving.

## Layered Table Elegance

Not many of us have the time, wherewithal or patience to constantly change decorations to fit the moment's mood. We suggest that instead of ignoring decorating altogether, you start with objects that echo the fall season and slowly build on them, so that by the time the holidays arrive, your table and home reverberate with the lavishness of the holiday season.

First step, consider autumn's local bounty, such as pinecones, nuts, gourds, vegetables, branches, corn stalks, wheat sheaves, pumpkins, vines, fallen leaves, pods, cattails and green boughs. Target those items that will have the longest indoor survival rate, can easily be restocked or have the potential to be enhanced later on with gilding, ribbons or fresh flowers.

Next, look at the items in your home with new eyes. The basket that stores guest towels may be a perfect container for pinecones, the footed vase a wonderful stand for a pumpkin, or how about a row of candleholders in the center of the table holding decorative corn instead of candles?

For the most impact, decorate the dining room table first, and then as time allows, move on to the front door, living room and beyond.

## Floral Arrangements

Of course, fresh flowers always provide pleasure. And the best way we know to bring bug-free flowers into the home and keep cost to a minimum is to scope out the seasonal offerings in Costco's cut-flower kiosks.

If time is really short, purchase massive bouquets of roses or Costco's grower's bunches that echo the colors of the changing leaves, and place them in vases scattered around the house, especially in the guest bedroom and bath. ∾

## Costco's Autumn Harvest

No one can deny the popularity of seasonal cooking. Products that have been newly harvested are not only a treat to eat but also a pleasure to cook with. Who wouldn't be thrilled with the deep-orange flesh of a newly harvested yam or the crunch and juiciness of a just-picked apple?

So it is that Costco's buyers search the world's markets seeking the finest in seasonal offerings. Here is a sampling of Costco's autumnal bounty:

New Crop Washington Apples
Large Baking Potatoes
Bananas
Grapefruit

Pomegranates
Medjool Dates
Mini Pumpkins
Indian Corn
Ornamental Gourds
Mixed Nuts
Persimmons
Halibut
Rib Roast
Tom Turkey
Kirkland Signature Spiral Ham
Fall Fruit and Pecan Pies
Pumpkin Pie and
    Pumpkin Cheesecake
Loaf Breads such as
    Pumpkin, Apple Crumb
    and Praline Pecan
Fruit and Cheese Danish
    Pastries
Dried-Fruit Trays
Panettone

# Savoring the Season with David

**David Andrew**
**Costco Global Wine Director**

## Season of Mists and Mellow Fruitfulness

Mellow fruitfulness? Keats must have been thinking of Burgundy (Pinot Noir), or perhaps Rioja, or even Chianti Classico. The combination of ripe, mellow fruit and the earthy aromas of autumn makes these gentle reds the perfect choice for the season.

Burgundy, France, is the home of Pinot Noir, and when it's good there, it's unforgettable. Gentle and refined, the wines can reach unbelievable levels of complexity. Pinots from Australia, New Zealand and the USA are usually bigger, brighter and fruitier, but perhaps not as seductive: Bardot to Burgundy's Deneuve.

Spain's ruby-hued beauties from Rioja and Navarra have a similarly mellow disposition. Tempranillo, the great grape of Spain, is perhaps one of the most underrated of all the reds. These beautiful wines show real nobility.

The October sun setting over the Tuscan hills … aah, Chianti. The top wines come from Chianti Classico, and in this region it's worth spending a few dollars more for the real thing.

Malbec from Argentina straddles the seasons. It has a delicate perfume, supple body and just a touch of feisty spice.

Alsace whites are a good choice in the fall, as they tend to have a subtle underpinning of earth and mushroom beneath their pure, clear fruit flavors. Riesling from this northeastern corner of France is perhaps the perfect food wine. Gewürztraminer, which smells of rose petals and lychees, is a great turkey wine and the classic accompaniment to spicier Asian dishes. Pinot Blanc marries well with practically anything, and for something a little different, try a Tokay (Pinot Gris).

A personal favorite of mine is one of the great Chenin Blancs from the Loire: Savennières. This is one of the longest-lived whites in the world. Its high acidity preserves it as it develops over the years toward rich, nutty, honeyed, hedonistic maturity.

Sherry: Often overlooked and misunderstood, this is truly one of the wine world's gems. From the bone-dry Finos through nutty and complex Amontillados to the rich, concentrated and sometimes sweet Olorosos, these wines have something for everyone.

# Harvest Dinner

*It's* time to polish the good silverware, set the table for casual abundance, and gather family and friends to welcome the season's guest of honor: nature's abundant harvest.

Whether outdoor entertaining is still an option or the dining room table must be dusted off, you can capture the harvest mood by setting the table in a mix of classic formality and relaxed elegance. Use cloth napkins and tablecloth, fine crystal, lustrous silverware, glass canning jars filled with flowers, and golden fall leaves coupled with just-harvested shiny red delicious apples scattered near each place setting.

## MENU

## Tree Top Quick Hot Spiced Cider

As nights turn chilly, warm cider and just-out-of-the-oven sweet bread create a wonderful welcome for your guests.

64 ounces (8 cups) Tree Top Apple Cider or Juice*

2 tablespoons brown sugar

1 teaspoon whole allspice

1 teaspoon whole cloves

8 cinnamon sticks (optional)

**1.** Combine first 4 ingredients in a large pot. Bring to a boil. Let simmer 15 minutes.

**2.** Strain and serve. Add cinnamon stick to each mug before serving. Makes 8 servings.

*Brands may vary by region; substitute a similar product.*

## Dean Specialty Foods Fried Dill Pickles

The Dean pickle family, including Farman's, Nalley's and Peter Piper, adds a zing to any occasion.

8-10 Dean large dill pickles, sliced in 1/4-inch-thick rounds*

1 box tempura batter mix

2 tablespoons Dijon mustard

2 eggs, beaten with a fork

2 tablespoons milk

1 box panko bread crumbs

Vegetable oil

Dry pickle slices with paper towel. Dip slices in tempura batter mixed with mustard and then into a mixture of eggs and milk. Generously toss to coat with panko breading. Heat 4 inches vegetable oil in pot over medium-high heat. Gently place 5-10 battered pickles in hot oil. Fry in batches 1-2 minutes, or until golden. Drain on paper towel. Serve warm with mustard. Makes 12 servings.

*Brands may vary by region; substitute a similar product.*
*Developed by Linda Carey and Pat Volchok.*

## Tree Top Mom's Apple Sauce Bread

This recipe has been in the Tree Top family for at least three generations.

2/3 cup shortening

2 cups sugar

3 cups Tree Top Original Apple Sauce*

4 cups flour

2 teaspoons baking soda

1 teaspoon salt

1 teaspoon cinnamon

1/2 teaspoon ground cloves

1/2 teaspoon ground allspice

1 cup raisins or cut-up prunes

1 cup chopped nuts, if desired

1 cup candied fruit, if desired

**1.** Preheat oven to 350°F.

**2.** Cream shortening and sugar together. Add apple sauce.

**3.** Combine all dry ingredients in a separate bowl and then add to the apple-sauce mixture. Mix until moistened.

**4.** Stir in fruit and nuts.

**5.** Put in 2 well-greased 9-by-5-inch bread pans, filling 2/3 full. Bake 1 hour and 20 minutes, or until a toothpick inserted in the center comes out clean. Makes 2 loaves.

*Brands may vary by region; substitute a similar product.*

## Fletchers Devils on Horseback

The name alone is enough to give any party a little jump start.

Wrap 1/2 strip of Fletchers (raw) bacon* around a bay scallop (raw). Secure with a toothpick. Broil on both sides until bacon is cooked thoroughly, using metal tongs to turn "devils" over. The scallop will be lightly browned. Serve with dipping sauce.

FLETCHERS BIT O' BACON AND HONEY DIPPING SAUCE:

Mix 4 parts honey mustard with 1 part mayonnaise and 2 parts cooked, diced Fletchers bacon.

*Brands may vary by region; substitute a similar product.*

## Lori Vaughters' Log Cabin Corn Bread

Friends have been trying to get this Melbourne, Florida, member to market her recipe for almost 20 years! Instead, she is sharing it with us.

1 cup butter, softened

1 cup sugar

4 eggs

1 14.5-ounce can creamed corn

1 cup flour

1 cup cornmeal

4 teaspoons baking powder

1/2 cup grated Monterey Jack cheese

1/2 cup grated Cheddar cheese

**1.** Preheat oven to 350°F.

**2.** Cream butter and sugar. Add eggs and corn.

**3.** Combine flour, cornmeal and baking powder. Add dry mixture to butter mix. Lightly stir. Fold in cheeses.

**4.** Pour batter into a greased and floured 9-by-13-inch pan.

**5.** Place pan in oven, lower temperature to 300°F and bake 1 hour, or until a toothpick inserted in the center comes out clean. Serve warm with butter and honey or plain. Makes 12 servings.

*Costco Member*
*Lori Vaughters*

## L & M Curried Apple Soup

This velvety soup has no cream, and the small amount of curry enhances the sweet apple flavor. Garnish with sautéed apples and snipped chives.

4 tablespoons unsalted butter

6 L & M Gala apples (about 2 1/2 pounds), peeled, cored and diced

1 large onion, diced

3-4 fresh thyme sprigs

1 teaspoon curry powder

6 cups chicken stock (or low-salt canned)

Salt

Freshly ground black pepper

**1.** In a large saucepan, melt butter over medium heat. Add apples, onion and thyme. Cook, stirring frequently, until soft and golden brown, about 15 minutes. Stir in curry powder and cook until fragrant, about 30 seconds.

**2.** Add stock and bring to a boil. Reduce heat to low and simmer until apples are very soft, about 25 minutes. Remove from heat and cool slightly.

**3.** Puree soup in a blender. Add salt and pepper to taste. Serve hot or at room temperature. Makes 8 servings.

### Floral Arrangements

Sometimes, simple arrangements have the most impact. Fill a large vase with whole fruits such as small apples, lemons or cranberries. Add water and then flowers for a spectacular presentation that's perfect for a buffet or sideboard and just as pretty below the water as above.

## Tanimura & Antle Pear and Feta Salad with Port Vinaigrette Dressing

Who better than the largest independent lettuce grower/ distributor in the United States to share a favorite salad recipe?

*2 cups extra-virgin olive oil*

*3 shallots, minced*

*1 cup port wine*

*1/4 cup balsamic vinegar*

*2 tablespoons honey*

*2 tablespoons fresh lemon juice*

*4 whole SaladTime Hearts of Romaine, chopped**

*1/2 cup crumbled feta cheese*

*2 ripe pears, cored and sliced*

*Red onion, sliced, to taste*

*1/2 cup chopped pecans*

*Salt and pepper*

**1.** Pour oil over minced shallots in a sauté pan and cook over medium heat until oil begins to sizzle. Reduce heat and simmer 2 minutes. Remove from heat.

**2.** Whisk together port, vinegar, honey and lemon juice. Whisk in the hot oil and shallots.

**3.** Toss romaine, feta, pears, onion and pecans with just enough dressing to coat the salad. Season to taste with salt and pepper. Serve immediately.

**4.** The dressing yields 3 cups. Keep the remaining dressing for your next salad. Makes 8-12 servings.

*\*Brands may vary by region; substitute a similar product.*

## Eat Smart Broccoli Parmesan Soufflé

Broccoli, originally a food of the Roman Empire, is an excellent source of vitamin C and folacin (folic acid).

*2/3 cup grated Parmesan cheese*

*3 cups Eat Smart broccoli florets**

*1 1/2 cups milk*

*6 tablespoons butter*

*1 cup minced scallions*

*1 clove garlic, minced*

*2 tablespoons minced fresh parsley*

*5 tablespoons flour*

*6 egg yolks*

*1/2 teaspoon salt*

*7 egg whites*

*1/4 teaspoon cream of tartar*

**1.** Preheat oven to 450°F. Butter 8 1-cup soufflé cups or an 8-cup soufflé dish and sprinkle with 1/3 cup Parmesan cheese.

**2.** Steam broccoli 3 minutes, or until tender. Drain and run under cold water. Puree in food processor.

**3.** Bring milk to boil in saucepan. Meanwhile, melt butter in skillet. Add scallions and garlic. Sauté 1 minute. Whisk in parsley and flour; stir until bubbling. Add milk and cook 2 minutes, stirring constantly. Remove from heat and stir in egg yolks, one at a time. Add broccoli puree, remaining cheese and salt. Stir well.

**4.** Beat egg whites until foamy. Add cream of tartar and beat until stiff. Add 1/3 of beaten egg whites to broccoli mix and stir until incorporated. Fold in remaining egg whites.

**5.** Pour batter into prepared cups or dish. Place in oven and reduce heat to 375°F. Cook cups 20-25 minutes, or dish 45-50 minutes, or until soufflé has risen and top is golden brown. Makes 8 servings.

*\*Brands may vary by region; substitute a similar product.*

## Tyson/Kirkland Signature
### Harvest Moon Chicken Chesterfield

More than 60 years have passed since John Tyson drove his battered truck to Chicago to deliver a load of 500 Arkansas chickens. He sold the birds for a profit of $235, of which he wired home $220 to pay his debts and buy another load of birds. Out of that trip sprang the foundations of a company that would revolutionize the poultry industry.

1 cup mayonnaise

1/2 cup prepared horseradish

1/2 cup spicy brown mustard

1 tablespoon Worcestershire sauce

1/4 teaspoon cayenne pepper

8 Tyson/Kirkland Signature Boneless, Skinless Chicken Breasts (frozen)*

4 cups shredded white Cheddar cheese

1 cup coarsely chopped crisp-cooked bacon

8 cups frozen green beans, steamed and seasoned

1 teaspoon paprika

**1.** Preheat oven to 375°F.

**2.** Combine mayonnaise, horseradish, mustard, Worcestershire sauce and cayenne in a bowl and mix thoroughly. Cover and chill.

**3.** Lightly spray a foil-lined baking pan with cooking spray.

**4.** Place frozen chicken breast fillets on a baking pan and bake 45-55 minutes. To ensure that the chicken has been properly cooked, insert an instant-read thermometer into the thickest part of the chicken. Internal temperature should read 170°F.

**5.** When chicken is done, place on an ovenproof serving platter in a linear pattern. Top the breast fillets with the horseradish-mustard sauce. Sprinkle with the cheese and then the bacon pieces.

**6.** Broil 1-1½ minutes, or until the cheese is blended with the sauce and lightly browned.

**7.** Serve fillets with sauce and green beans. Sprinkle chicken with paprika. Makes 8 servings.

*Brands may vary by region; substitute a similar product.*

## Canlis Restaurant Pumpkin Risotto

Selected in 2001 by *Gourmet* magazine as one of America's 50 Best Restaurants, Seattle's Canlis continues its 52-year tradition of dining excellence.

*1 tablespoon olive oil*

*1 tablespoon butter*

*1 cup diced onion*

*3-4 cloves garlic, peeled and thinly sliced*

*2 cups diced dense, sweet pumpkin or kabocha squash*

*1 cup short-grain rice*

*1/2 cup white wine*

*3 cups light chicken broth, boiling hot*

*1/2 cup grated Parmigiano-Reggiano cheese*

*1 tablespoon butter, optional*

**1.** In a heavy saucepan over medium-high heat, warm the olive oil and butter. Sauté the onion briefly and add the garlic. Stir in the diced pumpkin and cook until the pumpkin is hot and just beginning to brown. Stir in the rice and cook 1 minute, or until it is translucent.

**2.** Stir in the wine. When it has boiled off, add 1/2 cup of the chicken broth. Stir until the broth is absorbed, then add another 1/2 cup broth. Continue stirring and slowly adding broth for 20 minutes, or until the rice and the pumpkin are tender.

**3.** When the last of the broth has been added, stir in the cheese and, if desired, the extra tablespoon of butter. Serve the risotto hot, followed by a green salad. Makes 4 servings.

**Celebrity CHEF**
**GREG ATKINSON**

Greg Atkinson, Canlis executive chef, is an authoritative voice on Northwest cuisine and author of The Northwest Essentials Cookbook.

## Monterey Mushrooms Grilled Portabellos

*4 Monterey Portabello Mushroom Caps\**

*1 1/4 cups prepared vinaigrette (balsamic or Italian)*

Quickly rinse mushroom caps in cold water and pat dry. Place in vinaigrette, stem side up. Spoon dressing into caps and let stand 5-10 minutes. Grill mushrooms over medium heat, stem side up, 8-10 minutes. Turn and grill another 8-10 minutes, or until cooked through. Slice into individual servings. Makes 8 servings.

*\*Brands may vary by region; substitute a similar product.*

## Nestlé After Eight Truffles

These two desserts are not only brilliant, they are real showstoppers. Need we say more?

*2 (3.5 ounces each) milk or dark chocolate Perugina Bars, finely chopped*

*1 box (8.81 ounces, 30 mints total) Perugina After Eight Chocolate Mints\**

*1/2 cup whipping cream*

*1 1/2 cups finely chopped walnuts or almonds, toasted, or cocoa for coating truffles*

Place chocolate and mints in medium bowl. Heat cream to gentle boil in small saucepan. Pour over chocolate mixture; let stand 1 minute. Stir until smooth. Cover bowl and refrigerate 15-20 minutes, or until slightly thickened. Drop chocolate mixture by rounded teaspoonful onto baking sheet lined with waxed paper. Refrigerate 10-15 minutes. Shape into balls; coat with nuts or cocoa. Store in airtight container in refrigerator. Makes about 36 truffles.

*\*Brands may vary by region; substitute a similar product.*

## Nestlé Baci Soufflés

*12 Perugina Baci Hazelnut Candies\**

*4 (3.5 ounces each) dark or bittersweet chocolate Perugina Bars, broken into pieces*

*1/2 cup butter*

*4 large eggs, separated*

*3/8 cup hazelnut liqueur*

*1/2 cup granulated sugar*

*Confectioners' sugar*

Preheat oven to 400°F. Spray 12 6-ounce ramekins with cooking spray; coat lightly with granulated sugar. Place 1 Baci candy in each ramekin. Melt chocolate and butter, stirring until smooth. Stir in egg yolks and liqueur. Beat egg whites until soft peaks form. Gradually beat in 1/2 cup granulated sugar until stiff peaks form. Fold egg whites into chocolate mixture. Divide batter among prepared ramekins. Place on baking sheet. Bake on center oven rack 13-15 minutes, or until puffed and center still moves slightly. Sprinkle with confectioners' sugar; serve immediately. Makes 12 individual servings.

## Walkers Shortbread Parfait

How fun, not to mention convenient and stunning, to offer this luscious dessert in crystal goblets on a silver platter at the end of the meal.

*16 ounces raspberries*

*16 ounces canned/jarred peach slices, chopped*

*2 teaspoons medium sherry (optional)*

*16 ounces Greek-style plain or vanilla yogurt*

*2 5.3-ounce packets Walkers Shortbread, coarsely crumbled*

Two hours before serving, mix fruit with sherry, reserving a few raspberries for garnish. In 8 crystal goblets, parfait glasses or sundae dishes, arrange the fruit and yogurt (reserving some for topping) in alternate layers with the shortbread crumbs. Chill. Top with remaining yogurt and raspberries. Makes 8 servings.

Family Night

*V*acation is over, school begins, night wrestles with day and calendars start to fill again. What better time than fall to sit the family down and reconnect?

Make it a special occasion. We're not suggesting taking out the heirloom china, but with a few diversions such as our Jelly Belly centerpiece and doggie treats, family night can become a dinner filled with laughter, great food and togetherness.

And now that shoes have replaced flip-flops, this might be the time to present a little refresher course on manners. Then finish on a festive note with ice cream treats.

Who knows, by the end of the meal, you just might receive a very polite thank-you.

**MENU**

## Seeking Comfort

*Life isn't static and neither are comfort foods. For example, a 1989 survey by Prepared Foods reported the top consumer comfort foods to be beef or pork roast (52%), fried chicken (35%) and mashed potatoes (29%). By 2001, Bon Appétit's How America Eats Reader Survey found that favorite comfort foods included pasta (46%), mashed potatoes (41%), ice cream (38%) and pizza (36%). Just one year later (March 2002), this annual reader survey detailed yet another change, with ice cream (35%), cookies (29%) and pasta (28%) leading the pack.*

*What's the bottom line? There's no set rule on comfort foods, other than that they be delicious.*

Costco Employee
Mark Bjorkman

### Earthbound Farm California Salad

*¹/4 cup tarragon or white wine vinegar*
*1 tablespoon Dijon mustard*
*2 teaspoons honey*
*³/4 cup extra-virgin olive oil*
*¹/2 cup canola oil*
*¹/4 teaspoon salt*
*2 teaspoons dried tarragon*
*1 pound Earthbound Farm Organic Mixed Baby Greens\**
*1 cup sliced almonds, toasted*
*4 ounces mild goat cheese, crumbled*
*1 avocado, peeled and sliced*
*30 dried apricots, preferably Turkish, sliced*

**1.** To make the dressing, combine vinegar, mustard, honey, oil, salt and tarragon in a glass jar and shake vigorously.

**2.** Place the greens in a very large salad bowl. Add most of the dressing and toss thoroughly to coat. Add the remainder of the dressing if necessary.

**3.** Transfer the salad to a large platter and scatter the almonds and goat cheese over the greens. Arrange avocado slices around platter. Sprinkle apricots over salad.
Makes 8-12 servings.

*\*Brands may vary by region; substitute a similar product.*

## Mark Bjorkman's Cream Cheese Wontons

Many of our Costco employees are renowned for their cooking prowess. Such is the case with Mark, who was asked to contribute this recipe. He recommends serving this dish as a first course with barbecued pork.

*16 ounces cream cheese, room temperature*
*1 cup sugar*
*2 tablespoons snipped chives, fresh if available*
*4 dozen wonton wrappers*
   *(available in the produce section of your local grocery)*
*4 cups peanut oil*

**1.** In a large bowl combine cream cheese, sugar and chives, mixing well until smooth.

**2.** Place a small spoonful of the mixture in the center of each wrapper. Follow folding instructions on the wonton package.

**3.** Preheat peanut oil to 375°F in a deep pan. Deep-fry wontons until golden brown. Serve hot.
Makes 48 wontons.

## Ling Ling's Hearty Chicken Potsticker Soup

Established within the San Francisco Bay Area in 1986, Discovery Foods brings generations of Asian culinary experience with their Ling Ling products.

2 packets Ling Ling Potsticker Sauce (included), thawed*

1/4 cup cornstarch

12 cups chicken broth

2 cups water

40 frozen Ling Ling Chicken Potstickers*

8 cups of your favorite frozen mixed vegetables

2 tablespoons grated fresh ginger

2 teaspoons chopped scallions, plus more for garnish

Salt and pepper to taste

**1.** Mix Ling Ling Potsticker Sauce with cornstarch in a small bowl. Set aside.

**2.** In a large pot combine broth and 2 cups water. Bring to a boil. Add frozen Ling Ling Potstickers. Return to a boil and cook 4 minutes, stirring occasionally.

**3.** Add frozen vegetables, ginger and scallions. Cook 4 minutes.

**4.** Add sauce mixture and bring to a simmer. Season with salt and pepper. Garnish with scallions. Makes 8 servings.

FOR HOT AND SOUR, ADD:

1/4 teaspoon ground white pepper

2 tablespoons hot sauce

## Ling Ling's Gourmet Chicken Potsticker Stir-Fry

20 frozen Ling Ling Chicken Potstickers*

1 tablespoon vegetable oil

5 cups of your favorite frozen stir-fry vegetables

Ling Ling's Stir-Fry Sauce (see recipe below)

Salt and pepper

**1.** Cook Ling Ling Potstickers according to boiling instructions on bag and set aside.

**2.** Heat vegetable oil in a 13-inch nonstick frying pan over high heat 1 minute. Add vegetables and stir-fry 3 minutes.

**3.** Add Ling Ling Potstickers and stir-fry 3 minutes. Add Ling Ling's Stir-Fry Sauce and mix well. Bring to a simmer. Season with salt and pepper to taste. Makes 4 servings.

**Note:** To make 8 servings, prepare recipe twice for best results.

LING LING'S STIR-FRY SAUCE

1 cup water

2 tablespoons cornstarch

1/4 cup sugar

1 packet Ling Ling Potsticker Sauce*

2 tablespoons toasted sesame or vegetable oil

1 teaspoon grated fresh ginger

2 tablespoons chili sauce (optional)

2 teaspoons minced garlic (optional)

1 tablespoon oyster sauce (optional)

In a medium bowl, combine water, cornstarch and sugar, and mix well. Add Potsticker Sauce, oil and ginger, mixing until well blended. Add optional ingredients if desired.

*Brands may vary by region; substitute a similar product.

Costco Member
Wendy Peterson

## Wendy Peterson's Hoisin Baby Back Ribs

"This family dish, passed down to me by my mother, is a real crowd-pleaser," reports this Irvine, California, member.

5 pounds baby back ribs

2-inch piece of fresh ginger, sliced, plus
   1 teaspoon grated fresh ginger

1 cup sugar

1 cup ketchup

1/2 cup soy sauce

1/2 cup oyster sauce

1/3 cup hoisin sauce

1 clove garlic, crushed

3 tablespoons sake

Cilantro for garnish

**1.** Cut racks into individual ribs. Place in a large pot and cover with water. Add slices of ginger. Boil gently 1-1 1/2 hours. Drain ribs, discarding ginger.

**2.** Combine sugar, ketchup, soy sauce, oyster sauce, hoisin sauce, grated ginger, garlic and sake. Marinate the cooked ribs in this mixture 4-5 hours in the refrigerator.

**3.** Preheat broiler. Place ribs in roasting pan and broil 15 minutes, turning if necessary.

**4.** Garnish with sprigs of cilantro. Serves a crowd.

## Mann's Stringless Sugar Snap Peas with Toasted Sesame Seeds

So flavorful and so easy to make!

1 tablespoon toasted sesame oil

2-pound bag Mann's Stringless Sugar Snap Peas*

2 teaspoons sesame seeds, toasted

In a large wok or sauté pan, heat sesame oil over medium-high heat. Add peas and sauté 4-6 minutes, or until crisp-tender and bright green. Transfer peas to serving bowl and sprinkle with toasted sesame seeds. Makes 8 servings.

**Costco Tip:** These succulent peas are also wonderful served alongside grilled teriyaki chicken or beef and steamed rice.

*Brands may vary by region; substitute a similar product.*

## Jelly Belly Bark

We guarantee that everyone will stay at the table until this treat is devoured.

*1 bag (12 ounces) white or milk chocolate chips*

*3/4 cup (6 ounces) Jelly Belly jelly beans, fruit flavors*

**1.** Pour chocolate chips into a 2-cup glass measuring cup and microwave 2-4 minutes, or until barely melted; be careful not to overcook. Or melt chocolate in a double boiler. Stir to be sure that all the chips have melted.

**2.** Pour chocolate onto waxed paper in 2-inch puddles, spreading to about 1/4-inch thickness. While the chocolate is still hot, sprinkle about 15 Jelly Belly beans on each, pressing beans lightly into the chocolate. Let cool completely on the counter. Do not refrigerate or freeze.

**3.** Store in an airtight container. To serve, press into bark. Makes 16-24 pieces.

### Vase

We suggest a whimsical Jelly Belly flower arrangement. Take two vases of similar height but one smaller in circumference. Fill the smaller container about halfway up with water and seal the opening with plastic wrap. Carefully position the sealed vase inside the larger container. Pack the space between the two vases with Jelly Bellies. Unseal and add flowers. When dinner is over, offer the Jelly Bellies to whoever does the dishes.

FROM THE MEMBER'S KITCHEN

Costco Member
Jane Brookman and Henry

### Henry's Meatball Doggie Treats

And speaking of family, Jane Brookman of Seattle is passionate about her 185-pound pooch named Henry and prepares all his food, including these veterinarian-approved treats.

*3/4 cup green peas*

*2 pounds lean ground beef (9% fat)*

*2 eggs*

*1/2 cup plain bread crumbs*

*2 tablespoons veterinarian-approved bone meal powder*

**1.** Preheat oven to 350°F.

**2.** Boil peas and puree in a food processor. Add to rest of ingredients. Mix well.

**3.** Shape mixture into a large rectangle and divide evenly into about 68 pieces. Shape into meatballs and place in baking pans.

**4.** Bake for about 25 minutes. Cool and refrigerate. Freeze if unable to use within 4 days. Ground lamb or turkey can be substituted for beef; other pureed veggies also can be used.

Jane adds, "Remember to never serve onions or chocolate to a dog! Both are poisonous to them."

# Drop-In
# Open House

*s Jack Frost begins to visit ever more
frequently,* nothing feels better than flinging the
doors wide one last time and hosting an open house
for neighbors, colleagues and family. The key is to
keep the event simple so guests can drop by or stay as
time dictates, and the host and hostess are free to
meet, greet and converse.

Fashioning one table for drinks and another laden
with no-fuss food is the solution. That's why this
menu works so splendidly. And then there's the pièce
de résistance—a harvest basket centerpiece filled
with vegetables and dips.

# Harvest Basket Centerpiece

By Pat Volchok, Editorial Director

On a rather crowded buffet table, what could be better than a centerpiece that also functions as a food station?

Start with a dress rehearsal. Lay out the serving platters around the buffet table and then measure the space left vacant in the table's center. Then search the house for a handled basket to fit the space, the bigger the better. Clean the basket, line it with plastic, and add two or three cans that are taller than the basket and numerous others that are slightly shorter than the basket.

The shopping list should include whole heads of curly lettuces, red, yellow and orange bell peppers (one for each dip), baby carrots, radishes, small mushrooms, celery, asparagus, snap peas, broccoli, cauliflower, string beans, tiny cooked potatoes, hardy flowers, ivy and the ingredients for two or three favorite dips.

On the day before the party, clean the lettuces, leaving most of them whole. Hollow out the peppers, wrap and refrigerate. Blanch any vegetables that need to be softened, cool in an ice bath, slice if desired, bag by type and refrigerate. Prepare dips. An hour before the party, distribute the numerous lettuce heads to act as filler in the basket. Drape lettuce leaves over the cans and position peppers on top. Group the vegetables and snuggle slightly into the leaves of the lettuces, always considering colors and textures. Add the dip.

The basket should appear to be bursting, so if there are thin spots, fill them with flowers, more lettuce leaves, greens and even garden herbs. Twine ivy around the basket's handle and into the arrangement.

During the party, replenish as necessary. ❧

## Diamond Fruit Growers *Pears and Cheese Platter*

*A stunning platter of pears and cheeses is a very compatible marriage of tastes and textures. Whether used as an appetizer or dessert, cheeses ranging from Cheddar, Gorgonzola, blue or Swiss to the soft cheeses such as Camembert or Brie are a splendid complement to summer or winter pears.*

*Be sure the pears are perfectly ripe. If need be, a day or two before the party, put them in a paper bag at room temperature with the top folded down. When they give slightly at the stem end, they will be sweet, juicy and flavorful.*

*To retard browning (oxidation) of pear slices, brush the cut surfaces with a mild solution of lemon juice and water.*

## Trapper's Creek Kippered Wild King Salmon Caesar Salad

Wild king salmon, also known as Chinook, is the largest of the Pacific salmon species and is highly prized for its rich flavor, high oil content and red flesh.

---

2 large garlic cloves, peeled

5 anchovy fillets (packed in olive oil)

1/2 cup plus 2 tablespoons olive oil

1/2 teaspoon Worcestershire sauce

1 1/2 teaspoons salt

1/4 teaspoon dry mustard

Generous grating of black pepper

2 tablespoons red wine vinegar

1 raw egg or 1/4 cup egg substitute

Juice of 1 lemon

2 heads romaine lettuce, torn into bite-size pieces

1 cup seasoned croutons

1/4 cup grated Parmesan cheese

8 ounces Trapper's Creek Kippered Wild King Salmon, flaked*

---

**1.** Slice 1 clove of garlic in half and rub it well over the interior of a large wooden salad bowl.

**2.** Mash remaining garlic into a paste. Add anchovies and continue to mash. Drizzle in 2 tablespoons olive oil, continuing to stir and mash; add Worcestershire sauce, salt, mustard and pepper. Whisk in vinegar and remaining olive oil.

**3.** Drop the egg into the mixture, add lemon juice and whisk until creamy.

**4.** Add lettuce, croutons and Parmesan, tossing to coat well.

**5.** Sprinkle salmon over the salad. Makes 8-10 servings.

*\*Brands may vary by region; substitute a similar product.*

## Mama Cardile's Crab-Stuffed Mushrooms Florentine

The Cardiles have been growing mushrooms for four generations, and this recipe is a family favorite.

---

16 Cardile's Silver Dollar Mushrooms, stems removed*

2 tablespoons butter

1 tablespoon chopped shallots

1/4 cup white wine

Salt, pepper and Chesapeake Bay-style seafood seasoning

1 cup cooked, chopped spinach, preferably fresh

1 small red bell pepper, cored, seeded and diced

1 pound cream cheese, softened

1 pound crabmeat

1/2 cup bread crumbs

---

Preheat oven to 350°F. Sauté mushroom caps in butter until golden brown and set aside. Finely dice mushroom stems and cook with shallots, white wine, salt, pepper and a touch of seasoning. Cook until dry, 15-20 minutes. Mix spinach, bell pepper and mushroom stems into cream cheese. Gently fold in crabmeat and bread crumbs. Fill caps and bake 10-15 minutes, or until browned. Makes 16 hors d'oeuvres.

*\*Brands may vary by region; substitute a similar product.*

## Café NewStar Citrus Spinach Salad

2 teaspoons white wine vinegar

2 tablespoons freshly squeezed lemon juice

2/3 cup freshly squeezed orange juice

3/8 cup olive oil

Approx. 20 ounces Café NewStar Young & Tender spinach*

2 large oranges, peeled, pith removed and sectioned

2/3 cup thinly sliced red onion

Coarsely ground black pepper

1 cup crumbled goat cheese (optional)

2/3 cup toasted pine nuts (optional)

In a small bowl, whisk together vinegar, lemon juice, orange juice and olive oil. Place spinach, orange slices and red onion in a large salad bowl. Add dressing and toss gently until evenly coated. Add pepper to taste. Top with goat cheese and pine nuts, if desired. Makes 8 servings.

*Brands may vary by region; substitute a similar product.*

## Keystone Fruit Sweet Onion Bisque

A big pot of onion soup is an easy first course.

1/4 cup butter or margarine

3-4 pounds Mayan Sweet onions, diced*

2 tablespoons flour

5 cups chicken stock

1 cup light cream or milk

Salt and pepper to taste

Melt butter over medium heat in stockpot; add onions and cook until soft, approximately 15-20 minutes. Stir in flour and then add remaining ingredients. Bring to a boil, stirring occasionally. Makes 8-10 servings.

**Options/Additions:** 4 medium potatoes, diced; 15 ounces canned or frozen white corn; 1 pound cooked shrimp or crabmeat.

*Brands may vary by region; substitute a similar product.*

## Mercer Ranch Herbed Carrot Salad

Mercer Ranch, of Prosser, Washington, takes advantage of the hot days and cool nights in southeastern Washington and Southern California to produce the best-tasting carrots. They are not only colorful and tasty but also loaded with beta-carotene and fiber.

2 pounds Mercer Ranch baby carrots*

1/2 cup snipped fresh dill

1/2 cup minced fresh oregano

2 tablespoons minced fresh thyme

3/8 cup lemon juice

1/4 cup olive or vegetable oil

2 tablespoons sugar

2 teaspoons grated lemon peel

16 cups torn romaine lettuce

**1.** In a saucepan, bring 1 cup water to a boil; add the carrots. Reduce heat, cover and simmer 5-6 minutes, or until crisp-tender. Drain; cool slightly.

**2.** Meanwhile, in a bowl, combine the dill, oregano, thyme, lemon juice, oil, sugar and lemon peel. Add carrots and toss to coat. Cover and refrigerate.

**3.** Serve over romaine. Makes 8 servings.

**Costco Tip:** Also look for Mercer Ranch corn.*

*Brands may vary by region; substitute a similar product.*

**Editorial Director
Pat Volchok**

## Pat Volchok's Butterflied Leg of Lamb

If there is some of this grilled lamb left over, plan on stuffing it the next day into pita bread along with cucumbers and a drizzle of garlic-infused plain yogurt.

*1/2 cup soy sauce*

*3 cloves garlic, chopped*

*1 tablespoon curry powder*

*1/2 cup Burgundy wine*

*2 tablespoons ketchup*

*2 tablespoons dried oregano*

*2 tablespoons dried thyme*

*2 tablespoons dried rosemary*

*2 tablespoons dried minced onion*

*1/2 cup olive oil*

*1 boned and butterflied leg of lamb*

*TESTED AND APPROVED*

To make the marinade, combine soy sauce, garlic, curry powder, wine, ketchup, oregano, thyme, rosemary, dried onion and olive oil. Massage and marinate the lamb at least 48 hours in the refrigerator. Grill the lamb over indirect medium-high heat for approximately 45 minutes. Thoroughly boil any excess marinade. Serve the lamb thinly sliced, drizzled with the cooked marinade. Makes 12-16 servings.

## Uncle Ben's Wild Rice and Herb Salad with Toasted Pecans

*3 packages Uncle Ben's Long Grain and Wild Rice Original Recipe*

*1 1/2 cups chopped pecans*

*9 green onions, chopped*

*3/4 cup chopped parsley*

*6 ribs celery, finely diced*

*1 tablespoon dried thyme*

*1 tablespoon dried marjoram*

*3/4 cup olive oil*

*3 tablespoons lemon juice*

**1.** Prepare rice according to package directions and chill.

**2.** Place pecans on a baking sheet and toast at 325°F 15 minutes.

**3.** Combine all ingredients except pecans and mix well.

**4.** Top with toasted pecans. Makes 12 servings.

## Uncle Ben's Rice Pilaf

Converted Brand Rice is parboiled while in the husk, then dehydrated. This ingenious technique boosts nutritional value since the heat drives nutrients and proteins into every grain.

*3-4 tablespoons butter or margarine*

*1 cup chopped onion*

*2 cups Uncle Ben's Original Converted Brand Rice*

*5 cups chicken broth*

*1 teaspoon salt, or to taste*

*Dash pepper*

**1.** Melt butter or margarine in a heavy saucepan over medium-high heat.

**2.** Add onion and sauté.

**3.** Stir in rice and sauté until golden.

**4.** Add chicken broth, salt and pepper. Bring to a boil. Cover and simmer 20 minutes. Makes 12 servings.

## Multifoods Four Seasons
## Sliced Pound Cake

What could be better for an Open House dessert than a beautiful Costco butter pound cake, made fresh daily in each Costco warehouse bakery? It will stay fresh for a decent period of time on a buffet, needs only a fork to eat and will allow you to spend time on other food preparations that require more babysitting. It's a winner for guests and cooks alike.

*FRESH FRUIT*

Blend your own combination of fruit to equal 4 cups. Choose from seasonal fruit such as:

*Strawberries, hulled and sliced*

*Kiwi, peeled and sliced*

*Mango and pineapple, peeled, sliced and diced*

*Blueberries, raspberries or grapes*

*RASPBERRY COULIS*

Place 1 cup of sugar and 1 cup of water in a saucepan and bring to a boil. Add 2 cups of fresh raspberries (or frozen, thawed). Cook over moderate heat 2-3 minutes. Whisk with wire whip until smooth and then chill.

*CRÈME ANGLAISE*

In a bowl, whisk 1 cup of sugar into 6 egg yolks for several minutes, until thick and pale yellow. Heat 2 1/2 cups of whole milk in a heavy saucepan until bubbles form around edges (do not boil). Gradually whisk milk into eggs in a thin stream. Return to saucepan and cook over low heat, stirring slowly with a wooden spoon, 4-5 minutes, or until sauce thickens enough to coat the spoon. Add 1 whole vanilla bean (slice the bean open down the middle) and chill.

*PRESENTATION*

Place 1/2-inch slice of pound cake in the center of each plate. Top with 1/3 cup of fruit. Place 1/4 cup raspberry coulis on one side of the plate and 1/4 cup crème anglaise on the other. Decorate the plate with fresh mint leaves and whipped cream. *Bon appétit.* Makes 12 servings.

# Tailgate Party

*At one time, tailgating was just a simple impromptu picnic set up on the back end of the family station wagon before a big fall football game. While recreational and sport-utility vehicles have in many cases replaced the station wagon, tailgating has not lost its allure. If anything, it has become even more popular, with most sporting and outdoor venues embracing this casual form of pre-event partying.*

*As with a winning team, the key to a great tailgate party is a well-executed game plan. Which is precisely why we've created this uncomplicated yet hearty tailgate meal, packed with deli and make-ahead foods, as well as easily grilled fare. So grab a blanket, fire up the coals and let the game begin.*

## MENU

Just because you've never played football, that doesn't mean you don't know a thing or two about a winning game plan. So tear a page out of the football handbook and put it to work as you design a successful tailgate party.

# A Winning Tailgate Party

By Pat Volchok,
Editorial Director

### Cook's Playbook

The first priority is to reserve a parking space for a home game. Then attempt to purchase extra tickets for anyone you'd like to invite who doesn't have season tickets. Collect recipes, prepare the equipment list, invite your "team," check weather reports and establish a decorating theme.

Decorations are easy: Just use the home team's colors. For example, a football tailgate party could include a tablecloth made from sheets of Mylar in team colors. It's fun and waterproof. Add a football flower vase. To make, start with an old, inexpensive football, slice an oval hole along one side and nail to a board. Carve floral foam to fit the inside of the ball, soak it in water and pack in a resealable bag for easy transport to the game.

On tailgate day, set your table, add the colorful Mylar and place the football vase attached to the board slightly off the table's center. Weight the board down with some rocks if needed. Remove the soaked floral foam from the bag and stuff it into the football centerpiece. Add bunches of flowers in team colors. We guarantee no penalty whistles.

Pat's Advice: You still can invite friends without game tickets to the tailgate. After all, it's going to be a great party, and you just never know when an extra ticket might pop up.

### Fundamentals
#### Huddle

In football, the huddle has to be called eight yards from the ball. All tailgate party planning should be completed at least eight days prior to the party.

#### Offensive Line

Set up your party using manageable folding tables and chairs, coolers, at least one grill, lots of ice, a battery-operated radio or CD player, clock, sports whistle, thermoses and of course lots of food and drinks.

Pampering could include an awning or, depending on the weather, portable fans or heaters.

### Strategy Pointers
#### First Down

Your appetizers should be easy to make, easy to refill and weather flexible. If someone asks what to bring, request an appetizer, as that's the easiest for most tailgate guests.

#### Second Down

Score big with marinated, room-temperature salads versus greens, which will wilt and get soggy.

#### Third Down

Heat up the action with an abundant offering of grilled items. Grilling is an activity in which everyone has an opinion, even armchair quarterbacks.

#### Time-Out

Guests will be thirsty, so be sure to offer many non-alcoholic beverages, including bottled water and at least one hot drink, as well as an assortment of beers and wines.

#### Two-Minute Warning

A few minutes before the start of the game, the mad scramble begins. Why not assign someone the job of watching the clock and blowing the whistle for a 20-minute warning. As a special treat, give a bag of goodies such as Kirkland Signature Snack Packs to each departing guest.

### Defense
#### The best offense is a good defense:

- Provide a separate cooler for drinks.
- Blankets and umbrellas just may save the day.
- Napkins, napkins, napkins and then more napkins.
- Keep hot foods hot, cold foods cold. Even room-temperature food should not stay out for more than 2 hours. Never leave food in the sun.
- Remember aluminum foil, plastic wrap and plastic storage containers for leftovers. And, of course, lots of heavy-duty disposable garbage bags.

#### Touchdown! ∾

## Tom Douglas' Hot Pepper Wings with Cilantro Sour Cream

"Either grilled or broiled, what really makes these
wings is their time in the marinade. I have found that
two days is even better than one."

2 cups soy sauce

1 cup Dijon mustard

1 cup water

3/4 cup hot sauce

1/4 cup chopped garlic

2 tablespoons chopped fresh Italian parsley

2 teaspoons chopped fresh thyme

2 teaspoons chopped fresh sage

2 teaspoons chopped fresh rosemary

18 whole chicken wings

**1.** Whisk soy sauce, mustard, water, hot sauce, garlic and
herbs together in a large bowl. Reserve 1/2 cup of marinade
for basting and sauce. Add chicken wings to remaining marinade, cover and refrigerate overnight, turning occasionally.

**2.** Fire up your grill or preheat your broiler. Remove chicken
wings from marinade, discarding marinade. Grill wings on
medium-low heat, turning often, until cooked through, about
15 minutes. Heat reserved marinade and baste the wings a
few times. You want them to cook slowly so the glaze doesn't
burn. Cut into one of the wings to make sure no pink
remains near the bone.

**3.** To serve, spoon Cilantro Sour Cream on 6 plates, top each
with 3 wings, and drizzle with a teaspoon of warm reserved
marinade. Don't use more than a drizzle, though—it's really
strong. Serve remaining reserved marinade on the side for
heat lovers. Makes 18 wings.

### Cilantro Sour Cream

You also can use this
flavorful sour cream in
burritos or on tacos. The
chicken wings are quite salty
and hot, so we don't add
salt or pepper here. For
other dishes, add salt and
pepper to taste.

1/2 cup sour cream

2 tablespoons heavy cream

2 teaspoons
chopped cilantro

Kosher salt and freshly
ground pepper to
taste (optional)

Combine all ingredients
in a small bowl.

### A Step Ahead

You can make the marinade
a few days ahead. It will keep,
covered in the refrigerator,
for up to a week.

## Unilever Best Foods Recipes

From tea to ice cream, Unilever Best Foods has one of the most comprehensive portfolios of brands to meet the everyday needs of consumers.

## Bertolli Bruschetta with Portobellos

2 tablespoons Bertolli Extra-Virgin Olive Oil*

1 pound small portobello mushrooms, stems removed and thinly sliced

2 loaves French or Italian bread, diagonally cut into 3/4-inch slices

2 large cloves garlic, peeled

1 26-ounce jar Bertolli Tomato and Basil Pasta Sauce*

Freshly ground black pepper

In a 12-inch skillet, heat olive oil over medium-high heat and cook mushrooms, stirring occasionally, 4 minutes, or until tender. Meanwhile, broil bread slices until golden; rub with garlic. Evenly spoon unheated pasta sauce over bread, then top with mushrooms and black pepper to taste. Garnish, if desired, with sliced fresh basil. Makes 24 servings.

*Brands may vary by region; substitute a similar product.

## Ragú Chili

2 pounds ground beef

1 large onion, chopped

2 cloves garlic, finely chopped

1 26-ounce jar Ragú Robusto! Pasta Sauce*

1 15-ounce can red kidney beans, rinsed and drained

2 tablespoons chili powder

In a 12-inch skillet, brown ground beef with onion and garlic over medium-high heat; drain. Stir in remaining ingredients. Simmer uncovered, stirring occasionally, 20 minutes. Pour hot chili into a thermos for transportation to the game. Serve, if desired, with shredded Cheddar cheese. Makes 8 servings.

**Note:** For a spicier Ragú Chili, stir in 1/2 teaspoon ground cumin and 1/2 teaspoon dried oregano before simmering.

*Brands may vary by region; substitute a similar product.

## Skippy Chicken Saté with Peanut Sauce

1/4 cup Bertolli Pure Olive Oil Classico*

2 tablespoons soy sauce

2 tablespoons apple cider vinegar

2 tablespoons sugar

2 teaspoons grated fresh ginger

2 cloves garlic, finely chopped

2 pounds boneless, skinless chicken breast halves, cut in strips

**1.** For marinade, blend olive oil, soy sauce, vinegar, sugar, ginger and garlic.

**2.** In a large, shallow non-aluminum baking dish or plastic bag, pour marinade over chicken, turning to coat. Cover, or close bag, and marinate in refrigerator, turning occasionally, up to 3 hours.

**3.** Discard marinade and thread chicken on skewers. Grill or broil chicken, turning once, 6 minutes, or until fully cooked and no longer pink. Serve with Peanut Sauce. Makes 8 servings.

*Brands may vary by region; substitute a similar product.

### Peanut Sauce

2 tablespoons Bertolli Pure Olive Oil Classico*

2/3 cup finely chopped onion

2 cloves garlic, finely chopped

1/2 teaspoon crushed red pepper flakes

2/3 cup Skippy Creamy or Super Chunk Peanut Butter*

2 tablespoons packed dark brown sugar

2 tablespoons soy sauce

2 tablespoons apple cider vinegar

1-2 teaspoons grated fresh ginger

1 cup water

**1.** In a small saucepan, heat oil over medium heat and add onion, garlic and crushed red pepper. Cook, stirring frequently, 3 minutes, or until onion is tender.

**2.** Stir in peanut butter, brown sugar, soy sauce, vinegar and ginger. Gradually stir in water until blended. Serve warm. Makes about 2 cups.

*Brands may vary by region; substitute a similar product.

## Grimmway Two-Way Garden Party Dip

Given all the hearty fare at this party, this lighter dip is an excellent idea. In fact, we liked the seasoning options so much that we suggest you prepare both and put at opposite ends of the table. Serve with Grimmway baby carrots and tortilla chips.

*1/2 pint light sour cream (50 percent less fat
   and 1/3 fewer calories)*
*4 ounces (1/2 package) Neufchatel cheese (1/3 less fat), softened*
*1/4 cup finely shredded Grimmway carrots\**
*1/4 cup each finely chopped red bell pepper and green onion*
*Freshly grated peel of 1/2 lemon*
*2-3 tablespoons bottled salsa or 1 teaspoon dried
   salad herb blend and 1/4 teaspoon garlic salt, or to taste*

**1.** In a medium bowl, whisk together sour cream and Neufchatel cheese until smooth.

**2.** Stir in vegetables and lemon peel.

**3.** Add either salsa or herb blend and garlic salt.

**4.** Cover and chill. Makes about 1 1/2 cups.

*\*Brands may vary by region; substitute a similar product.*

## Wisconsin Potatoes Pesto Potato Salad

Alsum Produce, Anthony Farms, Russet Potato Exchange and Wisconsin Potato and Vegetable Growers Association have joined together to share one of their favorite potato salads. This salad is particularly good for outdoor events because there is no mayonnaise in the recipe. Nonetheless, keep it out of direct sun and nestled in a bowl of ice, and refrigerate after 2 hours.

*12 pounds Wisconsin russet potatoes\**

*1 cup minced green onions*

*2 ounces anchovy fillets, minced*

*2 teaspoons sugar*

*1 teaspoon salt*

*3/4 cup balsamic vinegar*

*1/2 cup vegetable oil*

*1 1/2 cups prepared pesto*

*4 cups sliced celery*

*1/2 cup minced fresh parsley*

Cover potatoes with water in large saucepan. Bring to boil, reduce heat and simmer, covered with lid tilted, 20-30 minutes, or until tender. Drain potatoes and slice 1/2 inch thick. Combine green onions, anchovies, sugar, salt, vinegar and oil in a small bowl; mix well. Add pesto and blend well. Pour dressing over warm potato slices; mix gently and cool to room temperature. Add celery and parsley; mix gently. Serves a crowd!

*\*Brands may vary by region; substitute a similar product.*

*H.J. Heinz Company, manufacturer of a wide array of condiments, offers products that can easily be adapted to most occasions, including a tailgate party.*

## Heinz Zesty Walnut Spread

It's always a good idea to pack a little punch in an appetizer or two, especially if the weather is cold and dreary.

*1 8-ounce package cream cheese, softened*
*1/4 cup Heinz Tomato Ketchup*
*1/2 teaspoon lemon juice*
*1/4-1/2 teaspoon hot pepper sauce*
*1/2 cup toasted walnuts, coarsely chopped*

**1.** In a small bowl, beat cream cheese, ketchup, lemon juice and hot pepper sauce with electric mixer until well blended; stir in walnuts.

**2.** Cover; chill. Serve with crackers or vegetable dippers. Makes about 1 1/2 cups.

## Yoshida Gourmet Meatball Appetizers

Appetizer-size meatballs are a perfect food choice when tables and chairs are scarce. Remember to pack toothpicks.

*18 ounces of frozen cooked meatballs, thawed*
*1 cup Yoshida Original Gourmet Sauce*

**1.** Combine ingredients in large skillet.

**2.** Simmer 5 minutes, or until meatballs are glazed, stirring to coat evenly. Makes 30-36 appetizers.

## Classico Pizza Rustica

*1 16-ounce package hot roll mix*
*1 pound bulk Italian sausage*
*1 26-ounce jar Classico di Napoli (Tomato & Basil) Pasta Sauce*
*1 1/2 cups (6 ounces) shredded mozzarella cheese*
*1 10-ounce package frozen chopped spinach, thawed and well drained*
*1 egg, slightly beaten*
*Milk to brush loaf*
*2 teaspoons sesame seeds (optional)*

**1.** Preheat oven to 350°F.

**2.** Prepare hot roll mix according to package directions through the kneading step. Cover and let dough rest 5 minutes.

**3.** In large skillet over medium-high heat, brown sausage; pour off fat. Stir in 1 1/2 cups pasta sauce and heat through.

**4.** Coat bottom of 9-inch springform pan with vegetable cooking spray. On lightly floured surface, roll 3/4 of dough into 14-inch circle. Fit into bottom and up sides of pan, allowing dough to extend over edges. Pleat dough as necessary to fit.

**5.** Sprinkle dough with 1/2 cup mozzarella. Spoon meat mixture over cheese. Combine drained spinach, egg and remaining cheese; spread over meat mixture.

**6.** Roll remaining dough into 9-inch circle; place on top of filling. Moisten edge of bottom crust with water; fold over edge of top crust to seal. Brush top with milk; sprinkle with sesame seeds, if desired. Bake 40-45 minutes, or until golden brown. Cool 10 minutes. Makes 8 servings.

### Tarantino's Italian Sausage Sandwich with Peppers and Onions

Forty years ago, Pete Tarantino Sr. traveled the world looking for just the right sausage recipes. Today, Tarantino Sausage Company still uses these now tightly guarded recipes from the world's master sausage-makers to prepare their succulent offerings. Made from only the finest meats from our country's heartland, Tarantino's sausage is another way to spell party success.

*8 mild or hot Tarantino's Italian Sausages\**

*4 medium onions, cut in half and sliced*

*2 large green bell peppers, cored, seeded and sliced*

*2 large red bell peppers, cored, seeded and sliced*

*6 tablespoons olive oil*

*1 tablespoon salt*

*2 teaspoons ground black pepper*

*1/8 teaspoon dried oregano*

*3/8 cup white or red wine*

*1 cup shredded Parmesan, mozzarella or
 provolone cheese (or a combination)*

**1.** Poach raw sausages in 1/2 cup water in a covered skillet, simmering until almost done. This takes about 8-10 minutes and can be done a day ahead.

**2.** Also the day before, sauté onions and peppers with olive oil, salt, pepper and oregano 4 minutes on medium-high heat. Add wine, cover and cook 3 minutes more; uncover and cook until moisture is absorbed. Store in foil.

**3.** At the tailgate, grill poached sausages over medium-hot coals, turning often to ensure even browning, 7-10 minutes. Meanwhile, place the foil packet of onions and peppers on the grate to warm.

**4.** Serve on rolls or crusty Italian bread, garnished with shredded cheese and condiments. Makes 8 servings.

*\*Brands may vary by region; substitute a similar product.*

## Kraft Foods

Kraft is the largest branded food and beverage company in North America and the second largest in the world. In more than 145 countries, Kraft Foods markets the world's favorite food and beverage brands in five product sectors: snacks, beverages, cheese, grocery and convenient meals. Brands include Kraft cheese, Jacobs, Yuban and Maxwell House coffees, Nabisco cookies and crackers, Philadelphia cream cheese, Oscar Mayer meats, Post cereals and Milka chocolates.

### Kraft Foods Dynamite Dogs

*Oscar Mayer Cheese Dogs\**

*Hot dog buns*

*Claussen Bread 'N Butter Sandwich Slices\**

*Bull's-Eye Spicy Hot Barbecue Sauce\**

Grill cheese dogs until thoroughly heated (160°F), turning frequently. Serve in buns and top with pickles and barbecue sauce.

### Kraft Foods Layered Taco Dip

*1 16-ounce can Taco Bell Home Originals Refried Beans\**

*1 cup Breakstone's or Knudsen Sour Cream\**

*1 cup guacamole*

*1 cup Taco Bell Home Originals Thick 'N Chunky Salsa\**

*1/4 cup chopped green onions*

*1/4 cup sliced pitted ripe olives, optional*

*1/4 cup seeded and sliced jalapeño peppers, optional*

*Grated Cheddar cheese*

*Wheat Thins Snack Crackers or Big Wheat Thins Snack Crackers\**

Spread beans onto a large serving plate; top with layers of sour cream, guacamole and salsa. Sprinkle with onions, olives and peppers. Garnish with cheese. Cover and refrigerate several hours, or until chilled. Serve as a dip with crackers. Makes 12 servings.

*\*Brands may vary by region; substitute a similar product.*

### Hebrew National
#### Franks and Toppings

The ideal way to serve a Hebrew National hot dog is simple: grilled and placed in a standard roll, with a streak of Hebrew National mustard. Here are a few of the most popular "dog creations" from around the country:

##### NEW YORK CITY DOG
In a hot dog roll with Hebrew National Deli Mustard and Hebrew National Sauerkraut.

##### CHICAGO DOG
Comes on a poppy seed bun. Served with mustard, relish, peppers, chopped raw onion, tomato slices, a pickle spear and a dash of celery salt. (In other words, everything but the kitchen sink!)

##### SLAW DOG
In the South, they ask for the hot dog to be "dragged through the garden." The garden (slaw) is made with chopped cabbage, onions, mayonnaise, spices and a touch of carrot for color. It's served on a hot dog bun.

##### KANSAS CITY DOG
Kansas City is famous for its Reuben dog. Like the Reuben sandwich, it comes in a sesame seed roll, topped with sauerkraut and non-dairy melted cheese.

Costco Member
Vivian Berry

## Vivian Berry's Pumpkin Cake

The note on the recipe page read, "Everyone's favorite." We couldn't agree more with this Salinas, California, member's assessment of her Berry good cake.

2 cups sugar

1 1/4 cups oil

4 eggs

2 cups flour

2 teaspoons baking soda

1 teaspoon salt

1 1/2 teaspoons cinnamon

1 1/2 cups pumpkin puree

**1.** Preheat oven to 350°F.

**2.** Combine sugar and oil in a bowl. Add eggs one at a time, beating well after each addition.

**3.** Combine dry ingredients and add gradually to batter along with the pumpkin puree. Mix well.

**4.** Pour into a greased tube pan or 2 loaf pans. Bake 1 hour, or until a toothpick inserted in the center comes out clean. Ice with Cream Cheese Frosting when cool. Makes 16 servings.

CREAM CHEESE FROSTING

1/2 cup butter or margarine, softened

8 ounces cream cheese, softened

1 16-ounce box confectioners' sugar

1 tablespoon vanilla extract

Cream butter and cream cheese together. Add confectioners' sugar and beat until smooth. Add vanilla and blend well.

## Shultz Foods Tex-Mex Pretzels

1 stick butter

1 package taco seasoning

2 tablespoons Worcestershire sauce
   or 1 tablespoon prepared mustard

1 10-ounce bag Shultz mini pretzels*

Preheat oven to 250°F. Melt butter in saucepan. Add taco seasoning and Worcestershire sauce. Spread pretzels on baking sheet. Pour seasoning mixture over pretzels and toss to coat well. Bake 30 minutes, turning every 10 minutes to ensure even toasting.

*Brands may vary by region; substitute a similar product.*
*Recipe developed by Linda Carey and Pat Volchok.*

## Kirkland Signature Trail Mix Brownies

Imagine gooey chocolate brownies topped with large
Virginia peanuts, roasted nonpareil supreme almonds,
Thompson natural seedless raisins, M&M's, roasted
cashews and thick caramel. Talk about a winning salty-
and-sweet combination!

*1 package brownie mix*

*3 cups Kirkland Signature Trail Mix*

*50 light-colored caramels*

*1/3 cup evaporated milk*

*6 ounces chocolate chips*

**1.** Assemble the brownie mixture, following directions
on the box.

**2.** Place 1 cup of trail mix in a plastic bag and gently break
the large nuts. Stir into the brownie mixture.

**3.** Pour into a lined and greased 9-by-13-inch pan. Bake
according to instructions on the box.

**4.** In a heavy medium-sized saucepan, combine caramels
and evaporated milk. Warm over low heat, stirring
occasionally, until melted.

**5.** Remove brownies from the oven and pour half of the melted
caramel on top, spreading evenly. Sprinkle the chocolate chips
over the caramel and let melt slightly. Add the remaining trail
mix and press lightly. If desired, drizzle on more melted
caramel sauce to hold the trail mix on the brownies.

**6.** When cool, cut the brownies into squares, cover and
transport in the pan to prevent drying. Serve on a disposable
platter and stand back while the guests devour them.
Makes 24 brownies.

### Kirkland Signature Snack Packs:

If you're running short of time, hand out individual
Kirkland Signature Snack Packs, offered in a 12-pack
assortment of four 3-ounce bags of Rice Crackers with
Nuts, Fruit & Nut Medley and Trail Mix. These snack
packs are also good for school lunches, hiking, car-
pooling and on-the-go snacking.

# Frightfully Delicious Halloween Dinner

*I*rish immigrants arriving in this country in the 1800s brought with them the traditions of a harvest festival originated by their Celtic ancestors 2,000 years before. Pumpkins, native to America, replaced turnips and beets, and groups of costumed revelers walked their neighborhoods at night showing off their fanciful attire. Neighbors awarded treats to those whose costumes were exceptional. And the lively, whimsical American Halloween was born.

Today, Halloween is a night full of amusement, neighbors and most definitely fun. It's a time to indulge in eating a few sweets, dressing up in the absurd, and filling the night air with laughter. After all, as most trick-or-treaters have learned, laughter is truly the best way to shoo all those naughty spirits away.

## MENU

Costco Member
Christie Meacham

## Christie Meacham's Carrot Salad

What could be better on this traditional orange-and-black day than a yummy, colorful carrot salad? We thank this Oakland, Oregon, Costco member for taking the time to share it with us.

*6 cups grated raw carrots*
*1/4 cup packed brown sugar*
*1 teaspoon salt*
*1 tablespoon real apple cider vinegar*
*1/2 cup finely chopped onion*
*1 large green pepper, cored, seeded and finely chopped*
*1/2 -1 teaspoon ground pepper*
*1 jalapeño pepper, seeded and finely chopped (optional)*
*1 cup mayonnaise*
*1 clove garlic, minced*

**1.** Mix all ingredients and refrigerate overnight for best flavor.
**2.** You also can add 1/2 cup grated broccoli, 1/2 cup small apple cubes, 1/2 cup raisins, or 1/2 cup pineapple chunks or crushed pineapple (drained). Makes 10-12 servings.

### A Catering Trick ... the Costco Party Platters

It's been rumored for years that professional caterers and many savvy home cooks purchase the Costco party platters already prepared with assorted fresh veggies, whole cooked and peeled shrimp, and sliced meats and/or cheeses and then rearrange them on their own handsome plates to serve for parties. Who can blame them? Not us.

Colorful order brochures for party platters are available in every Costco Deli. While most Costco warehouses have basic party platters that are made fresh daily and that are available in the cooler cases, the only way to guarantee a party platter is to order it at least 48 hours in advance.

Costco Member
Erika Feuer

## Erika Feuer's Gardenburger Meatballs

"This is my recipe for vegetarian meatballs," writes this member from Cerritos, California. "They are good in a spaghetti sauce, as a snack, with a dip or for juggling." Initially we thought juggling was a little extreme, but then we've heard of stranger things happening on Halloween.

*6 frozen Gardenburgers*
*1/4 cup flour*
*1/2 cup egg substitute or two eggs, beaten*
*2 teaspoons spice of your choice*

Preheat oven to 400°F. Defrost Gardenburgers for 2 minutes on high in microwave. Mix all ingredients (easiest done by hand). Form 30 meatballs. Place on greased cookie sheet. Bake 20 minutes. Serve with your favorite barbecue sauce. Makes 30 meatballs.

**Costco Member
Shelby Snider**

## Shelby Snider's Molasses Baked Beans

"This dish has become a favorite with all of my family and friends. Each time there is a holiday, a party, and especially a backyard barbecue, I am always *told* what I will bring," writes this good sport and Costco member from Chino, California.

4 15 1/4-ounce cans pork and beans

2 15 1/4-ounce cans BBQ beans

1 pound lean ground beef, cooked and drained well

1 large onion, diced

1 cup diced green bell pepper

1/2 cup ketchup

1/2 cup molasses

1 cup packed brown sugar

1/4 cup prepared mustard

2 tablespoons Worcestershire sauce

2 teaspoons seasoned salt

1 teaspoon lemon pepper

6-8 slices bacon, cut in 1-inch pieces

Preheat oven to 275-300°F. Mix all ingredients except bacon and pour into a large casserole dish. Place bacon pieces on top. Cover with foil and bake 2 1/2-3 hours. (Bean mixture should be bubbling.) Remove foil, adjust oven to 325°F and bake 30-60 minutes longer, or until bacon and top of beans are a deep golden brown. Check often. Makes 12 servings.

### Milton's All-American PB&J

Sometimes the anticipation of the night ahead is just too much for a child to bear. Be prepared by having a platter of these adorable peanut-butter-and-jelly sandwiches made with Milton's healthy breads on hand. You also might want to pack up a few of them for the night's adventures.

**DIRECTIONS:** Spread your favorite jelly on a slice, and peanut butter on another. Use a cookie-cutter to stamp a shape out of the peanut butter slice. Place the remaining slice on a jelly slice so you can see jelly in the cutout window. Make a stack of little PB&Js with the leftover cutouts.

**COSTCO TIP:** Have the sandwiches fit the theme by using pumpkin cookie-cutters for Halloween and shamrocks for St. Paddy's Day.

## Nabisco Oreo Peanut Butter Frogs

Either presented on a plate or hopping around the table, these little critters are the perfect Halloween treat!

2 squares Baker's Semi-Sweet Baking Chocolate

2 tablespoons butter or margarine

12 Oreo Chocolate Sandwich Cookies

4 tablespoons creamy peanut butter

24 miniature pretzel twists

24 candy-coated milk chocolate candies

Melt chocolate and butter in pan over low heat. Spread bottom of each cookie with 1 teaspoon peanut butter; dip in melted chocolate. Press 2 pretzels on chocolate for "legs," with wide part facing outward. Place on waxed paper, pretzel side down. Attach candies for "eyes" using remaining chocolate. Makes 12 frogs.

**FRIGHTFULLY DELICIOUS HALLOWEEN DINNER**

## Celestine Johnson's Sweet Potato Pudding

The Halloween orange food theme continues with this recipe from a member in Hampton, Virginia. She writes, "Whenever I am asked to bring something to church, senior meetings and parties, my famous Sweet Potato Pudding is always requested."

4 large sweet potatoes or yams, peeled, cooked and pureed

1 14-ounce can sweetened condensed milk

1 cup milk

1/2 teaspoon cinnamon

1 teaspoon vanilla extract

1 stick butter or margarine, melted

1 cup sugar

1 cup packed dark brown sugar

1/2 teaspoon nutmeg

Pinch of salt

3 eggs

**1.** Preheat oven to 350°F.

**2.** Mix all ingredients together. Pour into a well-greased 9-by-13-inch baking dish or individual ramekins.

**3.** Bake 45-60 minutes, or until pudding is set in the center.

**4.** Serve warm with whipped cream. Makes 12 servings.

Costco Member
Celestine Johnson

Costco Member
Christy Hall

## Christy Hall's Pam's Caramel Corn

Walla Walla, Washington, is the home of this Costco member, whose caramel corn is great freshly popped and out of this world when placed back in the oven.

Popcorn

2 sticks butter

2 cups packed light brown sugar

1 teaspoon salt

1 cup light corn syrup

1 teaspoon baking soda

**1.** Pop enough corn to fill a very large bowl 2/3 full. Sort to remove any unpopped kernels.

**2.** In a 2-quart saucepan, mix butter, brown sugar, salt and corn syrup. Cook until boiling and then time it to boil exactly 4 minutes. Remove from heat and add soda, stirring thoroughly. Mixture will foam up.

**3.** Pour syrup over popcorn and mix well. It can be eaten sticky or baked on a cookie sheet in a slow oven (150-200°F) 1/2 hour, turning to dry. Makes 12-14 servings.

# Halloween Tips and Treats

*By Pat Volchok,*
*Editorial Director*

Besides the traditional Halloween activities such as bobbing for apples or watching a scary movie, we'd like to suggest a few additional ideas.

### Dinnertime Treats

Children love Tootsie Pop ghosts. Cut inexpensive white cotton into 8-by-12-inch rectangles. Drape over the pops and tie each with a length of black cord to fit snugly under the candy and around the stick. Draw triangle eyes on the "ghost heads" and big O's for the mouths. (If these are offered to small children, we strongly suggest adult supervision.)

Party cups full of nuts and candy corn are a nice dinnertime favor. Or better yet, provide diners with their own popcorn hands. To create, fill each finger of an unpowdered see-through plastic glove with one candy corn (white tip pointing down) "finger nail," add freshly popped corn and tie with black ribbon at the wrist.

*See-through shallow glass containers filled with water and gently bobbing apple votives, sporadically placed around the main centerpiece, are a nice festive touch.*

Decorate the dinner table with candy spiders. Take individually wrapped hard candies, glue dots on the edges for eyes, and bend 4 pipe cleaners into furry legs and attach with tape to the undersides.

To roast pumpkin seeds, toss with vegetable oil and a little salt. Bake at 350°F for 10 minutes. For a sweeter treat, toss the seeds with a little melted butter, brown sugar and cinnamon and then bake. (Sugar has a tendency to burn, so check sporadically.)

### Scary Stories

What could be better than a little poetry from the master of fright, Edgar Allan Poe. Just light a fire in the family room, turn off the lights, gather the group and have someone, with flashlight in hand and perhaps some scary face paint, read first "The Haunted Palace" and then "The Raven."

### Goody Bags

While it may be impossible to create goody bags for all the little creatures that visit your home on Halloween, it's always nice to craft special treat bags for the children you know.

The creation of the bags can be a family affair, with members of all ages decorating brown paper lunch bags with stars, stickers and faces.

Finally, don't forget the half-frozen adults who stand back in the shadows accompanying the little trick-or-treaters. Prepare steaming pots of apple cider and serve in disposable hot cups to these brave souls. ❧

*Thanksgiving Gathering*

*I*n an uncertain world, it's a comfort to embrace a holiday that has changed little over several hundred years. Then (1621) as now, Thanksgiving has been a time to gather together to give thanks for family, friends and the land's plentiful harvest.

It is a time of golden moons, crackling leaves, old and new faces, shared stories, childhood memories and hands around the table.

This year when the family sits down at the Thanksgiving table, be reminded that in the grand scheme of life, it matters little whether the turkey leans to one side, the gravy has a few lumps or the cornbread is burned. What is important is that loved ones are gathered together, and for that we should all give thanks.

## MENU

### Kirkland Signature/ Newman's Own
## Grape Cooler

A festive non-alcoholic drink is always a nice touch.

---

1/2 cup Kirkland Signature 100% Grape Juice
1/2 cup prepared iced tea chilled
1/2 cup lemon-lime soda chilled

---

In a large glass with ice, mix grape juice and iced tea. Slowly stir in soda and garnish with lemon.

## Jane Schuelein's Sweet Dill Pickles

We were intrigued by this recipe and then sold on the taste of these sweet dill pickles created by a Costco member from Fox Island, Washington.

---

32-ounce jar dill pickles
2 cups sugar
2/3 cup white vinegar
1/3 cup water

---

**1.** Drain pickles, cut them in chunks and put back in the jar.

**2.** Bring the sugar, vinegar and water to a boil. Pour over the pickles. Refrigerate. They will be ready to eat in 3 days.

**3.** Try adding freshly sliced onions to the jar before pouring in the brine. They pickle nicely. Serves a crowd.

**Jane's Tip:** "I double this recipe for the big Costco jar of pickles and keep a jar of them in the refrigerator at all times."

*Costco Member Jane Schuelein*

---

### *Costco Dinner Rolls*

*What would a Thanksgiving dinner be without a fresh basket of dinner rolls, especially those made in the Costco Bakery? Costco dinner rolls are the perfect combination of sweetness, creamy flavor and softness, with a golden crust. Made fresh each morning, Costco dinner rolls are baked with wholesome ingredients and traditional techniques and sold in groups of 36.*

*They can be frozen for up to a month in their plastic bag. To reheat, place frozen rolls on a cookie sheet in a preheated 380°F oven for 10 minutes, then put in a bread basket and enjoy.*

### Meridian
## Lobster Stuffing

---

2 8-ounce Meridian lobster tails, cooked and finely chopped
1/2 cup melted butter or olive oil
1/3 cup finely chopped onion
1/3 cup finely chopped green pepper
1/3 cup finely chopped celery
1/4 teaspoon black pepper
1/4 teaspoon garlic powder
1/2 teaspoon seasoned salt
1/2 pound crushed Ritz crackers (2 stacks)
1/2 cup grated Parmesan cheese
1/3 cup sherry (or substitute water)
1/3 cup water

---

Heat butter or olive oil in sauté pan over medium heat. Sauté chopped onion, green pepper and celery until soft and onions are translucent. Add black pepper, garlic powder and seasoned salt. Cook 1-2 minutes. Remove from heat. Put crackers in a medium-sized bowl and crush until all pieces are uniform in size. Add the cooked lobster, Parmesan cheese and sautéed seasoned vegetables. Mix thoroughly. Add Sherry and water. Stir until moistened. (Additional water may be added if needed.) Place mixture in a glass-baking dish, cover and bake at 400°F for 20-25 minutes.

### Giorgio Foods
## Mushroom Stuffing

---

1/4 cup butter
3 medium onions, chopped
4 stalks celery, chopped
4 4-ounce cans Brandywine, Giorgio or Penn Dutch pieces and stems mushrooms, drained, broth reserved*
3 cloves garlic, minced
1/4 cup chopped fresh parsley
2 teaspoons chopped fresh basil
8 cups bread cubes or 2 8-ounce packages unseasoned stuffing mix
Salt and pepper

---

In large skillet, melt butter and sauté onions, celery and mushrooms. Add garlic, parsley and basil and cook 3-5 minutes, stirring frequently. In a bowl combine bread cubes and mushrooms. Heat reserved broth and add to bread cubes as needed. Add salt and pepper to taste. Use to stuff turkey, chicken or pork chops. Can also be baked, covered, at 375°F 30-40 minutes. Makes 10-12 servings.

*\*Brands may vary by region; substitute a similar product.*

## Karin Van Valkenberg's
## Grilled Thanksgiving Turkey

Costco's Pat Volchok smelled the luscious aroma of a turkey cooking in her neighbor's yard last Thanksgiving and begged for the recipe. Graciously responding to the request, this Seattle member wrote, "I've been cooking turkeys this way for a long time. It's so easy that I now do it all year round."

*1 cup rock salt*

*2 cups brown sugar*

*14- to 16-pound turkey, trussed*

**1.** Prepare brine of rock salt, brown sugar and at least 2 quarts of water. Place bird in a deep bucket or pot. Add brine and more water if needed to cover the turkey completely. Cover and let soak in the refrigerator for 2 days.

**2.** Heat lots of coals in a barbecue kettle. When hot, move the coals to evenly distribute around the perimeter. Make an aluminum pan from foil and place in the cleared-out center. This is called the indirect heat method.

**3.** Place the turkey (discard the brine) breast side down in the pan and cover the kettle. You can add alder chips that have been soaked in water to the coals every so often for a smoked taste. Turn the turkey after it has browned. Karin notes, "Usually, a 14- to 16-pound turkey takes 2-plus hours to cook." Makes 10-12 servings.

Costco Member
Karin Van Valkenberg

*FOSTER FARMS TURKEY TALK*

*PREPARATION:*

- Remove wrapper from turkey. Remove hock lock from legs; pull neck and giblets from cavities. Rinse turkey inside and out with cold water. Pat dry.
- Stuff cavities lightly with stuffing, if desired. Stuffing expands as it cooks.
- Skewer cavity openings to secure stuffing. Tie legs together or return to hock lock; twist wing tips under the back.

*ROASTING:*

- The turkey is cooked when the meat thermometer reads 180°F to 185°F at the thigh, or 170°F to 175°F at the breast, and the center of the stuffing reaches at least 165°F. Drumstick should twist easily in socket, and juices should run clear, with no traces of pink when pierced with a fork.
- For easy slicing, let turkey stand 20 minutes after removing from oven.

### Costco Fresh Turkeys Gobbled Up

The better taste and convenience of a ready-to-cook turkey is something that is highly appealing to Costco members. More than 350,000 of the fresh (never frozen) 100 percent natural turkeys from Foster Farms and Butterball were sold last Thanksgiving in Costco warehouses and business-delivery centers.

The birds usually arrive in most locations 10 days ahead and are available until the holiday. The vast majority of these fresh turkeys are toms (males) ranging from 18 to 24 pounds. The smaller hens (females), in the 10- to 16-pound range, are also brought in for Thanksgiving and carried again for the December holidays.

## Micah Wyzlic's Horseradish **Basin Gold** Mashed Potatoes

It would be close to sacrilegious not to serve mashed potatoes for Thanksgiving. This Gilbert, Arizona, member's version is about the best we have ever tasted.

3 pounds Basin Gold russet potatoes

1 cup sour cream

1/2 cup half-and-half or milk

1/4 cup butter

1 tablespoon kosher salt

1/2 teaspoon freshly ground black pepper

1/4 cup prepared horseradish (bottled)

**1.** Boil the potatoes until fork tender. Drain well.

**2.** Add all the ingredients in a pot and mash.
Makes 8-12 servings.

### Costco Tips:

• Store potatoes in a cool, dry place away from light.

• Do not store potatoes in the refrigerator, as the starches will turn to sugar.

*Costco Member
Micah Wyzlic*

## **Pacific Fruit** Bonita Banana and Sweet Potato Casserole

What a brilliant way to give new life to a Thanksgiving family favorite.

4 pounds sweet potatoes

1 teaspoon salt

6 medium Bonita bananas*

1/4 cup orange juice

1/2 cup packed brown sugar

1/2 teaspoon cinnamon

4 tablespoons butter, melted

Preheat oven to 350°F. Bring sweet potatoes to a boil in water to cover. Add salt and simmer 30-35 minutes, or until tender. Peel and slice about 1/4 inch thick. Slice bananas and combine with orange juice. Mix sugar and cinnamon in a separate bowl. In a greased deep baking dish, layer 1/3 of sweet potatoes, 1/3 of bananas, 1/3 of brown sugar and 1/3 of butter. Repeat layers. Bake 45 minutes, or until hot and bubbly. Makes 12 servings.

*Brands may vary by region; substitute a similar product.*

## Joyce St. Amand's Herbed Edamame

This Temecula, California, member says that her herbed soybeans are particularly wonderful in salads. We say forget the salad and just eat them as soon as possible.

100 soybeans

1 tablespoon butter

1 teaspoon dried basil or 1 tablespoon chopped fresh basil

Salt to taste

Shell soybeans after cooking in boiling water 10 minutes. Sauté cooked beans in butter, basil and salt to taste. Makes 8 servings.

*Costco Member
Joyce St. Amand*

### Domex Apple Salad

Crisp apples and miniature marshmallows go hand in hand with Thanksgiving.

4 Domex apples, cored and cubed

4 celery stalks, diced

1 cup pineapple tidbits

1 cup golden raisins

1/2 cup chopped dates

1 cup miniature marshmallows

2 teaspoons celery seed (optional)

1 cup chopped pecans/walnuts (optional)

1 cup mayonnaise

1 cup sour cream

1/4 cup sugar

4-6 tablespoons orange juice

Combine apples, celery, pineapple, raisins, dates, marshmallows, celery seed and nuts in a bowl. Mix together mayonnaise, sour cream, sugar and orange juice. Pour over salad and stir gently to combine. Makes 12 servings.

**Costco Tip:** Adding orange juice to the dressing will help keep the apples from browning.

### Ocean Spray White Cranberry-Apple Chutney

This chutney is a nice addition or alternative to traditional cranberry sauce.

1 cup Ocean Spray White Cranberry Juice Drink

3/4 cup red wine vinegar

1/4 cup packed brown sugar

4 medium apples, peeled, cored and diced

1 medium onion, diced

4 garlic cloves, finely chopped

2 tablespoons finely chopped fresh ginger

1/4 teaspoon salt

1/4 teaspoon grated orange peel

Combine all ingredients in medium saucepan. Bring to a boil over medium heat. Reduce heat to low and cook, stirring occasionally, about 40 minutes, or until apples are tender and sauce has thickened slightly. Serve with poultry, pork or fish. Makes about 5 cups.

### Mariani Cranberry Cream Pie

1 cup Mariani Dried Cranberries*

1 cup sugar

1/2 cup all-purpose flour

1/8 teaspoon salt

21/4 cups milk

2 eggs, lightly beaten

1/2 cup sour cream

1/4 cup butter, diced

1 9-inch piecrust, baked

1 cup heavy whipping cream

3 tablespoons confectioners' sugar

1 teaspoon vanilla extract

Cover dried cranberries with boiling water. Let stand 5 minutes and drain. In a medium heavy-bottomed saucepan, combine sugar, flour and salt. Gradually stir in milk and eggs. Cook over medium heat, stirring constantly, until the mixture thickens and boils. Boil and stir 2 minutes. Remove from heat. Stir in sour cream, butter and cranberries; pour mixture into baked pastry shell. Cover with plastic wrap and refrigerate overnight. Whip cream until soft peaks form; fold in confectioners' sugar and vanilla. Swirl over top of pie. Makes 8 servings.

*Brands may vary by region; substitute a similar product.

# Setting the Table

A Thanksgiving dining table should provide a comfortable entertaining ambience, one that is functional as well as attractive.

### Noritake Fine China

If you are seeking one set of fine china for today's many entertaining styles, then Noritake's boxed china service for eight (dinner plates, salad plates, bowls, cups with saucers and accent plates) is the perfect choice. It comes with an additional seven-piece service set: oval platter, oval serving bowl, creamer, sugar container with lid and gravy bowl with tray.

Each piece is made of fine white translucent porcelain and features gold- or platinum-etched metallic designs. It lends itself to mixing and matching, and Noritake has included the two latest fashion trends: accent plates and all-purpose bowls.

The accent plates are nine inches in diameter and can be placed on the dinner plates to serve a first course with dramatic flair. They can also be used later as dessert plates. The all-purpose bowl can be used for soup, salad, and even fruit.

### Charger Plates

Chargers are large shallow plates or platters that have an enhanced lip and are used as an elegant frame for dinner plates. Charger plates first became popular in the United States around 1900. The first ones were ceramic, but in the 1950s metallic accents were first produced in Italy.

This exclusive set of eight 13-inch chargers is made by artisans who hand-apply individual paper-thin sheets of hammered aluminum leaf to create gold or silver chargers. The plate is then rubbed and sealed with a minimum of four to six coats of the highest-quality clear lacquer to protect against moisture and oxidation. Chargers also look lovely lining the center of your table holding centerpieces or candles. A 14-by-14-inch tray is included for serving or storage.

### Newport-Layton Table Runners

Table runners add elegance to your table, sideboard or hutch. Runners come in a wide range of decorative fabrics, colors and trims, from traditional jacquards to woven country French designs.

Newport-Layton, the leader in the decorative-accessory industry for 48 years, suggests purchasing runners in multiple sets so that you can extend them across the width of your table instead of along the length and use as placemats.

Newport-Layton runner fabrics range from heavyweight 100 percent cotton to 100 percent finely woven silks. All products are handmade in the Portland, Oregon, factory to the highest quality standards.

### Godinger Crystal

Godinger, well known for its fine hand-finished, European-crafted, 24 percent lead crystal glassware, reports that candles are now an integral part of life, no matter what the time of day.

This pair of Godinger 10-inch candleholders are hand-finished and enhanced with such niceties as ridges carved into the glass of the bowls to better secure candles. They will hold standard tapers or 3-inch pillar candles or more unusual items such as pineapples or pears.

Godinger's footed centerpiece bowl is also hand finished with old-world techniques and is made of brilliant 24 percent lead crystal.

Also look for Godinger hurricane lamps, photo frames and crystal vases.

### Over and Back Ceramic Platter Set and Bowl

Platters are a mainstay of food presentation. The decorative rim is particularly important, as the food tends to cover much of the rest of the surface.

Over and Back commissioned a century-old manufacturer in Italy to produce the handsome, antique-design Savannah two-piece platter set and matching bowl. Unrefined natural clay is fixed with an Italian white glaze to produce an heirloom-quality work of art with a wonderfully intricate and delicate filigree border.

The platters offer year round use.

We suggest that you squirrel away some of these pieces for wedding, anniversary and birthday gifts and, of course, Mother's Day.

### Hampton Signature Silverware and Serving Pieces by Hampton Silversmiths

While silverware is part of everyday life, there are those sets of knives, forks and spoons that instantly add enjoyment to any meal. Such is the case with Hampton Signature Silverware.

Made of 18/10 stainless steel alloy with 18 percent chromium for an enduring finish and 10 percent nickel for an unmistakable rich luster and appearance, this heirloom-quality silverware will delight your eyes and palate. Designed in classic European-style and double-sided patterns, pieces are oversized, for a substantial and perfectly balanced feel, as well as proportioned for efficient use.

This classic 65-piece set of flatware consists of 12 five-piece place settings and a five-piece hostess set, which includes sugar spoon, butter knife, serving spoons and a serving fork.

Also offered is a six-piece entertainment set that's perfect for large buffets and dinners. It has two buffet serving spoons, buffet serving fork, buffet ladle, pierced buffet serving spoon and buffet cake server.

A stainless steel knife-and-fork carving set, presented in a latched wooden mahogany-stained box with dark blue velvet lining, makes a wonderful holiday gift.

All Hampton Silversmiths flatware is warranted to be free of defects in material and workmanship for 30 years from the date of purchase, but you should nevertheless treat it as you would any fine collectible.

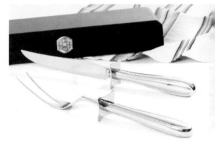

**The silversmiths suggest:** While this flatware is dishwasher safe, its brilliance will dull over time, so if you want to maintain luminosity, wash it by hand with a non-abrasive sponge and mild detergent. Also, be wary of any detergent that contains lemon, as it can cause corrosion on stainless steel. Do not leave the pieces soaking in water for a long time, and dry with a clean, soft towel.

Replacements and completer pieces can be ordered from the company. ❧

*Winter Wonderland*

# Winter Reflections

**Winter can be fierce. Winter can be chilly. Winter can be dark. And winter can be wonderful. It's all in how you approach it.**

**One of the best ways we know to see the wonders of this most beautiful season is through good food and good friends—whether it be a festive buffet with an edible centerpiece, a luxurious holiday dinner or the gathering of friends to watch a bowl game, eat Italian or be warmed by the fire.**

## Food for the Soul

Weekends are the perfect time to prepare the unhurried foods of winter—sweet-potato and creamy broccoli soups, standing rib roasts and warm garlic spinach spread, cheesecakes and roasted vegetables, scampi risotto and warm Brie. This is when you can slow down to spend some leisurely time in the kitchen.

Fill your cupboards with foods that instantly add depth to any meal—canned tomatoes, rice, lentils, dried peas and beans, and pastas. Make rich, flavorful stocks for risottos and soups.

Bring on the desserts. They don't have to be complicated, just good. James Beard, the master of good food and taste, once expressed his fondness for a dessert that was nothing more than roasted bananas topped with butter, brown sugar, rum and vanilla ice cream.

## Layered Decorating Elegance

The multi-layered decorating approach that was started in autumn is continued, but now in a much grander fashion. We suggest embellishing nature's colorings with gold, bronze or silver.

Try metal leafing; it's easy. Inexpensive kits can be found in most craft shops, but be forewarned that once you get a taste for gilding, you may never want to stop. If gilding seems like too much work, there are also jars of rubbing gel in every color imaginable. While not as showy, they definitely are an easy way to lend a hint of elegance to evergreens, pinecones, nuts, vegetables, fruits and dried flowers. Just remember that whatever you gild or rub with color is no longer edible. For a festive look, nestle inexpensive tiny white lights among the decorations, and add that unexpected splash of color with gorgeous red poinsettias. (Costco brings in 10-inch poinsettias, two-gallon rosemary cones and 25-foot cedar garlands for the holiday season.)

Once the New Year's celebrations are over, remove all fall decorations and start with a clean slate. The goal is an elegant simplicity that fights the gloom of winter, which is why we suggest filling your home with vibrant blooming plants. (Costco's phalaenopsis and cymbidium orchids are breathtaking and available during this season.)

## Costco's Wonderful Winter Offerings

If winter doldrums has set in, why not take a trip to Costco, where you'll find a treasure chest of winter delights? While all products may not be available everywhere, be sure to look for:

Halibut

Hen Turkeys (smaller than Toms)

Standing Rib Roast

Rack of Pork

Navel Oranges

Northwest Pears

Chilean Grapes

Yams

Clementine Oranges

Tangerines

Mixed Nuts

Medjool Dates

Chestnuts

Japanese Mandarins

Korean Mandarins

Pummelos

Blood Oranges

Oso Sweet Onions

Persimmons

And, of course, mushrooms, salads, carrots, hothouse tomatoes, peppers, garlic and onions.

Costco's prepared foods include fresh stuffed salmon, meat loaf, flank steak with portobello mushroom, chicken enchiladas, manicotti with spinach or cheese, Take-N-Bake pizzas and rotisserie chicken.

Absolute essentials for cold winter nights are our seasonal fruit pies, cheesecakes, loaf breads, holiday cupcakes, fruit-cakes, holiday and Valentine candy, and dried-fruit trays.

# Savoring the Season with David

**David Andrew Costco Global Wine Director**

### Hearty, Spicy Reds and Some Heady Whites

As the mercury drops and the nights draw in, it's time for heartwarming reds: something rich and ripe, deep and dark, spicy and seductive, something to sip by the fire. It's also the best time to bring out those long-lived wines—Bordeaux, Barolo and anything else with the tannin and acidity to last for decades.

**Cabernet Sauvignon:** Bordeaux, although a blend, is the benchmark for Cabernet-based wines, especially in its top wines: the classified growths. These are not wines to be drunk young, and if you're lucky enough to taste a great one from an old vintage, you'll never forget it. Cabernets for more immediate drinking are made just about everywhere grapes will successfully ripen. Australia delivers rich, ripe, delicious Cabernets, often without the attack of tannins the grape is famous for. Chilean examples are a great value, and Californians, especially at the high end, can be very serious, indeed.

**Merlot:** It has more flesh and less muscle than Cabernet Sauvignon. Think plush red velvet.

**Syrah:** This is a personal favorite. From spicy and peppery in the northern Rhone to thick and lush from Australia (where it is known as Shiraz), Syrah never disappoints. Washington State and California also offer some good examples.

**Zinfandel:** A true California original, Zinfandel soaks up that warm state's sunshine all summer long and offers it up to us when we most need it: in the depths of winter. It should be spicy, with juicy blackberry fruit, lots of body and no shortage of alcohol. Après ski, anyone?

**Italians:** Big, muscular Brunello di Montalcino and lean, aristocratic Barolo make wonderful accompaniments to winter menus with meat or game.

**Pinotage:** A meaty, hearty wine from South Africa, this is a match for any stew.

**White Burgundy:** When it snows in Seattle, in my house we hunt down the oldest White Burgundy we can find, usually a Puligny-Montrachet. This is Chardonnay at its best— elegant and refined in youth, becoming rich, nutty and honeyed with age. Let it snow!

**Port:** These fortified wines from Portugal are wonderful winter warmers. Usually enjoyed at the end of a meal at any time of the year, they provide a warm welcome after winter activities in the cold outdoors.

**Champagne:** It's truly a wine for all seasons. Don't wait for a special occasion; Champagne delivers some of the best value imaginable. For around $20 a bottle, you can add a very special sparkle to any occasion.

# *Perfect Holiday Buffet*

*$\mathscr{W}$hile the weather outside may be frightful,* your holiday party will always be delightful if you keep in mind the three P's:

**Plan** foods that can be prepared ahead and appeal to both the nose and the taste buds.

**Proof** your party the day before. Walk down the street and then come back as if you were a guest. How does the front door look? Can the doorbell be heard from the kitchen? Where do the coats and umbrellas go?

**Present** at least one showstopper—our edible "flower" arrangement, for example.

Finally, don't forget the first rule of entertaining: Enjoy!

## MENU

## Sugar Foods Raspberry-Peach Sparkler

This festive rose-colored drink made with Sweet'N Low will be appreciated by everyone on the holiday buffet party circuit.

*2 cups boiling water*

*4 peach tea bags*

*4 cups bottled unsweetened raspberry juice blend*

*1/4 cup lemon juice*

*6 packets (or 2 teaspoons bulk) Sweet'N Low\**

*4 cups cold club soda*

In a large pitcher, pour the boiling water over the tea bags. Steep 10 minutes; remove tea bags and discard. Stir in the raspberry juice, lemon juice and Sweet'N Low. Refrigerate until well chilled. Just before serving, mix in the club soda. Makes 10 servings.

*\*Brands may vary by region; substitute a similar product.*

## Grace Baking Bruschetta

Grace bread is baked daily in Costco Bakeries.

*16 1/4-inch-thick slices Grace Baking Bread (Pugliese, potato rosemary or garlic)\**

*2 garlic cloves, cut in half*

*10 tablespoons olive oil*

*8 tomatoes, cut into cubes (or 2 pounds sliced mushrooms)*

*2 tablespoons chopped fresh garlic*

*Pinch of red pepper flakes*

*2 tablespoons chopped Italian parsley*

*6 tablespoons chopped fresh basil*

*Salt and pepper*

**1.** Toast or grill the bread. While warm, rub with garlic halves, and brush with 4 tablespoons olive oil.

**2.** Cook the tomatoes and chopped garlic in 6 tablespoons olive oil in a sauté pan over medium heat for about 5 minutes. Add red pepper flakes, parsley, 4 tablespoons basil, and salt and pepper to taste and remove from heat.

**3.** Place tomato mixture on bread slices. Sprinkle with basil and serve. Makes 12 servings.

*\*Brands may vary by region; substitute a similar product.*

### Spooning

*Another fun idea is to create "spoon hors d'oeuvres," filled with a tasty treat and presented on a tray. Guests select a filled spoon, just as they would a piece of cheese on a cracker.*

## Warm Spinach and Artichoke Dip with Carr's Crackers

Understated elegance is the message you'll send when you serve crispy, golden-baked Carr's crackers with dip.

*1 1/2 cups mayonnaise*

*1 12-ounce can or jar artichoke hearts, drained and slightly mashed*

*1 10-ounce box frozen spinach, thawed, chopped, drained and dried with paper towels*

*1 1/2 cups grated Parmesan cheese*

*Dash of hot sauce*

*1 package Carr's Table Water Crackers*

**1.** Preheat oven to 350°F.

**2.** Mix together mayonnaise, artichoke hearts, spinach, Parmesan cheese and hot sauce. Place in a small oval baking pan.

**3.** Bake approximately 10 minutes, or until slightly bubbly. Do not overbake, as the mayonnaise will separate.

**4.** Serve immediately with Carr's Table Water Crackers. Makes 12 servings.

**Costco Tip:** If you have any dip left over, refrigerate and within a day or two, smear it on a fillet of Costco salmon and bake or grill. You won't believe that something so easy could be so delicious.

## Swift Grilled Pork Loin Chops with Yams and Apples

Swift & Company traces its ancestry back to 1855, when 16-year-old Gustavus Franklin Swift used $20 he received from his father to buy his first head of livestock to start his meat-marketing business.

That modest beginning nearly 150 years ago was the forerunner of one of the largest meat processors in the nation, and Costco's main pork supplier. Fresh pork is an outstanding source of many vitamins and minerals, providing high-quality protein, vitamin $B_1$ (thiamine), $B_2$, $B_6$, $B_{12}$, iron and zinc. With its mild and versatile flavor, pork goes with everything.

Costco's Swift pork loin has been specially trimmed for more meat and less fat. This recipe suggestion of grilling the chops for quick flavor enhancement and then popping them into the oven offers a dish that's well suited for a buffet.

*12 Kirkland Signature/Swift boneless pork loin chops*

*Olive oil*

*Salt*

*White pepper*

*Granulated garlic*

*10 yams, peeled and cut into 1-inch chunks*

*4 red onions, cut into 1-inch chunks*

*8 Gala or other red apples, cored and cut in chunks*

*1 1/3 cups olive oil*

*2 teaspoons black pepper*

*1 cup brown sugar*

*2 bunches green onions, cut into 4-inch pieces*

*4 teaspoons cornstarch*

*Prepared mustard*

**1.** Preheat oven to 450°F. Preheat grill or start charcoal.

**2.** Rub chops with olive oil to coat. Sprinkle both sides with salt, white pepper and granulated garlic to taste.

**3.** Place chops on grill to achieve grill marks on both sides, approximately 2 minutes per side. Remove chops from grill and set aside.

**4.** Place yams, onions, apples, olive oil, 2 teaspoons salt, black pepper, brown sugar, green onions and cornstarch in roasting pan. Toss well to coat evenly and top with chops.

**5.** Place roasting pan in oven, lower heat to 425°F and roast for 30 minutes, or until chops reach an internal temperature of 160°F. Brush chops with mustard to taste. Makes 12 servings.

## Golden Russet/Atlantic Advantage/Pacific Pride
# Crab-Stuffed Potatoes

Crab is always an elegant touch.

6 large Western-grown Russet potatoes*
6 tablespoons butter
3/4 cup milk
5 finely chopped green onions
3/4 cup crabmeat
6 tablespoons sour cream
Paprika
Grated Cheddar cheese

Preheat oven to 400°F. Bake potatoes until tender. While still warm, cut potatoes in half lengthwise and gently scoop out pulp. Mash the pulp and add butter, milk, green onions, crab and sour cream. Fill the potato skins with the mixture. Sprinkle with paprika and cheese. Return to oven until cheese melts. Makes 12 servings.

**Costco Tip:** Potatoes are naturally high in vitamin C and potassium and are a good source of vitamin $B_6$ and dietary fiber.

*Brands may vary by region; substitute a similar product.*

## Gold-n-Soft Scalloped Corn

Corn is a classic, understated vegetable that imparts a natural sweetness to a dish.

2 eggs
16 ounces cream-style corn
16 ounces whole kernel corn, drained
1/2 cup Gregg's Gold-n-Soft margarine, melted
1 cup sour cream
1 8 1/2-ounce package corn muffin mix
1 cup shredded Cheddar cheese

Preheat oven to 350°F. Beat eggs in a medium-size bowl. Stir in corn, margarine and sour cream. Fold in muffin mix. Pour into a greased 9-by-13-inch pan. Sprinkle with cheese and bake 35 minutes, or until a toothpick inserted in the center comes out clean. Makes 12 servings.

## Tam Produce Stuffed
# California Tomatoes Mediterranean

Serve these beautiful tomatoes at room temperature.

8 large California tomatoes
1/2 cup sliced green onions
2 1/2 tablespoons lemon juice
1 tablespoon chopped fresh mint or 1 teaspoon dried mint
1 teaspoon finely chopped garlic
1 teaspoon salt
1/4 teaspoon pepper
1/3 cup olive oil
3 cups cooked rice
1/3 cup raisins, soaked in boiling water for 20 minutes and drained

Cut slice from stem ends of tomatoes. Scoop out center with spoon; reserve. Remove seeds and turn tomatoes cut side down on paper towel to drain. Meanwhile, seed and chop reserved centers. Combine with next 6 ingredients. Stir in oil, rice and raisins. Stuff tomatoes with rice mixture. Makes 8 servings.

## Nancy Stanton's Costco-Coded Supper Dish

We decided to have a little fun and test members' knowledge of our products by converting the ingredients of this Highland, Michigan, member's recipe into Costco item number code. We have no doubt that some of our dedicated Costco shoppers won't even have to visit a warehouse to decipher this cooking teaser.

12-15 small #83505

1/3 cup or more #22863 if available, otherwise any good-quality product

1 tablespoon butter

2 large #67245, chopped

1 each yellow, orange and red #60357, seeded and chopped

1/4 cup #433677

Dash of #848038

1 large bag #5685

1 cup crumbled blue cheese, or to taste

1/4 cup #23402

*(TESTED AND APPROVED)*

**1.** Place #83505 in boiling water and cook until just getting soft. Drain and return to burner until all water evaporates.

**2.** Heat a large skillet and add 3 tablespoons #22863 and butter. Add #67245 and #60357 to skillet and season with #433677 and #848038. Sauté, adding more #22863 if necessary. Cook 5-7 minutes.

**3.** Toss in 6 handfuls of #5685. Keep turning, adding a little more #22863 if sticking occurs.

**4.** Add #83505 to the skillet—make room for them by sliding #5685 mixture out of the way—so that #83505 touch the bottom of the pan and are seasoned with #22863 and bits from pan.

**5.** Now mix everything together in the pan. Add blue cheese to your liking. Turn off heat and leave on stove, covered, and the cheese will just melt into the mixture.

**6.** To serve, top with #23402. Makes 8 servings.

*The solution to this delicious recipe also is provided in this book; you'll just have to hunt for it!*

**Costco Member Nancy Stanton**

### Tips for Better Buffets

- Food preparations positioned at different levels add visual interest. Rather than using a glass container that could tip, we suggest making ledges on the table out of stacks of books and covering with cloth remnants, additional linen and even towels.

- To allow the guest to have one hand free, place plates at the beginning of a buffet and utensils and napkins at the end.

- If at all possible, create a bar and a dessert station away from the buffet table.

- The more room-temperature or cold foods, the better for the host and guests.

- To promote grazing, run easily accessible streams of nuts, candies or breads on the tablecloth from the centerpiece to the edges of the table.

- Rather than serve an entire fillet of salmon or beef, cut your entrée into serving portions, with sauce drizzled on top.

- If you have one dish that was a budget-buster, place it at the end of the buffet; most plates will be full by the time it's discovered.

- Stuff the bottom two-thirds of a bread basket with apples and then position numerous loaves of bread on top. Less bread will be needed, and the apples will be available if all the bread is eaten.

- Use only unscented candles near food.

- Fashion name cards for each dish. They answer the "What is it?" question and generate conversation.

## Fruitful Offerings

Costco offers members a wide range of fruits throughout the year. These helpful hints may come in handy.

### Berries

- Do not stem or wash berries until they are to be eaten.
- Keep refrigerated until served.
- When purchasing, smell the fruit first. You want a fruity aroma with no decay odor.
- Strawberries contain more vitamin C than oranges.
- Many berries will create their own syrup if they are sprinkled with a little sugar 30 minutes to an hour before serving time.

### Cherries

- Cherries should be firm and dark, with green stems.
- If there's a way, present cherries on a bed of crushed ice— decadently delicious.

### Grapes

- Grapes should be firm and consistent in size, with no browning at the stem attachment.

- Remove any spoiled grapes, as they will spread their decay to others.
- Refrigerate.
- Grape bags can hide poor grapes. To make sure grapes are still attached to the vines, hold the bag up and check for loose fruit.

### Melons

- Smell the fruit; there should be a slight aroma.
- Look for melons that have a smooth indentation where the stem was attached.
- Wash and brush any produce that grows on the ground with cool, fresh water before cutting.
- Plan ahead; it takes up to 12 hours to chill a watermelon.
- Watermelon seeds are edible. However, besides being a nuisance, they are high in fat. Costco's seedless watermelon variety is definitely the answer.
- Although cantaloupes do not continue to ripen once they are picked, they can at least get softer and juicier if left at room temperature for a few days.

## D'Arrigo Brothers
## Caesar Salad

California's D'Arrigo Brothers, with their full line of fresh vegetables, offer their favorite Caesar salad from the family kitchen.

4 cups thinly sliced
    Andy Boy Romaine Hearts*
3 cups halved cherry tomatoes
1 cup finely chopped green onions
1 cup thinly sliced fresh basil
2/3 cup fat-free Caesar dressing
1 cup chopped fresh parsley
8 ounces crumbled feta cheese
2 garlic cloves, minced

Combine ingredients in a large serving bowl. Toss well to coat. Serve and enjoy! Makes 8 servings.

**Costco Tip:** For a meal in itself, the family suggests adding 6 cups shredded cooked chicken breast and 6 cups cooked *penne* or *radiatore* pasta.

*Brands may vary by region; substitute a similar product.*

## Van Diermen Vanilla Cream Puffs
## with Caramel Sauce

You choose: four hours in the kitchen making your own cream puffs or 30 minutes thawing out Van Diermen's* glorious domes of pastry and cream. Drizzle this caramel sauce over 24 cream puffs.

1 1/2 cups sugar
1/2 cup water
3/4 cup light corn syrup
Pinch of salt
1 cup heavy cream
1 teaspoon vanilla extract

In a heavy saucepan simmer sugar, water, corn syrup and salt, stirring until sugar is dissolved. Boil over medium-high heat without stirring until mixture is caramel-colored (320-338°F). Remove from heat and add cream and vanilla, stirring until combined, about 1 minute. Cool to room temperature (sauce will thicken). Makes about 1 1/2 cups.

*Brands may vary by region; substitute a similar product.*

## Wilcox Family Farms Eggnog Cheesecake

It is thought that eggnog was originally a 17th-century punch made in England with milk, eggs and ale or wine that was given a new twist with the use of rum (grog) by American colonists. Over time, the popular wintertime egg grog became known as eggnog. Wilcox Farms reports that this eggnog dessert recipe is often requested.

2 1/2 cups graham cracker crumbs

1 1/2 cups sugar

2/3 cup melted butter

4 Wilcox eggs*

1/8 teaspoon salt

1 1/2 tablespoons lemon juice

1 1/2 teaspoons grated lemon rind

1 cup Wilcox eggnog*

1 1/2 pounds Wilcox cottage cheese*

4 tablespoons flour

1/4 cup chopped walnuts

**1.** Preheat oven to 350°F.

**2.** Combine graham cracker crumbs, 1/2 cup sugar and melted butter. Reserve 3/4 cup of mixture and press the remaining amount into a 9-inch springform pan.

**3.** Beat eggs with the remaining sugar until light; add salt, lemon juice, rind, eggnog, cottage cheese and flour. Beat thoroughly and strain through a sieve.

**4.** Pour into graham cracker crust; sprinkle with remaining crumbs and nuts.

**5.** Bake about 1 hour (until center is firm), turn off heat, open oven door and let stand in oven until cool. Makes 12 servings.

*Brands may vary by region; substitute a similar product.*

Costco Member
Prudy Smithson

## Prudy Smithson's Pineapple Cake with Coconut Frosting

"I am always asked for this recipe. It comes from a friend of mine, who got it from her grandmother many years ago," wrote this Bellingham, Washington, member.

1 1/2 cups sugar

2 cups flour

2 teaspoons baking soda

1/2 teaspoon salt

2 eggs

1 20-ounce can crushed pineapple with juice

**FROSTING:**

1 1/2 cups sugar

1/4 pound butter

1 5-ounce can evaporated milk

1 cup chopped walnuts

1 cup coconut

1 teaspoon vanilla extract

**1.** Preheat oven to 350°F.

**2.** Combine sugar, flour, baking soda and salt. Blend in eggs and pineapple. Pour into greased 9-by-13-inch pan and bake 30 minutes, or until toothpick inserted in center comes out clean.

**3.** To make frosting, combine sugar, butter and evaporated milk in a saucepan. Boil for 6 minutes. Stir in walnuts, coconut and vanilla. Pour over warm cake. Serve warm or at room temperature. Makes 12 servings.

*Y*our guests will halt in their tracks when they first see—and then eat—this showstopping centerpiece.

## Supplies

*1 brick green floral oasis foam*
*Oasis adhesive tape*
*Deep oval dish*
*40-60 12-inch wooden skewers*

## Ingredients

Depending on the season, most produce will be available at Costco and can be prepared one day early.

- **Broccoli and cauliflower florets:** Clean and break heads into small florets with 1-inch stems. Bag and refrigerate.
- **Radish florets:** Using a small paring knife, trim the ends and then cut short slashes around each radish. Place in refrigerated ice water to "bloom."
- **Asparagus spears:** Cut the top 3 to 4 inches off each asparagus stalk and blanch in hot water for up to 3 minutes, or until barely limp. Cool in ice water, drain, bag and refrigerate.
- **Red and yellow pepper flowers:** Cut peppers into 2- to 3-inch triangle-shaped fans. Using a knife, scallop the side of the pepper opposite the fan point. Bag and refrigerate.
- **Cherry tomatoes:** Clean.
- **Olives:** Select pitted olives of all colors and shapes. Drain brine. Bag and refrigerate.
- **Jicama flowers:** Peel and slice into 1/4-inch disks. Use a cookie-cutter to make a flat flower. Bag and refrigerate.
- **Cucumber flowers:** Same as jicama, except you can opt to only partially peel. Bag and refrigerate.
- **Carrot flowers:** Peel a carrot and then, starting about 2 inches from the top, make 4 evenly spaced vertical cuts in toward the center. The individual cuts should meet at the center of the carrot. Give a quick twist and break off. Repeat. Bag and refrigerate.

# Edible "Floral" Bouquet

By Pat Volchok,
Editorial Director

- **Button mushrooms:** Clean.
- **Green beans:** Follow asparagus instructions, increasing cooking time slightly.
- **Scallion flowers:** Cut off all but 2 inches of the green of each scallion. Trim and then slice the white root end numerous times. Put in refrigerated ice water to "bloom."
- **Turnip flowers:** Same as jicama. Bag and refrigerate.
- **Scallion greens:** Cut to same length as skewers.
- **Rosemary branches, parsley and kale leaves.**

### Directions

Prepare the flower container by positioning the floral oasis in the middle of the dish and securing with the oasis tape. If necessary, fill the rest of the container with small, clean rocks to act as ballast. Place on the buffet. Create stems by inserting a wooden skewer down through the center of a scallion green. Bag and refrigerate.

### Before the Party

Place one or more of the prepared "flower" vegetables onto the pointed end of each skewer stem. Stick the flat end of the skewer into the oasis container. Continue to create flowers until you have a beautiful bouquet of individual skewers. Stuff rosemary branches, parsley or kale in and around the oasis to cover. Serve with dipping sauces and toasted pita bread.

### Pat's Tips

- Make the centerpiece crazy and whimsical. For example, take a flat jicama flower and top it with an olive to make a "black-eyed" Susan, or punch 3 thin green beans through the flat face of a cucumber flower to resemble stamens.
- Be sure to provide a tray for used scallion skewers. ∾

*CARROT FLOWERS: Starting about 2 inches from the top, make 4 evenly spaced vertical cuts in toward the center. The individual cuts should meet at the center of the carrot. Give a quick twist and break off.*

*JICAMA FLOWERS: Peel and slice into 1/4-inch disks. Use a cookie-cutter to make a flat flower.*

*SCALLION STEMS: Create stems by inserting a wooden skewer down through the center of a scallion green.*

# Hanukkah: The Festival of Lights

*R*eligious, secular and ethnic celebrations abound during this season of the year. That's why we were so pleased when Costco member Gerry Worth sent us a collection of Hanukkah recipes that she and her friends have collected over the years.

Considered very much a family festival, Chanukah, or Hanukkah (both spellings are correct), commemorates an ancient Judaic victory and the miracle of oil lasting in the Temple not one but eight days. A nightly blessing and candle-lighting ceremony using a special candelabrum called a menorah is a highlight of the eight-day celebration, as well as games, songs, gifts and foods prepared from recipes handed down through the generations.

It is traditional to eat items fried in oil such as potato latkes (potato pancakes) and deep-fried jelly doughnuts, called *sufganiot*.

Gerry enjoys celebrating Hanukkah with her three children, five grandchildren and many friends. She loves to travel, is very active in the Jewish community and volunteers at the Manchester airport. All this and she still finds time to cook and shop at Costco!

Costco thanks Gerry and her friends for sharing some of their cherished traditional recipes.

Costco Member
Gerry Worth

## Frankie Shapiro's Chopped Herring

*Hanukkah would not be complete without this Londonderry, New Hampshire, Costco member's recipe.*

4 hard-cooked eggs

1 medium onion

1 good hard sweet apple, cored, peeled and cut in chunks

1 32-ounce jar Vita Herring or another brand, drained and liquid reserved

**1.** Use a hand grinder or a food processor to grind eggs, onion, apple and herring to a moderately chunky consistency. Mix well and taste. If too tart, add a little sugar. If too dry, add herring liquid. Make a day or two ahead to allow ingredients to blend.

**2.** Serve with crackers or black or rye bread. Garnish with chopped egg. Makes 8-12 servings.

## Bernice Kesslen's Sour Cream Pancakes

This Manchester, New Hampshire, Costco member got this recipe from her aunt, who served it on Sundays during Hanukkah. Well-seasoned pans make the pancakes taste even better.

$1/2$ pound small-curd cottage cheese

$1/2$ cup sour cream

3 eggs, beaten

$1/2$ teaspoon salt

1 tablespoon sugar

$3/4$ cup all-purpose sifted flour blended with $1/8$ teaspoon baking powder

2 tablespoons butter

**1.** Beat cottage cheese and sour cream until well blended. Add beaten eggs and then dry ingredients and beat until smooth. If batter is too stiff, add 1-2 tablespoons of milk.

**2.** Melt 1 tablespoon of butter in frying pan on medium-high heat. Drop tablespoonfuls of batter into hot pan. Cook until golden brown on each side. Use more butter if needed.

**3.** Serve with applesauce. Makes 6 servings.

## Charles Shapiro's Spicy Potato Pancakes

Hot sauce adds some zip to these latkes. The recipe was contributed by another member from Londonderry, New Hampshire, who of course is a friend of Gerry's.

6 russet potatoes, peeled

1 large or 2 small onions

$1/4$ cup matzo meal

2 eggs

1 teaspoon salt

Dash of pepper, 3-4 shakes

4-6 drops hot sauce

3-4 shakes Worcestershire sauce

Oil, chicken fat or both

**1.** Grate potatoes by hand or use processor (fine). Drain if need be.

**2.** Grate onion fine.

**3.** Put potatoes and onion in a bowl. Add matzo meal, eggs, salt, pepper, hot sauce and Worcestershire sauce (all seasonings are to taste). Mix well, making sure there are no lumps.

**4.** Drop mixture by tablespoonful onto a greased hot skillet. Brown over medium heat on both sides. Drain on paper towels.

**5.** Serve with sour cream and applesauce. Makes 30-40 latkes.

## Gerry Worth's Chopped Liver

2-3 large onions, chopped
Oil or chicken fat
1 pound chicken livers
2-3 hard-boiled eggs

**1.** Sauté onions in oil over medium heat until brown. Remove onions and add chicken livers to pan. Sauté until slightly pink in the center. Save the oil in the pan.

**2.** Chop onions and livers in chopping bowl or blender. Chop in eggs. The texture should be between chunky and smooth. Add oil saved from pan while chopping the mixture to keep it moist. Additional oil and salt can be added to taste.

**3.** Chill. Garnish with chopped egg and serve with crackers or on toast. Makes 8 servings.

## Elisa Harris' Hanukkah Noodle Pudding

Our testers raved about this New York City Costco member's noodle dish. In fact, seconds were had by all.

8-ounce package egg noodles
1/4 pound unsalted butter
2 eggs, separated
1 teaspoon vanilla extract
8 ounces sour cream
8 ounces cottage cheese
Pinch salt
1 tablespoon lemon juice
1/4 cup sugar
1 8-ounce can crushed pineapple in its own juice, drained
Raisins (optional)
TOPPING
2 cups frosted or plain corn flakes
3-4 tablespoons unsalted butter, melted
Cinnamon

**1.** Preheat oven to 350°F.

**2.** Boil egg noodles according to package directions. Drain. Immediately add butter to noodles so that butter melts.

**3.** Add 2 egg yolks, vanilla, sour cream, cottage cheese, salt, lemon juice, sugar, pineapple and raisins. Beat egg whites. Fold into noodle mixture.

**4.** To make topping, put cereal into a plastic bag. Pour butter over cereal. Add cinnamon and crunch plastic bag to crumble cereal. If using plain corn flakes, add 2-3 tablespoons sugar.

**5.** Grease an 8-inch square baking pan. Pour in noodle mixture. Sprinkle cereal over top. Bake 50-60 minutes, or until done. Makes 8-12 servings.

## Pearl Molmed's Beer Brisket

This longtime friend of Gerry's lives in Manchester, New Hampshire, and has graciously shared her brisket recipe.

10- to 12-pound beef brisket
Garlic powder
2 12-ounce cans beer
2 bottles chili sauce
1 packet of onion soup mix
2 large onions, sliced

**1.** Preheat oven to 350°F.

**2.** Sprinkle the brisket with garlic powder to taste. Place brisket in a roasting pan.

**3.** Mix beer, chili sauce and onion soup mix. Pour over brisket. Strew sliced onions around brisket.

**4.** Cover with foil and bake until tender. Check after 3 hours. Continue cooking until done. It serves a crowd.

*Elegant Christmas Dinner*

*It's true that the simple pleasures of life* bring the greatest joy, but every once in a while it feels oh so good to pamper and be pampered in return. What better occasion than Christmas dinner to give and receive extra-special treatment?

Indulge in fine wines and cheeses, velvety soups, seafood and meat specialties, hearty winter vegetables and delicious desserts.

Spoil with gorgeous decorations, a formal dining table, personalized place cards and treats, mutual toasts, a roaring fire, traditional music and extraordinary party favors.

Let your guests know they are the most precious gift in the world.

## Kirkland Signature Pine Nuts

*Many people think of pine nuts as only as ingredient in pesto sauce or a topping for a salad, so we thought you might appreciate a few additional ideas.*

### Claudia Dossat's Pine Nut Brie Nibble

This Las Vegas member says, "This recipe for pine nut Brie dip is a favorite for everyone in my family."

*1 round loaf of bread (we like sourdough)*

*1 stick butter, melted*

*One round of baby Brie*

*3 cloves garlic, chopped, or 1 teaspoon from a jar of chopped or minced garlic*

*1/3 cup chopped sun-dried tomatoes*

*1/3 cup Kirkland Signature pine nuts, plus more for garnish*

*1/2 cup chopped fresh basil*

**1.** Preheat oven to 350°F.

**2.** Hollow out the bread round, reserving the top and insides.

**3.** Spread half of the butter in the hollowed-out round.

**4.** Remove the rind and chop the Brie into pieces. Layer the Brie, garlic, sun-dried tomatoes, 1/3 cup pine nuts and basil in the bread shell. Pour the remaining melted butter over the top and sprinkle with additional pine nuts.

**5.** Bake 30 minutes, or until the filling is thoroughly melted.

**6.** Use the reserved bread pieces to dip into the mixture. When all the cheese is gone, slice the bread bowl into sections and eat. This is the best part!

**Costco Tip:** Shelf life for pine nuts is 1 year. For optimum freshness, store in a sealed container in the refrigerator.

### Mike Sanchez's Buffalo Pine Nuts

Mike, a Costco food-safety trainer, says these are good at any time of year.

*1 cup Kirkland Signature pine nuts*

*3 tablespoons canola oil*

*4 tablespoons Buffalo wing seasoning*

**1.** Preheat oven to 300°F.

**2.** Toast pine nuts in a skillet over medium heat until aromatic.

**3.** Place nuts in a bowl with oil and stir to coat. Sprinkle in half the seasoning and toss. Add remaining seasoning, coating the nuts completely.

**4.** Spread nuts evenly on a lined cookie sheet and bake 15-20 minutes, or until lightly toasted. Toss every 5 minutes, keeping nuts in an even layer. Remove from oven, spread nuts on another cookie sheet and let air-dry.

### Carmina Tapia's Cinnamon-Sugared Pine Nuts

Carmina also uses these nuts for her buñuelos (see page 87).

*1/2-3/4 teaspoon cinnamon*

*1/2 cup sugar*

*1 cup Kirkland Signature pine nuts*

*2 tablespoons white corn syrup*

Combine cinnamon and sugar. Put pine nuts in a bowl and drizzle with corn syrup. Toss with cinnamon sugar until coated. Spread on a cookie sheet to air-dry.

## Royale Spinach Salad

The combination of protein-rich bacon and spinach, a good source of iron and vitamins A and C, might be just the power boost needed during the hectic holidays.

*1/2 cup sugar*

*1 cup safflower oil*

*1 teaspoon dry mustard*

*1 teaspoon salt*

*1/2 cup vinegar*

*1 teaspoon celery seed*

*4 generous bunches spinach, washed, drained, stems removed*

*2 red onions, sliced thin*

*12 slices Royale bacon, cut in 2-inch pieces and fried until crisp\**

*1/2 cup walnut halves*

*4 tomatoes, sliced*

*1/2 cup grated Romano cheese*

Combine sugar, oil, mustard and salt. Add vinegar and celery seed; shake or beat well. Chill. Combine spinach, onions, bacon and walnuts. Pour chilled dressing to taste over salad and toss until well coated. Arrange tomatoes on top. Chill well and sprinkle with cheese before serving. Makes 12 servings.

*\*Brands may vary by region; substitute a similar product.*

**Costco Member Peggy Alexander**

FROM THE MEMBER'S KITCHEN

## Peggy Alexander's Sweet Potato Jalapeño Soup with Lime Cream

This Scottsdale, Arizona, member wrote that her soup is absolutely delicious, very Southwest and tasty, and we have to agree. It *is* all of the above and scored a perfect 10 from our Costco testers.

*8 sweet potatoes*

*2 cups diced red onion*

*4 tablespoons unsalted butter*

*8 cups chicken stock*

*3-4 fresh jalapeño peppers, seeded and minced, or to taste*

*1 pinch salt, or to taste*

*2 teaspoons ground black pepper*

*8 sprigs cilantro*

*LIME CREAM*

*4 limes*

*1 cup sour cream*

**1.** Cook sweet potatoes, whole and unpeeled, covered in salted water, about 1 hour, or until tender. Drain, cool and peel.

**2.** Prepare lime cream: Stir the juice and grated peel of limes into sour cream to attain a pourable consistency. Refrigerate until ready to use.

**3.** In small skillet, sauté onion in butter until soft. Purée potatoes, onion and 1 cup of stock in a blender or food processor, adding more stock if necessary.

**4.** Place in a saucepan. Add remaining stock, jalapeños and salt and pepper. Cover and simmer over low heat about 30 minutes, stirring occasionally.

**5.** Ladle into bowls. Swirl a spoonful of the lime cream into each bowl. Garnish with cilantro. Makes 8 servings.

Costco Member
Carol Bigham-Perez

## Global Fishing Red King Crab Legs

Called the King for good reason, genus *Paralithoides* is indeed a very large crab, with records noting 10-foot extensions from claw to claw and weights of up to 25 pounds.

The crabs, sometimes known as Alaskan king crab, are harvested in the icy waters from Alaska to Japan and are immediately frozen to retain flavor and freshness. The large pieces of white meat tinged with red found in the spiny legs are very popular, as are the enormous claws.

Low in fat and calories and an excellent source of protein, this king of crabs is available year-round, especially through Costco's seafood roadshows.

*GLOBAL FISHING RED KING CRAB STEAMING SUGGESTION:* Put 2 inches of water in a large covered roasting pan and bring to a boil. Place the crab on a rack in the pan so it is not touching water. Cover and steam for 10 minutes if crab is defrosted and 15 minutes if frozen. Serve with drawn (clarified) butter.

*FROM THE MEMBER'S KITCHEN*

## Carol Bigham-Perez's Global Fishing Red King Crab Legs

Costco member Carol Bigham-Perez of Tacoma, Washington, says, "It wouldn't be a celebration or holiday at our house without Costco's king crab legs."

Preheat broiler. Partially defrost cooked king crab legs and use a small kitchen knife to cut a strip along the length of the legs about 3/4 inch wide and 4 inches long. Place legs on a foil-lined cookie sheet. Spoon a small amount of the sauce on the openings cut in the shells. Broil the crab legs 2-3 minutes, or until just heated and slightly browned on top. Serve with more sauce on the side.

*RED KING CRAB LEG SAUCE*
*1/2 stick unsalted butter, melted*
*2 tablespoons red wine vinegar*
*1 bay leaf*
*1 tablespoon lemon juice*
*2 pinches cayenne pepper*

Combine all ingredients. Makes enough for 12 legs.

### Carol's Tips:

*"I use the little ceramic pots over candles on a stand to keep the sauce warm. Be sure to supply cocktail forks to pull the crab out."*

### Costco Tip:

*Costco's red king crab legs have already been cooked, so a quick warming is all that's required. Additional broiling will toughen the meat and ruin the flavor.*

## Premio Italian Sausage and Potato Medley

Premio Sausage Company, founded by a family from Naples, Italy, uses secret recipes passed down through the generations to create their quality-cut pork sausages. This medley of roasted sausage, potatoes and onions is *fantastico*.

1/3 cup olive oil

4 Idaho baking potatoes, peeled and cut in chunks

8 Premio sweet (mild) Italian sausages,
    split in half lengthwise*

3 cups onions cut in 1/2-inch dice

Salt and freshly ground black pepper

3 ounces balsamic vinegar

1 cup grain or deli mustard

6 tablespoons fresh rosemary or 2 tablespoons dried

1/2 cup seasoned dry bread crumbs

**1.** Preheat oven to 375°F.

**2.** In a large, shallow ovenproof casserole or roasting pan, heat olive oil over medium heat. Add potatoes and coat well with oil. Add sausages and onions, and season to taste with salt and pepper. Bake 20 minutes.

**3.** Combine vinegar, mustard and rosemary and pour over contents of pan until coated. If the sausages and potatoes are cooked at this point, sprinkle with bread crumbs and return to the oven at 400°F to brown. If sausages and potatoes are not cooked, return to the oven to finish cooking, then sprinkle with bread crumbs and brown at 400°F. Makes 8 servings.

*Brands may vary by region; substitute a similar product.*

This is the time to pull out all the stops by adding elegant and rich metal leaf to natural decorations and strands of festive beads to mantel, door, stairway and table décor. Accent with fresh holiday greens, red, green and white berries and flowers, candles and perhaps a wreath or two partially placed under a dining centerpiece. It is a nice tie-in to suspend a wreath by festive ribbon from the table's chandelier, like a halo. If there is room, wreaths make stunning individual plate chargers as well.

For very lovely and personalized place cards, gild and then open one walnut per person; remove and discard the meat. Make a narrow roll of paper to fit the width of each shell. Add a personal note at one end of the paper tail and the person's name at the other. Roll up starting at the message end, place in a shell, and carefully unroll the paper until the guest's name is visible and hanging outside the shell. Dot the shell's edge sparingly with glue and reattach to the other half. Secure each with a rubber band for 24 hours, then remove the band and put a personalized name card at each person's place.

## Swift Standing Rib Beef Roast with Harvest Vegetables

Here it is, the crowning touch to a glorious dinner. And no one but the cook will know that it was probably the easiest part of the entire meal!

12- to 14-pound Kirkland Signature/Swift
    standing rib beef roast

25 garlic cloves, peeled

2 teaspoons kosher salt

2 teaspoons coarsely ground black pepper

2 cups red wine

1 teaspoon sugar

5 pounds carrots, peeled

3 pounds red-skinned potatoes, unpeeled

1 pound pearl onions, peeled

**1.** Preheat oven to 450°F.

**2.** Using a sharp paring knife, very carefully cut diagonal slices through the fat covering the roast at 1-inch intervals, 1/2 inch deep, leaving a diamond pattern across the top. Insert garlic cloves into the cuts, spacing evenly. Don't worry, 25 cloves will not overwhelm the roast—it will taste wonderful!

**3.** Season the meat with salt and pepper and place in large roasting pan. Roast for 20 minutes, then lower oven temperature to 215°F for the remainder of the cooking time.

**4.** Add wine, sugar, carrots, potatoes and pearl onions to roasting pan.

**5.** Roast for an additional 2 1/2 hours for a medium-rare roast. Add 1/2 hour for medium.

**6.** Turn off the oven and let the roast sit for 20 minutes without opening the oven door. This will give the meat a chance to relax and redistribute the juices.

**7.** Remove from oven. Slice and enjoy! Makes 12-14 servings.

*Recipe courtesy of Chef Forrest D. Waldo II, C.E.C. Corporate Executive Chef, Retail Foods.*

## Washington State Mashed Potatoes with Roasted Garlic

Valley Pride, Skagit Valley's Best and Wallace Farms of Washington State offer this superb mashed potato recipe made with high-solid, low-sugar spuds.

2 whole medium
    heads garlic

4 pounds Washington
    red or white potatoes,
    peeled and quartered

1/2 cup milk

1/4 cup mayonnaise

2 tablespoons butter
    or margarine

1 teaspoon salt

1/2 teaspoon ground
    white pepper

Preheat oven to 375°F. Bake garlic 45 minutes. Cut top 1/2 inch off heads, squeeze to remove pulp and mash. Boil potatoes about 30 minutes, or until tender. Drain well. In a mixing bowl, combine hot potatoes, milk, mayonnaise, butter, salt and pepper. Whip at low speed just until smooth. Add garlic and mix well. Makes 12 servings.

## Kevin Riordan's Herb-Inlaid Potatoes

1-2 8-ounce Washington russet potatoes
Italian parsley leaves
Vegetable oil
Salt and ground white pepper

Slice potatoes lengthwise paper-thin* and place on a cookie sheet. Place a parsley leaf in the center of a slice. Lay another slice of potato on top and press slices together to seal edges. Edges should be free of any parsley. Slices should be thin enough that the parsley leaf shows through. Fry potatoes in oil to cover (300°F) until crisp in the center. Drain on plate or tray lined with paper towels. Season to taste with salt and pepper. Store at room temperature. Makes about 18 pieces.

**\*Costco Tip:** For best results, use a mandolin (slicer).

*Kevin Riordan, executive chef at the Brooklyn Seafood, Steak and Oyster House in Seattle, was kind enough to share a wonderful potato treat that's perfect for this elegant dinner. It can be used as either a garnish for the standing rib beef roast or a showstopping appetizer when sprinkled with salt and pepper.*

*Celebrity CHEF* KEVIN RIORDAN

**Herb-Inlaid Potatoes**

**Mashed Potatoes with Roasted Garlic**

## Carmina Tapia's Cinnamon Pine Nut Buñuelos

Mexican fried cookies, called *buñuelos*, are a traditional Christmas treat. We thank this Madera, California, member for suggesting such a delightful grand finale to our traditional Christmas dinner.

*2 cups flour*

*¹/₄ teaspoon baking powder*

*¹/₄ cup shortening*

*Up to 1 cup hot water*

*¹/₃ cup cooking oil*

*1 cup sugar*

*4-5 teaspoons cinnamon*

*1 cup Cinnamon-Sugared Pine Nuts (see recipe, page 82)*

*¹/₄ cup light corn syrup*

**1.** Mix flour and baking powder in a large bowl. Rub in the shortening with fingertips until blended. Stir in water gradually, mixing until dough cleans sides of bowl and forms a ball. Knead dough on a lightly floured surface about 5 minutes, or until smooth.

**2.** Shape dough into a 12-inch roll. Cut into 12 slices and shape each slice into smooth ball. Cover with a damp towel and let rest 15 minutes.

**3.** Flatten each ball into a 4- to 5-inch circle on a floured surface. Roll from center toward edge, turning one-quarter turn at a time, until tortilla measures about 9 inches in diameter. Place tortilla between damp towels to prevent it from drying out.

**4.** Heat about ¹/₄ inch oil over medium-high heat in a medium skillet. Or use a deep-fat fryer at 375°F.

**5.** While the oil heats, mix the sugar and cinnamon and spread half of the mixture on a plate.

**6.** When the oil is hot, carefully place a tortilla in the pan. Cook until golden brown on both sides. Drain off excess oil on paper towels, dip the tortilla in the cinnamon sugar and let cool. Replenish cinnamon sugar on plate as needed.

**7.** Place the sugared tortilla on a plate. Top with a couple spoonfuls of Cinnamon-Sugared Pine Nuts. Then drizzle with corn syrup. Top with another sugared tortilla. Repeat the process. Serve warm, cut in wedges, or store airtight. Makes 16 servings.

**Costco Member Carmina Tapia**

## Camelot Desserts Chocolate Mousse Puffs Ganache

Chocolate Mousse Puffs* are a great treat anytime. Just remove them from the freezer and serve. For a simple garnish, dust them with powdered sugar. To make a gourmet treasure, drizzle with chocolate ganache.

*1 cup heavy whipping cream*

*1 pound semisweet,*
*bittersweet or white chocolate, chopped*

Bring cream to a boil over medium heat. Remove from heat, add chocolate and stir until melted and smooth. Drizzle over the puffs with a fork or spoon, letting it drip down the sides. Makes 12-24 servings.

*\*Brands may vary by region;*
*substitute a similar product.*

# Après Theater

*fter the hectic pace of the holidays, a night at the theater, where nothing more is demanded than to sit back and enjoy, can be a welcome winter relief. When entertaining after (après) the play, why not continue this relaxed atmosphere? A simple, made-ahead meal is the perfect ticket.

While dining at a table may be customary, we suggest eating casually and slowly in front of the fireplace. Prepare delicious hors d'oeuvres to stave off hunger pains while the meal cooks. Dessert is a must, as is a warm, soothing drink.

Flowers should be uncomplicated. A gorgeous blooming orchid plant or one lovely bouquet in a casual vase is perfect.

An unhurried and carefree evening in the middle of winter—now that's a night to applaud.

### M E N U

## Inhee Hwang's Shrimp Appetizer

This Palo Alto, California, member reports, "The taste of the crispy cucumbers and the soft shrimp make this recipe delightful. All ingredients can be purchased at Costco."

1 pound cooked shrimp

3 tablespoons extra-virgin olive oil

2 tablespoons vinegar or lemon juice

1 1/2 teaspoons French-style mustard

1 tablespoon diced red bell pepper

1 teaspoon chopped shallot

1 teaspoon chopped garlic

1 teaspoon chopped scallion

1 tablespoon chopped parsley

1/4 teaspoon salt

1/4 teaspoon sugar

1/8 teaspoon ground black pepper

1/2 cup thin half-moon slices of long English cucumber

**1.** Place shrimp in a bowl and pour in olive oil.

**2.** Add all remaining ingredients except cucumbers to the bowl. Mix well.

**3.** Place the cucumber slices in the bowl. Mix again.

**4.** Serve chilled. Makes 6 servings.

Costco Member
Inhee Hwang

Costco Member
Vivian Nishimoto

## Vivian Nishimoto's Steak Lettuce Roll

This Honolulu member reports that she cooks by looking, not tasting.

2 1/2 pounds tri-tip steak

2 cloves garlic, crushed

1 tablespoon grated fresh ginger

1/4 cup dry sherry

Iceberg lettuce leaves

1/2 cup hoisin sauce, teriyaki sauce or sweet & sour sauce

**1.** Poke the tri-tip with a carving fork or pound with a meat tenderizer so marinade can penetrate.

**2.** Combine garlic, ginger and sherry; rub on all sides of the steak and refrigerate overnight.

**3.** Grill over indirect medium-high heat until medium-rare.

**4.** Slice into 1/4-inch pieces. Place in iceberg lettuce leaves and top with hoisin sauce. Roll and eat with fingers. Easily feeds 6, with lots of leftovers.

## Aidells Chicken and Sausage Potpie

Assemble this hearty main dish ahead of time and refrigerate. Just turn on the oven the moment you walk in the door and bake the pie while you serve hors d'oeuvres.

1/4 cup butter

2 onions, chopped

1/4 cup all-purpose flour

4 cups chicken stock

8 ounces asparagus tips

8 ounces sliced green beans

8 ounces diced carrots

8 ounces button mushrooms, sliced

4 cups cooked chicken chunks

1 tablespoon finely chopped fresh tarragon or parsley

Salt and freshly ground black pepper

4 links Aidells Sausage (we recommend Chicken Apple Sausage, or Habanero & Green Chile Sausage for a spicier version)

2 unbaked refrigerated piecrusts or 1 14-ounce package frozen puff pastry, thawed

**1.** Preheat oven to 425°F.

**2.** In a saucepan over medium-high heat, melt the butter and sauté the onions until translucent, about 3 minutes. Add the flour and cook, stirring, 3-4 minutes. Whisk in the stock and simmer, stirring occasionally, until thickened, about 4-5 minutes. Add vegetables, chicken and tarragon or parsley. Season to taste with salt and pepper.

**3.** In a skillet over medium heat, sauté the sausages until lightly browned, about 5 minutes. Let cool, then cut into 1/2-inch slices. Add to the filling, then divide the mixture between 2 deep-dish pie plates or 8 individual heatproof bowls.

**4.** Roll and trim dough to about 1 inch larger than your pie plates (roll and cut out 8 circles of dough if using individual bowls). Transfer to the baking dishes or bowls, fold the excess edges under and crimp, sealing the crust over the dish. Cut a few steam vents in the crust.

**5.** Bake 25-30 minutes, or until the crust is golden brown. Allow to cool 10 minutes before serving. Makes 8 servings.

**Note:** Aidells sausage is made without binders, fillers or MSG.

## Microwave Magic

Microwaves revolutionized food preparation. Here are just a few suggestions.

- Select foods that are naturally high in moisture such as vegetables, fruit, poultry and fish.
- Use round plates for better distribution.
- Lemons: To release more juice, cook them for 30 seconds.
- Garlic cloves: Skins will slide right off if cooked for 30 seconds.
- Crystallized honey: A quick warm-up will return it to normal.
- Small amounts of food or sauces left in glass jars will come out quickly if heated 10 to 20 seconds at full power.
- Vegetables: Wash and while still slightly damp, add the juice of half a lemon and 1 teaspoon olive oil, seal in a plastic bag and cook for 1 to 2 minutes.
- To dry herbs, lay them in a single layer on a paper towel and cook for 2 to 3 minutes.

## Naumes Bosc Pear Sauté

Naumes Bosc pears are golden brown, aromatic, spicy, sweet long-necked pears that do not change color when ripe. An excellent choice for eating fresh out of hand or in salads, they are also good baked, broiled and poached, as they hold their shape well.

*¹/₂ cup margarine*

*¹/₂ cup packed brown sugar*

*3 tablespoons soy sauce*

*4 Naumes Bosc pears, cored, sliced, unpeeled*

Combine margarine, brown sugar and soy sauce in a skillet. Cook over medium heat to blend. Add pears. Sauté until tender and juice is reduced to caramelized sauce. Serve with pork or chicken, or as a side dish. Makes 6 servings.

**Costco Tip:** Bosc pears are generally considered ripe when they yield slightly to gentle pressure near the base of the stem.

## Crisp & Golden Potatoes à la **Finlandia Swiss**

In Finland this is called Rösti. Swiss cheese is the basic ingredient, but blue cheese can be used to give extra aroma. Make this dish a team effort. Earlier in the day, prepare stations for grating, forming and cooking the potatoes. Also chop the onion, crush the garlic, slice the Swiss cheese into thin strips, crumble the blue cheese and wash the potatoes. When everyone arrives after the theater, have one person grate the potatoes, another form the patties and someone else cook. This leaves you free to reheat the potpie, toss a salad and serve the cheese dip.

*6 large potatoes*

*4 ounces Finlandia Swiss cheese*

*1 large onion, chopped*

*Butter*

*Salt*

*2-4 garlic cloves, crushed*

*1-2 ounces blue cheese*

Grate potatoes and Swiss cheese separately with food processor. Mix potatoes and onion, and panfry slowly in butter until light brown. Add salt to taste. Blend in grated Swiss cheese and crushed garlic. Mix ingredients well. Using a spatula, form into 1 large or 4 small patties. Continue frying patties over low heat on both sides until golden brown. You can use a lid or a plate to help with the turning. Garnish the patties with blue cheese crumbles and fry until they start to melt. Serve immediately with green salad. Makes 4 main-course servings or up to 8 as an accompaniment.

**Costco Tip:** Rösti can be served as a starter, a small main course or a side dish.

## Dole Orange-Asparagus Salad with Raspberry Vinaigrette

Dole is the world's largest producer and marketer of high-quality fresh fruit, fresh vegetables and fresh-cut flowers and markets a growing line of packaged foods. The company does business in more than 90 countries and employs approximately 59,000 people worldwide.

1 pound extra-large or jumbo Dole Fresh Asparagus, trimmed and cut into 1-inch pieces

1 package (5-12 ounces) Dole Spring Mix, European Salad Blends, or any other variety

1/2 cup thinly sliced red onion

1 15-ounce can Dole Mandarin Oranges, drained

1/2 cup bottled raspberry dressing

**1.** Steam asparagus 4-6 minutes, or until crisp-tender. Rinse in cool water; drain well and set aside.

**2.** In a large serving bowl, combine salad blend, asparagus, onion and mandarin oranges. Pour dressing over salad and toss to evenly coat. Serve immediately. Makes 6 servings.

## Boskovich Farms Warm Spinach Salad

Here's a warm salad for a cold night.

8 slices bacon

4 teaspoons sugar

1/4 cup cider vinegar

1/4 cup water

1 teaspoon salt

2 pounds Boskovich Farms Fresh 'N' Quick spinach*

1 cup restaurant-style croutons

Place bacon in a large, deep skillet and cook until brown. Crumble and set aside. Pour off all but 2 tablespoons of bacon fat from skillet. Stir in sugar, vinegar, water and salt. Pour warm dressing and bacon over spinach and toss. Top with croutons. Serve warm. Makes 6-8 servings.

*Brands may vary by region; substitute a similar product.

### Elevate the Ordinary to Extraordinary

- Add fresh tomatoes or sun-dried tomatoes to a packaged marinara sauce.
- Puree a little fresh basil and add it to prepared pesto.
- Enhance canned soups with fresh vegetables.
- Top dishes with real shredded Parmesan cheese.
- Change the flavor of a mayonnaise-based salad by adding curry.
- Liven up old fruit by combining with the juice of half a lemon or lime.
- Puree fruits or herbs and add to bottled dressing.
- Use the marinade from marinated artichoke hearts as the foundation of a salad dressing.
- Top salads with nuts, crispy noodles, croutons, canned onion rings, fruits or soft white cheeses.

## Jean-Yves Mocquet's Gewürztraminer Parfait

Our own Costco Wholesale bakery buyer and French pastry chef shyly dropped off this recipe one day. We can only begin to wonder what other fabulous recipes he must possess.

*Strawberries, hulled and sliced*

*Kiwi, peeled and sliced*

*Mangoes, pears, mandarin oranges and pineapple, peeled, sliced and diced*

*Blueberries, raspberries and grapes*

*4 cups Gewürztraminer*

*3 egg yolks*

*1 cup sugar*

*1 1/2 cups whole milk*

*1 package unflavored gelatin*

*1 teaspoon vanilla extract*

*3 cups heavy cream, whipped*

**1.** Blend your own combination of fruit to equal 6 cups, combine with 2 cups of the Gewürztraminer in a bowl and chill.

**2.** Beat egg yolks and sugar with a wire whip several minutes until thick and pale yellow. Scald milk (do not boil) and gradually whisk into eggs in a thin stream. Return to saucepan and cook over moderate heat, stirring slowly with a wooden spoon, 4-5 minutes, or until sauce thickens enough to film spoon with a creamy layer. Add gelatin, vanilla and 2 cups Gewürztraminer, mix well with wire whip and chill.

**3.** When cream is cold, slowly add whipped cream with a wire whip until the texture is creamy.

**4.** To finish the presentation, place a layer of mousse in the bottom of a stemmed glass. Add a layer of soaked fruits and a layer of mousse. Repeat steps until glass is full. Place some soaked fruits on top and garnish with mint leaves. Refrigerate for 2 hours before serving. *Bon appétit.* Makes 6 servings.

*Costco Employee*
*Jean-Yves Mocquet*

## Dole Fruity Tulip Chocolate Shells

*1 1/3 cups semisweet chocolate chips*

*1/4 cup butter*

*1 8-ounce package light cream cheese, softened*

*1/4 cup butterscotch sauce*

*1 Dole Banana, sliced*

*2 cups assorted cut-up Dole Fruit such as canned or fresh Pineapple Chunks, Red or Green Grapes, Cantaloupe or Honeydew Melon*

**1.** Melt chocolate with butter in a small saucepan. Place 8 paper or foil baking-cup liners in muffin cups. Spread 3 tablespoons chocolate on bottom and up sides of each liner with back of spoon. Chill 1 hour.

**2.** Beat cream cheese and butterscotch sauce until smooth; refrigerate.

**3.** Remove chocolate shells and sauce from refrigerator. Let stand a few minutes. Carefully remove liners from chocolate shells. Arrange banana slices in bottom of shells.

**4.** Spoon cream cheese mixture into chocolate shells. Arrange favorite fruit combination on top. Makes 8 servings.

# Hot Drinks... the Costco Way

**The weather outside may be cold and damp, but the aroma and taste of a warm drink can brighten the dreariest moment.**

## Brewing the perfect pot of coffee

Heat, light, moisture and old age are the biggest enemies of a good cup of coffee. Loose grounds will lose their flavor within a week even if stored in a cool, dark place. Freeze so they will last longer. It should be noted that good water brews good coffee, so if you don't like the taste of your tap water, you won't like the taste of your coffee. Use filtered or bottled water instead.

Even though it seems so handy to keep the coffeepot full, brewed coffee should be transferred to a thermos within 15 or 20 minutes. The heating element of a coffeemaker can destroy coffee oils, leaving a bitter taste.

Brew your own café mocha by placing a piece of chocolate in the coffee filter before adding the ground beans.

## Starbucks Four Fundamentals of Brewing Coffee

Since 1971, we've been passionate about coffee. Over the years, we've developed the four fundamentals of brewing so you can enjoy a terrific cup of coffee, wherever, whenever.

**1. Water:** Start with cold, fresh, preferably filtered water, heated to just off the boil, to extract coffee's full range of flavor.

**2. Grind:** The coffee in Starbucks ground packages can be used in all automatic drip coffeemakers. When preparing our whole-bean coffee, refer to the grind recommendations on the package.

**3. Proportion:** The classic recipe: 2 tablespoons (10 g) of ground coffee for each 6 ounces (180 ml) of water. (Using less coffee makes for an over-extracted, bitter brew.) To adjust the strength, simply add hot water after brewing.

**4. Freshness:** Since oxygen, light and moisture are no friends to freshness, Starbucks coffee comes sealed in a signature FlavorLock bag. ∾

## Brewing the perfect pot of tea

There can be only one—one pot reserved just for tea, that is. Coffee leaves a residual flavor in a pot that tea can pick up. As with coffee, the water must be good. Pour very hot water into the teapot and set aside. Start with a kettle, preferably glass or enamel, of fresh, cold water and bring to a rolling boil.

Meanwhile, pour the hot water out of the teapot and toss 1 teaspoon loose tea or 1 teabag per cup (6 ounces) of water into the warmed steeping pot. Immediately pour the just-boiled water over the tea leaves, replace the lid and cover with a tea cozy or thick towel. Steep for three to five minutes. Pour the tea through a strainer into cups. Provide additional hot water on the side, in case the tea is too strong.

Traditional accompaniments:
• Black tea is served with milk, lemon or sugar. Remember that milk and lemon react adversely to one another, creating curdled milk.
• Green tea is supposed to be served plain, but we know of many people who add milk and sugar.
• Herb teas are enhanced by honey.

Bowl Game Party

*W*hile the Super Bowl may be the most heavily watched sporting event of the year, it's not the only game in town. There are so many others, including the Orange Bowl, Gator Bowl, Rose Bowl, Music City Bowl, Motor City Bowl, Tangerine, Las Vegas and Chick-fil-A Peach, that it's little wonder we've included a bowl game party.

This is a relaxed occasion for family and friends. A bowl game party is not the time for elaborate decorations, surprise dishes or fancy food; all eyes are on the game and not the table. The game plan is to provide maximum flavor with minimum work; only quick and hearty finger foods will do. All that's left is for the referee to blow the starting whistle.

## MENU

## Heinz Party Plate

Leave it to Heinz to take the guesswork out of preparing five snacks at once with this easy party platter plan. All that's required is a shopping trip to Costco, a warm oven and rabid fans.

INGREDIENTS:

**T.G.I. FRIDAY'S BACON & CHEDDAR POTATO SKINS**
*Loaded with creamy 100 percent real Wisconsin Cheddar cheese and hickory-smoked bacon. Ready to go from freezer to oven.*

**CREAM CHEESE POPPERS**
*Jalapeños are stuffed with 100 percent real cream cheese and then breaded in wheat flour and milled rice mixture. A rather spicy dip is also included. Poppers must be cooked before eating.*

**DELIMEX BEEF TAQUITOS**
*Precooked and made with real tortillas and cooked beef.*

**T.G.I. FRIDAY'S MOZZARELLA STICKS**
*Precooked smooth mozzarella surrounded by an outrageously crispy Italian breading, complete with a tangy marinara sauce.*

**BAGEL BITES**
*Deluxe-made with bleached wheat flour, mozzarella cheese and tomato puree, these bites will satisfy big snack cravings. Bagel Bites must be cooked before eating.*

### Arrangement on Cookie Sheet:

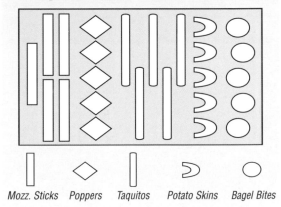

Mozz. Sticks    Poppers    Taquitos    Potato Skins    Bagel Bites

**1.** Preheat oven to 450°F.

**2.** Place 5 each of Potato Skins and Poppers on a 10 1/2-by-15-inch cookie sheet (don't use parchment paper). Avoid having the products touch.

**3.** Bake 7 minutes on middle rack of oven.

**4.** Remove from oven and add 5 each of the remaining products (Taquitos, Mozzarella Sticks and Bagel Bites). Bake 7 minutes longer.

**5.** Remove from oven and let sit 1 minute before serving. Makes enough servings to feed the offensive line.

## OSO Sweet's The Big Easy

Perfect for the easygoing atmosphere of a bowl game, this giant sandwich is the OSO Sweet version of the muffaletta, a tradition in the Italian groceries of New Orleans. Substitute other cold cuts, if you like.

*1 cup green olives, preferably Italian, pitted and chopped*

*1 cup chopped sun-dried tomatoes*
  *(packed in olive oil, drained)*

*1 1/2 tablespoons capers*

*3 cloves garlic, finely chopped*

*1 tablespoon chopped fresh oregano (1 teaspoon dried)*

*1/2 teaspoon freshly ground black pepper*

*2 tablespoons balsamic vinegar or other red wine vinegar*

*2 tablespoons olive oil*

*1 large, round loaf Italian bread, about 7 inches in diameter*

*1 OSO Sweet onion, thinly sliced, separated into rings*

*1/4 pound thinly sliced mozzarella*

*1/4 pound thinly sliced salami*

*1/4 pound thinly sliced ham*

*1/4 pound thinly sliced provolone*

*1/4 pound thinly sliced mortadella*

**1.** Mix the olives and the next 6 ingredients; stir in oil. Store, tightly covered, in the refrigerator at least 12 hours to marry flavors. Olive mixture can be made up to a week ahead.

**2.** Cut the bread in half horizontally; remove bread from inside crust (discard or save for bread crumbs) to form a thick shell.

**3.** Spread half the reserved olive mixture (with liquid) on the bottom half, then half the onion rings. Next, layer the cheeses and cold cuts in the order listed. Top with remaining onion slices, remaining olive mixture and top half of bread.

**4.** Sandwich can be made up to 6 hours ahead. Wrap tightly and store in the refrigerator. Return to room temperature before serving. Cut into 6 wedges. Makes 6 servings.

## Frito-Lay Scoops! Fiesta

No matter what the score, everyone will have the scoop on the game with this tasty snack.

*1/2 pound ground beef*

*1/2 pound sausage*

*1 large onion, chopped*

*1 9-ounce can refried beans*

*1 11-ounce jar Tostitos Restaurant-Style Mild Salsa*

*3 cups (12 ounces) shredded Cheddar cheese*

*9 green onions, chopped*

*1 cup sliced ripe olives*

*1 8-ounce carton sour cream*

*1 avocado, peeled, pitted and sliced*

*Fritos Scoops! Corn Chips*

**1.** Preheat oven to 350°F.

**2.** Cook ground beef, sausage and onion in a large skillet until meat is browned, stirring to crumble meat. Drain well.

**3.** Spread refried beans in a 9-inch pie plate; layer on the meat mixture and salsa; top with shredded cheese.

**4.** Bake uncovered for 15 minutes, or until cheese melts and mixture is thoroughly heated. Remove from oven.

**5.** Sprinkle green onions and ripe olives evenly over mixture. Top with sour cream and avocado slices. Serve warm with corn chips.

## Emmpak French Dip Sandwich

These sandwiches will add big points to the party.

16 slices Emmber Classic Sliced Roast Beef

3 cups water

4 beef-flavored bouillon cubes

2 tablespoons minced onion

1 teaspoon soy sauce

8 crusty rolls

**1.** In a medium saucepan, combine roast beef, water and bouillon cubes. Cook over medium heat until thoroughly heated, stirring occasionally.

**2.** Add minced onion and soy sauce. Cook 2-3 minutes.

**3.** For each sandwich, serve 2 slices of beef on a crusty roll. Divide hot bouillon mixture into 8 individual servings and use for dipping sauce. Makes 8 servings.

*Here are some other delicious sandwich variations to tickle your fancy:*

SWISS DIP

*On a toasted hoagie roll, combine 2 slices of your favorite Swiss cheese with warm roast beef. Spice it up with a little horseradish sauce.*

SAN FRAN DIP

*Add 2 slices of provolone to roast beef on grilled or seared sourdough bread.*

SOUTHWESTERN DIP

*Combine the hot roast beef slices with pepper-jack cheese and salsa rolled up in flat bread or a flour tortilla. Dip in the prepared au jus or your favorite queso sauce. If you like your food really spicy, add sliced jalapeño or habanero peppers.*

HOT OPEN-FACED POT ROAST SANDWICH

*Prepare a package of Morton's of Omaha Beef Pot Roast as described on the package (microwaves in about 7 minutes). Pull the heated pot roast into shreds using 2 forks. Mix the meat with the gravy so that it is evenly coated. Serve warm over your favorite sliced bread. Makes 6-8 sandwiches.*

SLT (SIRLOIN, LETTUCE & TOMATO) SANDWICH

*Prepare a package of Morton's of Omaha Steakhouse Classic Beef Tri-Tip by thinly slicing the meat across the grain. Place the thin slices of tri-tip in a preheated frying pan. Sauté over medium heat until cooked to your taste (approximately 2-3 minutes on each side for medium if sliced about 1/4 inch thick). Combine on your favorite bread with sliced tomatoes and fresh lettuce to create a variation of the classic BLT. Makes approximately 4 sandwiches per pound of uncooked roast.*

## La Brea Bakery French Baguette with Butter and Prosciutto

Fresh from the Costco Bakery oven, this bread is of uncompromising quality.

3-4 La Brea Bakery baguettes, cut into eight 7-inch pieces*

12 scallions, green part only, finely minced

1/2 cup finely minced Italian parsley

1 cup extra-virgin olive oil

1 teaspoon kosher salt

2-3 sticks (8-12 ounces) unsalted butter,
   slightly softened, but not greasy

12 ounces prosciutto, thinly sliced into about 48 slices

Slice each piece of baguette horizontally. Combine scallions, parsley, olive oil and salt in a medium bowl, and whisk to combine. Drizzle 1 tablespoon scallion oil on each piece of baguette. Smear 2-3 tablespoons of butter over the bottom half of each piece. Add 6 slices of rumpled prosciutto over the butter and cover with top half. Makes 8 servings, or can be cut smaller to feed a crowd.

*Brands may vary by region; substitute a similar product.

## Tillamook Beer Cheese Soup

This hearty soup is made with robust extra-sharp Cheddar from Tillamook County Creamery Association, a century-old farmer-owned cooperative in Tillamook, Oregon.

4 tablespoons butter

4 tablespoons flour

3 cups milk

1 tablespoon minced garlic

Salt and pepper to taste

1 teaspoon crushed red chilies, chopped

2 cups shredded Tillamook Extra-Sharp Cheddar

3/4 cup dark beer

**1.** Heat butter in sauté pan. Add flour and cook on low heat, stirring, until it starts to bubble. Do not allow it to brown. Remove from heat and set aside.

**2.** Heat milk in saucepan until ready to boil. Add garlic, salt, pepper and crushed chilies, and stir until nearly boiling.

**3.** Whisk in half of flour/butter mixture (*roux*) and stir until it simmers. Add more roux as necessary to thicken. Stir constantly to avoid burning.

**4.** Reduce heat and add cheese and beer, stirring until the cheese melts and texture is smooth. The soup can be gently reheated, but do not allow it to boil. Makes 8 small servings.

*Created by Billy Hahn, Executive Chef,*
*Jakes Famous Crawfish House, Portland, Oregon.*

## Unofficial Bowl Game Rules

- The fewer plates, the fewer dishes to be washed.
- A bowl party can harbor a score of remote-control junkies; hide the gadget before things get out of hand.
- Designate one room as the "quiet TV room," where serious football-watchers can gather.
- Stock up on paper towels, napkins, cups and bath tissue. Extra rug cleaner also is recommended.
- Those beverage commercials make thirst buds go crazy. Always purchase more beverages than you think you will need, and remember to provide nonalcoholic options.
- The cook gets to watch the game, too.

## Mrs. Dash/Molly McButter Chicken Fingers

If you're feeding a crowd, rotate cooking between two pans, so that one is always in service.

4 cups unseasoned bread crumbs

1/4 cup Mrs. Dash Original or Mrs. Dash Garlic & Herb

4 teaspoons Molly McButter Natural Butter

6 boneless, skinless chicken breast halves, cut in long strips

3 large eggs, beaten

Olive oil

Mix bread crumbs, Mrs. Dash and Molly McButter. Dip chicken in egg and then coat with bread crumbs. Sauté in olive oil for about 2 minutes on each side, or until brown. Makes 10-12 servings.

## Kellogg's Cheese and Mushroom Waffle Wedges

Kellogg Company, the world's leading producer of cereal and a leading producer of convenience foods, has been in business since 1906. Familiar Kellogg's icons include Tony the Tiger, Snap! Crackle! Pop! and Ernie Keebler. No doubt about it, these bowl game recipes are destined to be just Gr-r-reat!

1 1/2 cups shredded American cheese

1 2 1/2-ounce jar sliced mushrooms, drained

1/4 cup mayonnaise

1 tablespoon finely chopped onion

1/2 teaspoon salt

1/8 teaspoon cayenne pepper

2 teaspoons Worcestershire sauce

1/2 teaspoon prepared mustard

6 Kellogg's Eggo Homestyle Waffles

**1.** Preheat broiler.

**2.** Stir together cheese, mushrooms, mayonnaise, onion, salt, cayenne, Worcestershire sauce and mustard. Spread on each waffle to within 1/4 inch of edge. Place on a rack on a baking sheet.

**3.** Broil 4 inches from heat about 3 minutes, or until cheese has melted and waffles are thoroughly heated. Cut each into 4 pieces. Serve immediately. Makes 24 wedges.

## The Graze Craze

According to the Snack Food Association, 11.8 million pounds of potato chips were consumed during the 2000 Super Bowl. In the week leading up to the 2002 Super Bowl, salty snacks, crackers and snack nut/seed/corn nut sales all experienced a double-digit increase from the three previous weeks. The message? A bowl game party is one big graze, snack, graze, snack, graze, snack event.

## Kellogg's Cherry Almond Cookies

These are sure to hit the spot just about the time the fourth quarter rolls around.

1 1/3 cups all-purpose flour
1/2 teaspoon baking soda
1/4 teaspoon salt
1/3 cup margarine, softened
3/4 cup firmly packed brown sugar
2 egg whites
1 teaspoon almond flavoring
1/3 cup maraschino cherries, chopped
2 cups Kellogg's Low-Fat Granola or Low-Fat Granola with Raisins

**1.** Preheat oven to 375°F.

**2.** In a mixing bowl, stir together flour, baking soda and salt. Set aside.

**3.** In a large electric-mixer bowl, beat margarine and sugar until light and fluffy. Add egg whites and almond flavoring. Beat well. Stir in flour mixture until well combined. Add cherries and granola. Drop by level tablespoonfuls onto a baking sheet lightly coated with cooking spray.

**4.** Bake 10 minutes, or until edges start to turn brown. Cool on wire racks. Store in airtight container.
Makes 2 1/2 dozen cookies.

## Kirkland Signature Fresh-Baked Cookie Ice Cream Sandwich

What better way to wow the crowd than to make a big stack of these easy ice cream Costco Bakery cookie-wiches ahead of time and then just pull them out of the freezer and serve.

16 Kirkland Signature cookies, in assorted flavors
1 pint vanilla or chocolate ice cream, slightly softened
Garnishes as desired

**1.** Place a cookie with flat side up on a serving dish.

**2.** Place a bit less than 1/4 cup of ice cream on the flat side of the cookie.

**3.** Place a second cookie with flat side down on top of the ice cream to form a sandwich. Press down gently.

**4.** Apply garnishes and sauces as desired.

**5.** Serve immediately or wrap tightly in plastic and freeze.
Makes 8 servings.

**Serving Suggestions:** Roll the exposed ice cream in crushed nuts, mini semisweet chocolate morsels, coconut or crushed peppermints.

*An Italian Night:*
*Celebrating Life*

*Long before spring arrives, there's a welcome* event at Costco: the yearly winter arrival of our vibrant green, fruity, first-press (extra virgin) olive oil. If ever there were a reason to cook Italian, it would be when this harvest-dated Tuscan olive oil, at its peak of freshness, is first available to members.

We suggest starting the meal with cordial glasses set out on a silver tray, filled not with liqueur but with samplings of this phenomenal olive oil. Raise your glasses in a toast to life, then bring on the food: antipasti, roasted garlic pasta, seafood stew, delicate veal and espresso-laced desserts.

This is the dinner for extra-large white cloth napkins and an oversized tablecloth, small vases of fresh flowers, loaves of crusty bread, glasses stuffed with bread sticks, and wine in abundance.

It is a time to celebrate life. *Salute!*

## MENU

# Italy's Liquid Golds

## Italian Olive Oils

The use of olive oil in the United States nearly doubled from 1989 to 1999; sales of extra-virgin olive oil have increased 51 percent since 1995. Part of the reason is the oil's high level of unsaturated fats, which are believed to reduce cholesterol levels. (A tablespoon of olive oil contains only 2 grams of saturated fat and no cholesterol, whereas a tablespoon of butter contains 8 grams of saturated fat.)

Extra-virgin olive oil, the highest grade made, has harmonious fruity flavors and aromas, vivid green color and density. Its flavor is at its peak in the first two months after pressing, although it will keep well for a year. Store in a cool, dark place, but not in the refrigerator. If the oil gets chilled and becomes cloudy or solidified, bringing it to room temperature will restore it to its natural state.

Costco's Kirkland Signature limited-quantity, extra-virgin olive oil is made exclusively from Italian Tuscan olives that are harvested by hand and cold-pressed within 24 hours of picking under the watchful eyes of the Consorzio del Olio Toscano (Independent Association of Tuscan Olive Oil Producers). It is so valued by local harvesters of the Consorzio that many take bottles of this "liquid gold" home in lieu of payment.

The oil is magnificent drizzled over soups, tossed in pastas, or placed in a dish to be used for dipping with dense, crusty breads. ✎

## Italian Wines

It comes as a surprise to many people to learn that Italy is responsible for one quarter of all the wine produced in the world. Let's take a look at a few regions and the wines they produce.

Situated in Tuscany, Chianti has been waving the Italian flag in the United States for decades, although its identity has changed considerably over the years. Today's high-quality Chianti most likely will come from two distinct areas within the region: Chianti Classico (a hilly area south of Florence) and Chianti Rufina (the smallest and coolest area in the region).

In the northwest of the country is the Piedmont region. Here we find Barolo and Barbaresco, two of Italy's greatest wines.

To the south, in Puglia (the heel of Italy's boot), the less well-known Negroamaro and Malvasia Nera grapes are showcased, and from Molise comes the soft, juicy Sangiovese. In Umbria, northeast of Rome, there is Merlot being made that would put to shame some domestic offerings at twice the price.

Italy's white wines also have benefited greatly from improvements in the vineyard and the cellar. In the northeast, from Trentino and Veneto, look for light, delicate Pinot Grigio, with its lovely floral, almond scent, to quench your thirst. A good Soave Classico makes a wonderful alternative to Chardonnay. Veneto also is home to Valpolicella Classico and one of Italy's trademark wines, Amarone della Valpolicella. ✎

## Ottavio Olive Oil Antipasto

Antipasto means "before the pasta" and is usually an assortment of hot or cold hors d'oeuvres presented at the beginning of a meal. It is hard to imagine antipasto without olive oil.

### CROSTINI

*Grill 1/2-inch-thick slices of crusty bread. Rub fresh garlic on one side. Sprinkle with chopped oregano. Drizzle 1 tablespoon Ottavio Extra Virgin Olive Oil\* on each slice of bread. Season with salt and freshly ground pepper.*

### CAPRESE

*Layer a thick slice of tomato, a large fresh basil leaf and a slice of buffalo mozzarella. Season with salt and freshly ground pepper. Drizzle Ottavio Extra Virgin Olive Oil over the cheese and plate.*

Crostini

Caprese

Patates Frites

### GRIGLIATA DI VEGETALI

*Peel asparagus with a vegetable peeler. Cut bell peppers in quarters and seed them. Baste the vegetables with Ottavio Extra Virgin Olive Oil. Season with salt and pepper. Let stand for 10 minutes. Grill the vegetables over high heat until they are tender, turning to allow even cooking.*

**Costco Tip:** *Ottavio Olive Oil Company recommends using traditional olive oil for frying and extra-virgin olive oil as a finishing touch on salads or when grilling.*

*\*Brands may vary by region; substitute a similar product.*

## Ottavio Olive Oil Main Course

### PATATES FRITES

*Cut potatoes into 1/2-inch-thick wedges and keep them in a bowl of cold water to prevent oxidation. Chop fresh rosemary and mix with a small amount of olive oil. Deep-fry the wedges in Ottavio Traditional 100% Pure Olive Oil\* until golden. Drizzle the mixture of olive oil and rosemary over the fries. Season with salt. Garnish with crumbled feta cheese.*

### GRIGLIATA DI PESCE

*Brush a 6- to 8-ounce salmon steak with the following mixture: 1 tablespoon Ottavio Extra Virgin Olive Oil, juice of 1/2 lemon, salt and pepper. Marinate for 1 hour. Brush a little oil onto the grill to prevent sticking. Grill the salmon steak over high heat for about 4 minutes on each side, or until crispy and brown. Drizzle with more olive oil and serve.*

Grigliata di Vegetali

Grigliata di Pesce

### Kirkland Signature Gardenburger-Stuffed Portobello Mushrooms

Here's a way to create a quick, tasty, meatless hors d'oeuvre that's stuffed with flavor and crumbled Gardenburger.

*8 Kirkland Signature Gardenburger Gourmet Blend patties, heated according to package directions and crumbled*

*1/2 cup diced roasted red bell pepper*

*8 teaspoons chopped parsley*

*1/2 cup mayonnaise*

*8 teaspoons Dijon mustard*

*16 small portobello mushrooms, cleaned and cap/gills removed*

Combine crumbled Gardenburgers, red bell pepper, parsley, mayonnaise and mustard. Stuff into mushrooms. Place under preheated broiler 5-7 minutes, or until heated through. Makes 8 servings.

### *Arthur Schuman*
### *Cello Parmigiano-Reggiano Cheese*

*Parmigiano-Reggiano is exquisite served as an appetizer in chunky shavings with crusty Italian bread.*

*Shred it on salads, vegetables and pastas, or cut into small wedges and serve with fresh pears or apples as a dessert.*

*Note: True Parmigiano-Reggiano is aged for 2 years, made with special milk and imported from the Parma and Reggio Emilia provinces of Italy. Each wheel has a Consorzio (trade group) seal of authenticity (the name written in small dots) and an export stamp, and will give the date and the factory where it was produced.*

### Christopher Ranch Pan-Roasted Garlic Pasta

Garlic, a member of the lily family, is a gift from the earth, especially when mixed with pasta.

*6 tablespoons butter*

*1/3 cup olive oil*

*20 cloves Christopher Ranch Peeled Garlic*

*1 cup finely chopped yellow onion*

*2 cups shredded carrots*

*1 tablespoon Italian seasoning*

*2 tablespoons lemon pepper*

*1 1/2 cups white wine*

*1/2 cup chopped fresh basil*

*12 ounces vermicelli (thin) pasta, cooked al dente*

*Salt*

In large skillet, melt 2 tablespoons butter with oil over medium heat. Add whole garlic cloves and sauté 10 minutes, or until lightly browned, turning down heat if necessary. Add onion, carrots, seasonings and 2 more tablespoons butter and sauté until lightly browned and caramelized. Increase heat and deglaze pan with white wine. Turn heat to low, cover and cook 15 minutes, or until garlic is tender. Add a splash more wine if mixture gets too dry. Add basil and remaining butter, stirring until butter has melted. Add cooked pasta and toss until well coated and heated through. Salt if desired. Makes 6 small servings.

## Mazzetta's Zuppa di Pesce

This soup, made with versatile seafood, is both good-tasting and good for you. Shrimp, for example, are totally free of saturated fat and an excellent source of protein and minerals, providing important nutrients for fewer calories per ounce than chicken, turkey or beef.

The Mazzetta Company farm raises its shrimp so that the habitat of sea turtles and other marine animals is not endangered during the harvesting process.

---

*1 medium onion, finely chopped*

*3 garlic cloves, finely chopped*

*1/2 teaspoon shredded fresh thyme*

*1/2 teaspoon chopped fresh parsley*

*3 tablespoons olive oil*

*2 28-ounce cans crushed tomatoes in natural juice*

*2 cups white wine*

*6 cups fish stock*

*8 4- to 8-ounce Mazzetta's Rock Lobster Tails\**

*16 13/15-count Mazzetta's Black Tiger Raw Shrimp\**

*16 Mazzetta's Whole Greenshell Mussels\**

*Salt and pepper*

---

Sauté the onion, garlic, thyme and parsley in olive oil in a heavy 12-quart stockpot over medium heat until soft. Add the tomatoes, wine and fish stock. Simmer 20 minutes. Gently add the lobster tails and simmer 5 minutes. Add the shrimp and simmer 5 minutes. The mussels will cook in 2 minutes; add them at the end. Remember to stir during the cooking process. Add salt and pepper to taste. Makes 8 main-course servings.

**Serving Suggestions:** For those who like it spicy, add some crushed red pepper when the tomatoes, wine and fish stock are simmering. You also can serve this over spaghetti or linguine. It's nice to have a warm loaf of crusty bread rubbed with garlic to soak up the sauce. Enjoy with a bottle of Sauvignon Blanc.

*\*Brands may vary by region; substitute a similar product.*

### More Mazzetta Ideas:
### *Steamed Whole Greenshell Mussels*

*Greenshell Mussels are exclusive to the clean, cold waters of New Zealand. Within hours of harvest, each mussel is lightly steamed, snap-frozen in its shell and packed under the strictest quality control.*

*Melt 1 stick of butter or margarine in a covered stockpot. Add 2 cups of white wine and simmer 5-10 minutes. Steam Mazzetta's Greenshell Mussels in sauce 3-5 minutes.*

### *Grilled Shrimp Shish Kebob*

*Thread thawed Mazzetta's Black Tiger Raw Shrimp on skewers, alternating with bite-size pieces of onion, bell pepper, mushrooms and tomatoes. Marinate in your favorite marinade or salad dressing for 2 hours in the refrigerator, or simply brush with oil. Cook on a hot grill 3-5 minutes on each side.*

## Atlantic Veal and Lamb Veal Piccata

1/4 cup all-purpose flour

1 teaspoon salt

1/4 teaspoon paprika

1/4 teaspoon ground white pepper

2 pounds Atlantic Veal and Lamb veal leg cutlets,
   cut and pounded 1/8 to 1/4 inch thick*

2 tablespoons olive oil

1 1/3 cups dry white wine

1/4 cup fresh lemon juice

4 teaspoons drained capers

2 teaspoons butter

**1.** Combine the flour, salt, paprika and pepper, and use it to lightly coat the cutlets.

**2.** In a large nonstick skillet, heat 1/2 tablespoon oil over medium heat. Sauté cutlets in batches 3-4 minutes, turning once. Remove and keep warm. Repeat with remaining oil and cutlets.

**3.** Add wine and lemon juice to the skillet and cook, stirring, until any browned bits have dissolved and the liquid thickens slightly. Remove from heat and stir in the capers and butter. Spoon the sauce over the cutlets. Makes 8 servings.

*Brands may vary by region; substitute a similar product.*

### Jane Cohen's Garlic Tip

What to do with Costco's 3-pound plastic jar of freshly peeled garlic? This Aliso Viejo, California, member puts it right in the freezer. The garlic keeps well and doesn't even stick together. Take out as many cloves as you need and defrost in the microwave for about a minute. Add to soups, sauces and other dishes.

**Costco Tip:** The flavor of garlic may become stronger when it's frozen.

## Carter Thomas Pear and Sugar Pea Sauté

This melding of pears and peas offers the heartiness of winter with the lightness of spring.

4 shallots, thinly sliced

4 teaspoons olive oil

2/3 pound sugar peas, trimmed

4 Carter Thomas California Bartlett pears, cored,
   peeled and cut into 1-inch wedges

3/8 cup dry white wine

2 tablespoons unsalted butter

5-6 tablespoons fresh orange juice

Salt and pepper to taste

In a large skillet, cook shallots in olive oil over moderate heat for 3 minutes. Add the sugar peas, pears and wine and cook 4 minutes, stirring occasionally, until nearly tender. Add butter and orange juice and cook 1 minute. Season with salt and pepper and serve immediately. Makes 8 servings.

Culinary director of Washington's Chateau Ste. Michelle winery, Emmy-nominated cooking show host for Taste of the Northwest, author of numerous cookbooks and longtime Costco aficionado, John Sarich also travels the country sharing his recipes with Costco members.

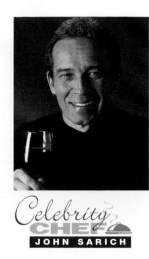

*Celebrity*
**CHEF**
**JOHN SARICH**

## John Sarich's Espresso Tiramisu

*6 egg yolks, slightly beaten*

*6 tablespoons sugar*

*Pinch salt*

*2 cups milk or half-and-half, scalded*

*1/4 cup Marsala wine*

*8 ounces fresh mascarpone cheese*

*24 ladyfingers*

*1 cup strongly brewed espresso*

*1 cup heavy cream, whipped firm*

*Solid bittersweet chocolate for garnish*

*Raspberries for garnish*

*Small fresh mint leaves*

*1/2 cup crumbled amaretto cookies*

**1.** Place a stainless steel bowl in a saucepan half full of water and bring water to barely boiling. Put egg yolks, sugar and salt into bowl and whisk until blended. Stir until eggs begin to thicken. Add scalded milk gradually and continue whisking until thick, about 7-8 minutes. Add Marsala and mascarpone and whisk until smooth. Place bowl in refrigerator until custard is firm, preferably overnight.

**2.** For the base, quickly dip ladyfingers in espresso. Turn each one face down and line bottom and sides of a glass serving bowl. Spread 1/3 cup whipped cream over ladyfingers. Pour firm chilled custard on top; bowl will be almost full. Top with remaining whipped cream and spread evenly.

**3.** Use a potato peeler to shave delicate twirls of the chocolate and sprinkle on top. Dot with berries and mint. Sprinkle with amaretto cookie crumbs. Makes 6-8 servings.

## Nonni's Biscotti

The company was delightful, the food sublime, and now the night is drawing to a close. So cap the evening with a cup of decaf espresso and a plate of Nonni's biscotti. Be sure to remind guests to "dunk" to their heart's content.

Biscotti, a twice-baked Italian cookie, is made by first baking the dough as a loaf, then slicing and baking again. It is full of crunchy texture, rich flavor and delicate sweetness.

Nonni's Biscotti* come in two flavors: walnut and almond, dipped in bittersweet chocolate, and gingerbread macadamia nut, dipped in white chocolate. They are delicious all by themselves or can be enjoyed:
• Dunked in your favorite beverage
• Served with ice cream
• Crushed and then sprinkled in a dish of fresh fruit

*Brands may vary by region; substitute a similar product.*

# Sunday Supper Potluck with Friends

*M*any dual-working households are discovering the pleasures of early Sunday evening entertaining. The chores are done, bodies and spirits are re-energized, stress-free cooking is a possibility, and guests more than likely won't stay late.

Organizing a potluck with friends adds an element of surprise as well as a division of labor to a party. Many prefer to wing it, asking guests to just bring whatever they please. These are the kind of people who thrive on a meal of six desserts and one bowl of mashed potatoes.

We prefer a little more structure, with the host or hostess directing the supper. You decide what dish you want to prepare, then inform your guests and suggest other specific categories, such as "I'm making my mom's meat loaf, so we need a side dish, starch, dessert, salad and appetizer."

With a little luck— and teamwork— you'll have a great time and pots full of good food.

## MENU

Costco Member
Deona Tait

*EDITOR'S CHOICE*

## Orca Bay Shrimp in Avocado Halves

Orca Bay Salad Shrimp are harvested in the icy waters of eastern Canada and are cooked, peeled and ready to eat. No chemicals or preservatives are used in the processing of this shrimp.

4 ripe avocados,
    halved and pits removed

2 cups shredded lettuce

4 cups Orca Bay Salad Shrimp

1/4 cup finely chopped celery

1/4 cup diced mango

1 cup alfalfa sprouts

24 cherry tomatoes, halved

2 limes, cut into wedges

French dressing

On 8 salad plates, place each avocado half on bed of lettuce. Combine shrimp, celery and mango and spoon some into the cavity of each avocado. Arrange alfalfa sprouts and tomatoes on plate next to avocado. Garnish shrimp with lime wedges. Serve French dressing separately. Makes 8 servings.

## Deona Tait's Tomato Puff Pastry

When we called to chat with this Bronxville, New York, Costco member she said, "Cooking is my passion." Judging by this recipe, we'd say she's right on target.

1/2 package frozen puff pastry (1 sheet)

1 tablespoon pesto (2 tablespoons, if you prefer)

1/4 cup chopped sun-dried tomatoes (in olive oil and herbs)

1 cup shredded mozzarella cheese

1 beaten egg (for glazing)

1 tablespoon sesame seeds (optional)

*TESTED AND APPROVED*

**1.** Preheat oven to 400°F.

**2.** Unfold pastry and roll slightly on a lightly floured surface to ease out the folds. Spread pesto on the center of the pastry, leaving a 1/2-inch border free on either side and the ends. Sprinkle tomatoes on the pesto, followed by the cheese.

**3.** Cut the pastry along the sides of the filling diagonally into 1/2-inch strips. Fold the pastry at either end over the filling. Brush the side pastry strips with water and plait (braid) over filling. Brush with beaten egg and sprinkle with sesame seeds.

**4.** Bake for 30 minutes, or until the pastry is golden and crisp. Serve hot. Makes 4-5 servings. Plan on making 2 of these.

## Foxy Creamy Broccoli Soup

5 cups Foxy Broccoli flowerets*

1 1/2 tablespoons olive or vegetable oil

1 cup chopped yellow onion

1 clove garlic, minced

3 14 1/2-ounce cans vegetable broth

1/4 cup raw long-grain rice

1/2 teaspoon salt

1/4 teaspoon ground nutmeg

1/8 teaspoon pepper

Grated Parmesan cheese, bell pepper strips,
    fresh oregano sprigs (optional)

Blanch 1 cup broccoli for 3 minutes; drain and reserve. Heat olive oil in saucepan; sauté onion and garlic over medium heat until tender. Stir in remaining broccoli, broth, rice, salt, nutmeg and pepper. Bring to a boil, reduce heat and simmer, partially covered, 20 minutes. Puree in food processor or blender. Garnish with reserved broccoli, Parmesan, bell pepper and oregano. Makes 8 small servings.

*Brands may vary by region; substitute a similar product.*

## Contessa Shrimp Scampi Risotto with Asparagus

It's hard to think of anything more satisfying than a delectably creamy mixture of rice, asparagus, green peas, Parmesan cheese and gorgeous shrimp scampi.

*2 pounds Contessa Shrimp Scampi\**

*3 cups Arborio rice (or medium-grain rice)*

*8-12 cups warm water or fish stock*

*3 cups asparagus cut in 2-inch lengths*

*1/2 cup green peas*

*3 tablespoons grated Parmesan cheese*

*Salt and pepper*

*Basil leaves and lemon wedges for garnish*

**1.** Place frozen shrimp scampi in a single layer in a large skillet. Do this in 2 batches if the pan is too crowded. Sauté over medium heat until shrimp turns orange/red outside and becomes opaque inside, about 3 minutes each side. Remove shrimp to a bowl and set aside. Leave the sauce in the skillet.

**2.** Add the rice to the scampi sauce and stir over medium heat for 2 minutes, until the rice is coated with sauce and slightly opaque.

**3.** Add warm water 1 cup at a time, stirring well between intervals and waiting until liquid has been absorbed before adding the next cup of water. Continue until almost all the liquid has been absorbed, about 20-25 minutes.

**4.** Add the asparagus, green peas and Parmesan. Cook, stirring frequently, for 3 minutes, or until the vegetables are cooked. Add salt and pepper to taste. Remove from heat.

**5.** Add the shrimp. Serve immediately, garnished with basil leaves and lemon wedges. Makes 8 servings.

*\*Brands may vary by region; substitute a similar product.*

## Valley Fine Foods Pasta Prima
### Ravioli, Alfredo Style

Here's another main-course suggestion.

*1 pound chicken tenders (or chicken breast),*
  *pounded very thin*

*1 bag Italian Herb Cheese Mix (included in ravioli bag)*

*4 tablespoons butter*

*1/2 cup cream*

*1/3 cup grated Parmesan cheese*

*1/4 cup water*

*1 1/2 tablespoons fresh lemon juice*

*1 1/2 tablespoons capers*

*1 1/2 tablespoons chopped fresh parsley*

*Black pepper*

*4 tablespoons olive oil*

*2 cloves garlic, chopped*

*4 cups assorted vegetable pieces (zucchini, yellow squash,*
  *asparagus, bell peppers, mushrooms or your favorites)*

*3-4 dozen hot cooked Valley Fine Foods Pasta Prima*
  *Spinach & Mozzarella Ravioli (or Ravioli Trio or*
  *Sun-Dried Tomato Ravioli)*

*Grated zest of 1 lemon*

**1.** Season chicken with half of Herb Cheese Mix; set aside for 15 minutes.

**2.** To make sauce, cook butter, cream, Parmesan and water in medium saucepan over low heat for about 10 minutes, stirring constantly, until sauce has thickened slightly and cheese melts. Add lemon juice, capers and parsley. Season to taste with pepper; keep warm.

**3.** Heat 2 tablespoons of olive oil in large nonstick skillet over medium heat. Add garlic; sauté 1 minute. Add vegetables; sauté 4-5 minutes, or until they reach desired tenderness. Remove from skillet; keep warm.

**4.** In same skillet, heat the remaining oil over medium heat. Sauté chicken until cooked thoroughly, about 2-3 minutes on each side. Keep warm.

**5.** Serve freshly cooked ravioli topped with chicken and vegetables and a light coating of sauce. Sprinkle with lemon zest and additional Herb Cheese Mix and serve immediately. Makes 4-6 servings.

## Washington Apple Blue Cheese Slaw

What would winter be without crisp, juicy apples to keep the sunless days at bay? The Washington Apple Commission brings together a delicious side-dish slaw that can be made up to a day ahead and a quick yet spectacular dessert in case Sunday evening comes around before you're ready for it.

*4 Washington Red Delicious apples (about 6 ounces each),*
  *cored and julienned*

*1/2 cup thinly sliced red onion*

*1/2 cup dairy sour cream*

*1/2 cup mayonnaise*

*6 tablespoons chopped fresh parsley*

*2 ounces crumbled blue cheese*

*2 tablespoons lemon juice*

*1/2 teaspoon sugar*

*Salt and pepper*

**1.** Combine all ingredients; mix well.

**2.** For optimum flavor, refrigerate 6 hours or overnight. Makes 8 servings.

## Nicolin Hoffmann's **DNE World Fruit** Caramel Mint Oranges

When DNE World Fruit, a grower, packer and marketer of fresh citrus products, heard about this recipe from a member in Scarsdale, New York, they agreed that it must be included.

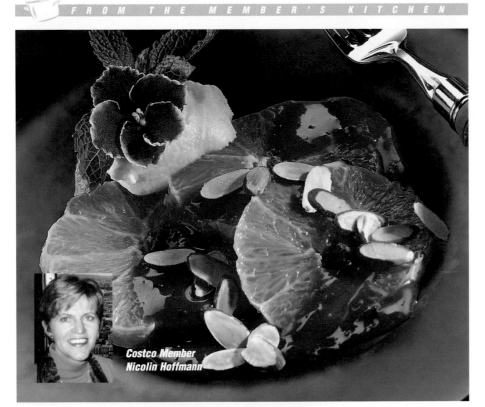

Costco Member
Nicolin Hoffmann

*5 DNE World Fruit oranges*

*¹/₃ cup sugar*

*¹/₄ cup water*

*1 small stick cinnamon*

*¹/₄ cup cream*

*3 tablespoons unsalted butter*

*2 teaspoons finely shredded orange rind*

*2 tablespoons chopped fresh mint*

*6-8 tablespoons mascarpone cheese*

*Ground nutmeg, toasted sliced almonds and mint leaves for garnish*

Peel oranges and remove pith. Cut in thin horizontal slices. Arrange, slightly overlapping, in 1 or 2 shallow pie dishes. Put sugar, water and cinnamon in small pan and cook over medium-high heat until sugar has dissolved. Don't stir; just shake occasionally. Increase heat and bring syrup to a boil. Remove cinnamon. Cook syrup to a caramel color. Remove from heat and gradually stir in cream. Return lumpy mixture to heat and stir until caramel dissolves. Whisk in butter, orange rind and mint. Transfer to bowl and refrigerate for 4 hours. Preheat broiler. Dot orange slices with caramel and place under the broiler until hot. Garnish with mascarpone, nutmeg, almonds and mint. Makes 8 servings.

## **Washington** Golden Apple Meringues

*4 (about 1¹/₂ pounds) Washington Golden Delicious or Rome Beauty apples, halved and cored*

*4 cups apple juice or water*

*1 cup orange marmalade*

*4 egg whites*

*¹/₄ cup sugar*

*¹/₄ cup chopped toasted almonds*

**1.** Preheat oven to 350°F.

**2.** Poach apples in apple juice about 5-7 minutes, or until barely tender; drain.

**3.** Spoon 2 tablespoons marmalade into center of each half.

**4.** Beat egg whites to soft peaks. Add sugar gradually and beat until stiff. Fold in almonds or sprinkle on top.

**5.** Cover tops of apple halves to edges with meringue. Bake 7-10 minutes, or until lightly browned. Makes 8 servings.

*The presence of color is one of the first signs of the season. Glorious spring showers us with apple-blossom pink, daffodil yellow, tulip red, robin's-egg blue and new-leaf green.*

*They are the signposts, reminding us that it is time to break out of our home's cocoon and venture forth once more to celebrate religious traditions, life's rejuvenation, family gatherings and whimsical fun.*

*As we throw open the windows to breathe the fresh air, sit outside to lap up the sun, listen to baby birds chirping in their nests, and eat delicate foods that defy the imagination—pencil-thin asparagus, sweet green peas, crisp beans, meadow greens, new potatoes, sun-kissed strawberries, tangy rhubarb and succulent lamb—our senses are slowly reawakened, blossom by blossom, breath by glorious breath.*

# Spring Reflections

## Dizzying Foods

Nature bestows her most luscious culinary pleasures at this time: flavors that are fresher, seasonings that are more intense, and foods that are bursting with energetic colors and shapes.

These three qualities—freshness, intensity and energy—are the hallmark of our spring menus. Our Ode-to-Spring Feast is colored with brilliant oranges, yellows and reds, hearts and roses are wedded at the Romantic Bridal Luncheon, traditions are reclaimed in the Cinco de Mayo Fiesta and Mother's Day. Diminutive delicacies fill the Tea Party, and in closing we offer family favorites.

## Dazzling Flowers

Gone is the need to cover, stuff or embellish, as simplicity takes center stage. Look to nature for your floral cues: bold clusters of bright yellow daffodils, lip-red tulips and cloud-white narcissi, budding branches and unfurling leaves.

Perennials can offer triple show power. When first purchased, they are hardy enough to be brought inside for a few days. We suggest groups placed in baskets or terra-cotta pots. As the flowers start to fade or the leaves turn yellow, quickly find a home for them in your flower beds, where with any luck some varieties, such as primroses, will grace your yard with a second bloom. The third showing will happen next year, when these hardy plants peek out of the dirt to say hello once more.

## Delightful Tablescapes

While it may still be too cold to entertain outside, we suggest bringing a little bit of the outdoors in.

For example, why not bring in half a dozen potted tulips and place them down the center of your table? Tip a couple of the pots over and let a little dirt fall onto the table. In an instant, your table has gone from the ordinary to a whimsical potting-shed scene.

Except for rare occasions, fancy linen, expensive china and Grandmother's crystal will simply overpower a centerpiece of fresh spring flowers. Instead, use everyday ware, crockery, pottery and informal glassware.

As for vases, we suggest clear, shiny glass of all shapes and sizes so that spring flowers can be enjoyed from the tips of their petals to the bottoms of their stalks.

### Costco's Spring Bounty Includes

| | |
|---|---|
| Halibut | Chocolate Cream Pie and Berry Tart |
| Copper River Salmon | Hass Avocados |
| Rib Roast | Artichokes |
| Lamb | Papayas |
| Ham | Asparagus |
| Driscoll Long-Stem and Regular Strawberries | Flank Steaks with Portobello Mushrooms |
| Mangoes | Sliced Roast Beef, Hams, Turkeys and Cheeses |
| Oso Sweet and Vidalia Onions | |
| Strawberry Cheesecake | Chicken Caesar Salad |

# Savoring the Season with David

**David Andrew
Costco Global
Wine Director**

Spring is the time to put away the heavy reds and enjoy something lighter and fruitier. It's also the time when white wine consumption takes off on its summer flight. Something bubbly to blow away the remnants of winter is always appropriate.

One of my own favorite reds for spring is Cabernet Franc, from the Loire region of France. It won't be called Cabernet Franc on the label, but rather it will have the name of the area or appellation that the wine comes from. Look for Chinon, Saumur-Champigny or Bourgeuil. The wines have a bright color and a distinctive juicy green, leafy quality that makes them the perfect accompaniment to spring lamb.

Beaujolais, made from the bright, fruity Gamay grape, is another good choice for spring. This one you can even serve chilled.

White wines of summer—Riesling, Sauvignon Blanc, Pinot Grigio—will, of course, be equally attractive in spring. But before the temperature gets too high, spring is a perfect time for fuller-bodied whites.

Chardonnay needs no introduction, but it comes in a variety of styles (or body types), from the big, round, ripe and tropical styles of Australia and California to the leaner, crisper examples from Chablis, in the north of Burgundy. Try a number of Chardonnays to find the level of oak, body and alcohol you like. Chablis makes a crisp, mineral style that is beautifully refreshing and is a classic match for oysters. The fuller, riper examples from the New World can stand up to much fuller-flavored fish, as well as poultry.

Here are a few others to add some variety to your spring sipping:

Muscadet: a bright mineral-scented wine from France (great with mussels and other shellfish).

Soave: the other Italian white. A good one is preferable to Pinot Grigio in my book.

Albariño: floral, peachy freshness from northwest Spain.

Viognier: beautifully scented, a mixture of peaches, flowers and gummy bears. The best comes from France.

Champagne is at home in any season, but spring and summer call for a special lightness and delicacy. One of my favorite sparkling sippers is Moscato d'Asti, a gently sparkling wine from Italy. Inviting aromas of Muscat grapes and flowers lead to a delicate, delicious lightness in the mouth. This wine works equally well on its own or as a light accompaniment to or replacement for dessert.

*Ode-to-Spring Feast*

*Blossoming flowers trumpet the season's arrival.* Days miraculously grow longer, nights warmer, bees begin to search for nectar and people shed their coats. The world is alive, and it is a perfect time to celebrate the passing of winter and the coming of spring.

Food is the star attraction. To showcase the gifts of the season, serve a dinner of tomato salad, savory lamb, spring asparagus, heirloom rice and citrus tarts.

The best backdrop for your party is the sun itself, so if you are lucky enough to catch a sunny day, start your feast a little early, with drinks and hors d'oeuvres served beside a sunny window. Otherwise, keep decorations simple, perhaps bouquets of spring flowers made whimsical with the addition of long asparagus spears in lieu of ferns.

Play Beethoven's Ninth Symphony, *Ode to Joy,* in the background as a toast is raised.

## MENU

## Joan Daciek's Decorative Ice Bucket

This Costco member from Highlands Ranch, Colorado, has a wonderful party decorating suggestion.

Stuff a two-liter plastic soda bottle with rocks and place in the middle of a clean mop pail. Fill the pail with spring flowers, berries and/or leaves, and then gently fill the bucket with water. Freeze, checking occasionally during the first three hours, as items may float to the surface and have to be pushed back down. Freeze for about 48 hours, then unmold by adding warm water to the soda bottle and the outside of the pail. Remove the bottle first.

Return to the freezer until ready to use. The floral ice bucket is perfect for wine, champagne or berries. It should last two to three hours; just remember to keep a plate underneath to catch the melting water.

Joan has used this same idea at Christmas with plastic holiday ornaments and artificial flowers. She even once made a personalized ice bucket for a party honoring her tennis-loving daughter. It was made out of—you guessed it—tennis balls!

If the floral ice bucket sounds like too much work, how about creating floral ice cubes? Place an edible flower in each compartment of a plastic ice-cube tray. Fill with water, making sure the petals are submerged. Freeze. Use as needed.

*Costco Member*
*Joan Daciek*

### BelGioioso *Cheese-Tasting*

*What could be more fun than a theme within a theme? This cheese-tasting concept is perfect for a celebration-of-spring dinner, as it keeps your guests happily occupied while you finish preparing other more involved hors d'oeuvres. It also will help establish a congenial mood for the rest of the evening.*

*Cheese-tastings are now a hot new serving concept. An elegant arrangement of BelGioioso Asiago, Aged Asiago,*

*Parmesan and American Grana will create a flavorful experience.*

*Established in 1979 by Italian cheese maker Errico Auricchio and based in Wisconsin, BelGioioso now makes 13 varieties of "Classic Italian Cheeses."*

*Always keep in mind: When tasting, start with the mildest cheese and make your way to the sharpest. Always serve cheese at room temperature for the best flavor.*

### Star Fine Foods
### Olive Bruschetta

*1 baguette, sliced*
*6-8 garlic cloves, peeled*
*1/2 cup Star Extra Virgin Olive Oil\**
*1 cup sliced Star Spanish Olives\**
*1 cup diced tomatoes*
*1/2 cup minced red onion*
*1 tablespoon Star Capers\**
*3 tablespoons Star Balsamic Vinegar\**
*Pepper*

Lightly toast baguette slices on both sides. While hot, rub with garlic cloves, then brush lightly with some of the olive oil. Combine olives, tomatoes, onion, capers, vinegar and remaining olive oil and toss. Season to taste with pepper. Spoon onto baguette slices and serve. Makes 8 servings.

*\*Brands may vary by region; substitute a similar product.*

Alpine Santa Tomato Salad

Costco Member
Julia Cabatu

Alpine Mango Bruschetta

Mango Bread

## Alpine Mango Bruschetta

The mango is a fragrant tropical fruit that blends
surprisingly well with basil and red bell pepper.

*1 baguette, sliced ¹/₂ inch thick*

*¹/₄ cup olive oil*

*1 Alpine mango, peeled, pitted and diced*

*¹/₄ cup diced red bell pepper*

*1 tablespoon minced fresh basil*

*1 cup grated Romano cheese*

**1.** Preheat broiler.

**2.** Arrange bread slices on baking sheet. Brush each slice lightly
on one side with olive oil. Broil until toasted, about 2 minutes.

**3.** In a bowl, combine mango, red pepper and basil.

**4.** Top each bread slice with the mango mixture and sprinkle
with Romano cheese.

**5.** Place under broiler. Broil 2-3 minutes, or until cheese is
melted and lightly browned. Serve hot. Makes 8-10 servings.

**Costco Tip:** Mangoes can be ripened in a paper bag.

*Recipe developed by Linda Carey and Pat Volchok.*

## Alpine Santa Tomato Salad

Grape tomatoes were developed seven years ago in Taiwan.
The Santa F1 variety is considered the sweetest of them all,
and is now recognized as one of the world's best tomatoes.
Alpine grows these tomatoes along the eastern seaboard from
Florida to New Jersey to ensure the freshest availability year-
round. The Alpine Santa F1 Grape Tomato is excellent in
salads, pastas, sauces, salsa and any tomato recipe.

*2 pounds Alpine Santa F1 Grape Tomatoes*

*¹/₄ cup extra-virgin olive oil*

*¹/₄ cup balsamic vinegar*

*¹/₂ cup thinly sliced sweet onion*

*Salt and pepper to taste*

*¹/₂ cup crumbled Gorgonzola, blue or other favorite cheese*

**1.** Wash, stem and dry tomatoes.

**2.** Mix all ingredients except cheese, which is added
immediately before serving. Makes 8 servings.

**Costco Tip:** Grape tomatoes are delicious on their own
as a quick, healthy snack.

### Julia Cabatu's Mango Bread

*This member reports
that she's worked for 26
years at the Hawaiian
Electric Company. This
recipe is one of thousands
that have been tested by
the consumer services
division. It obviously is
a standout.*

2 cups flour

2 teaspoons baking soda

2 teaspoons cinnamon

1¹/₄ cups sugar (can be
  adjusted according to
  sweetness of mangoes)

¹/₂ cup unsweetened
  coconut (if you have
  only sweetened coconut,
  cut down slightly on the
  sugar amount listed above)

¹/₂ cup chopped nuts
  (you can use walnuts)

2 cups chopped firm ripe
  Alpine mangoes

³/₄ cup salad oil

3 eggs, beaten

2 teaspoons vanilla extract

*1.* Preheat oven to 350°F.
Grease a 9-by-5-inch
loaf pan.

*2.* Sift flour with baking
soda and cinnamon into a
mixing bowl. Stir in sugar,
coconut and nuts. Add
remaining ingredients
and mix well.

*3.* Pour into prepared pan
and bake 1 hour and 15
minutes, or until a toothpick inserted in the center
comes out clean.

Costco thanks Hawaiian Electric
Company for allowing this recipe
to be reprinted.

## Celebrity CHEF
### GLENN OCHI

**Red Chamber Company**, one of the largest seafood suppliers in North America, offers its stun- ning colossal shrimp and scallops at Costco Seafood Road-shows. Red Chamber worked with California School of Culinary Arts Chef Glenn Ochi to create these two dishes exclusively for Costco members. Chef Ochi has received many Culinary Arts Salon awards for his food preparations. While no awards will be given out at your spring dinner, we suspect that guests will applaud when they taste these dishes.

## Red Chamber Grilled Spicy Scallops

3 pounds scallops

2 teaspoons finely chopped fresh ginger

2 teaspoons finely chopped garlic

2 teaspoons finely chopped cilantro leaves

2 tablespoons chili sauce

2 tablespoons low-sodium soy sauce

$1/2$ cup fresh-squeezed orange juice

Pinch of ground black pepper

$1/2$ cup peanut oil

2 teaspoons toasted sesame oil

20 ounces European salad mix

2 carrots, julienned

$1/2$ cup prepared raspberry salad dressing

1 pint fresh raspberries

$1/2$ cup crumbled Gorgonzola cheese

**1.** Clean scallops by removing side abductor muscle, and set aside.

**2.** Prepare marinade: combine ginger, garlic, cilantro, chili sauce, soy sauce, orange juice, pepper, and peanut and sesame oils and mix well.

**3.** Place scallops in the marinade and refrigerate for 1 hour, stirring from time to time.

**4.** Place scallops on a hot grill and cook approximately 2 minutes per side, depending on how well-done you like your shellfish.

**5.** Toss the salad greens and carrot with the raspberry vinaigrette, place on your favorite plate, set scallops around or on top of the salad, place a few fresh berries all around your plate, sprinkle with crumbled Gorgonzola and enjoy. Makes 8 servings.

**Red Chamber Shrimp Veracruz**

**Red Chamber Grilled Spicy Scallops**

## Red Chamber Shrimp Veracruz

4 tablespoons olive oil

3 pounds jumbo shrimp, peeled and deveined

1/2 cup finely diced onion

1/2 cup each finely diced green bell pepper and
    red bell pepper

8 cloves garlic, finely chopped

1 teaspoon crushed chili flakes

1 teaspoon dried oregano

2 Roma tomatoes, sliced

1/4 cup white wine

1/2 cup tomato sauce

1/2 cup sliced black olives

2 cups chicken broth

1/2 teaspoon salt

Pinch of black pepper

2 teaspoons each cornstarch and water, as needed

**1.** Heat oil in a large skillet. Sauté shrimp in batches for 30 seconds on each side. Remove and set aside.

**2.** Next sauté the onion, bell pepper, garlic, chili flakes, oregano and tomato until soft.

**3.** Add white wine and reduce by half.

**4.** Add tomato sauce, olives and chicken broth, bring to a boil, then simmer for another 5 minutes.

**5.** Adjust seasoning with salt and black pepper.

**6.** Thicken to taste with the cornstarch and water mixture.

**7.** Add shrimp to this scrumptious sauce and cook another minute. Serve over rice. Makes 6 servings.

### Balsamic Vinegar

So many balsamic vinegars have been introduced in this country over the past few years that it is sometimes hard to know which one to buy. Be reminded that traditional preparation of balsamic vinegar includes the must (the juice of crushed grapes) that results from the cooking and filtering of Trebbiano grapes, most specifically those found in Modena, Italy.

Costco's Kirkland Signature private-reserve, a distinctly sweet balsamic vinegar, is prepared in the old-world way with Trebbiano grapes, in Modena, using centuries-old recipes and techniques, including aging in wooden casks for up to 15 years before bottling. It is perfect for salads.

Remember to store *balsamico* in a cool, dry place. Use it to dress salads, marinate meats and vegetables, and top off finished dishes that call for an extra splash of flavor.

### Dressed to Perfection

While many cooks reach for prepared salad dressing, making your own is essentially an easy endeavor, especially if you remember 3:1, which is the ratio generally accepted for mixing oil and vinegar.

Oil and vinegar need one another. Oil has a subtle taste and needs vinegar to awaken its character. Conversely, vinegar needs oil to coat its acidic base so that it can be distributed evenly; otherwise, it would pool at the bottom of a plate.

Some prefer a stronger oil profile of 4:1 and even add a little wine or water to particularly strong vinegar to tone it down. By the way, salt, sugar and spices should be added to the oil before its introduction to the vinegar.

### Vinegar Vocabulary

- **Cider:** *All-purpose, usually made from fermented apple cider, with a rather pungent taste.*
- **White wine:** *Made from white wine. It is mild and mellow, and it works well with delicate flavors.*
- **Red wine:** *Made from red wine. It has a robust quality that is best paired with strongly flavored foods. Remember that this vinegar adds a delicate reddish cast to dishes.*
- **Champagne vinegar:** *Delicate, works well in infusions, in which herbs are cooked with the vinegar and then strained.*
- **Malt:** *All-purpose, suitable for chutneys and pickling.*
- **Rice:** *All-purpose, made from fermented rice; delicate, mild and slightly sweet.*
- **Sherry:** *Sweeter and more complex. Use it on substantial salads containing meats, poultry, cheeses or fruits.*
- **Balsamic:** *Dark, pungent, sweet and tart. This vinegar can go solo, without oil.*

## The Australian Lamb Company

*Fresh Australian lamb is naturally raised, low in fat and cholesterol and contains no additives. With its sweet and mild taste, this delicate meat can be prepared and served in many ways.*

*Costco imports 27 percent of Australia's fresh lamb. All lamb products are vacuum packed to preserve freshness.*

### Australian Lamb Loin Chops

Here are four great sauces for quick-cooking chops, which are perfect for busy weekday schedules.

*ROSEMARY & GARLIC SAUCE*

3 tablespoons olive oil

2 tablespoons chopped rosemary

Crushed garlic, to taste

*SATAY-STYLE SAUCE*

3 tablespoons peanut butter, crunchy or smooth

3 tablespoons honey

3 tablespoons light soy sauce

*BARBECUE SAUCE*

3 tablespoons soy sauce

1 1/2 tablespoons brown sugar

3 tablespoons olive oil

2-inch piece fresh ginger, grated

*HONEY & SOY SAUCE*

3 tablespoons honey

3 tablespoons light soy sauce

Crushed garlic, if desired

For all sauces, simply combine ingredients in a small bowl and use for basting. Extra sauce can be served for dipping. Recipes cover up to 8 lamb chops.

*GRILLING:*

Preheat grill or barbecue on high. Cook chops about 2 minutes, until just starting to brown, before basting with sauce (optional). Continue cooking 3-5 minutes on each side, basting occasionally.

*PAN-BROILING:*

In a heavy frying pan, sear chops over high heat 1 1/2-2 minutes each side, until just starting to brown, before basting with sauce (optional). Reduce heat to medium and cook 2-4 minutes longer, turning at least once.

**Costco Tip:** The firmer the feel of the meat, the more well-done.

## Australian Lamb Roast Leg of Lamb

A roast boneless leg of lamb is perfect when constant supervision is not possible.

*BASTES*

*CLASSIC SEASONING*

1 tablespoon olive oil

1 1/2 tablespoons dried rosemary

6 garlic cloves

Note: Cut small slits in leg and push in garlic cloves before placing in oven.

*MUSTARD & ROSEMARY*

1 1/2 tablespoons Dijon mustard

1 1/2 teaspoons dried rosemary

2 garlic cloves, minced

Salt and black pepper, to taste

*ITALIAN FLAVORING*

8 ounces Italian-seasoned tomato paste or plain tomato paste

1 teaspoon dried or 1 tablespoon chopped fresh oregano

1 teaspoon dried basil

2 garlic cloves, minced

Combine ingredients in a small bowl and spread over leg of lamb. Recipe covers 1 whole boneless leg (about 5 pounds).

*BASIC COOKING INSTRUCTIONS FOR BONELESS LEG:*

Preheat oven to 350°F. Season leg with salt and pepper to taste, or baste. Roast for about 1 hour and 20 minutes, or until the internal temperature is 135-140°F, for medium-rare. Remove from oven, cover loosely with foil and let meat rest 10-15 minutes. Carve and serve. Makes 8-10 servings.

## Australian Lamb Roast Rack of Lamb with Artichokes and Wild Mushrooms

Frenched (fat and tissue between the bones removed) and ready to roast, a rack makes an impressive presentation, yet is easy to prepare!

2 teaspoons salt

1 1/2 teaspoons ground black pepper

1 1/2 teaspoons dried thyme

2 teaspoons dried rosemary

4 Australian Range Lamb Frenched Racks
   (approximately 6 pounds)

3/4 cup olive oil

12 ounces wild mushrooms, cut in 1/2-inch slices

12 ounces artichoke hearts, quartered

1/2 teaspoon minced garlic

1/2 cup flour

6 cups rich beef stock

Salt and pepper

**1.** Preheat oven to 450°F.

**2.** Combine salt, pepper, thyme and rosemary and rub evenly over the lamb. In a skillet, brown the meat on both sides in 2 tablespoons of smoking-hot olive oil.

**3.** Place the lamb on a baking/roasting rack. Roast 13 minutes, or until the internal temperature is 135-140°F (medium-rare). Remove meat from oven and let rest 15 minutes.

**4.** Sauté the mushrooms in the remaining olive oil until golden. Reduce heat and add artichokes and garlic; sauté 3 minutes. Sprinkle with flour and mix in completely; cook 5 minutes over low heat. Add beef stock and simmer 10 minutes, or until slightly thickened. Season to taste with salt and pepper.

**5.** Divide mushroom mixture evenly among 8 plates. Slice lamb racks and place 3 or 4 chops on top of vegetables, spooning the remaining sauce over each portion. Makes 8 servings.

## Debi White's Capered Chicken

"My husband and I both love your Kirkland Signature boneless, skinless chicken breasts, and I was looking for a different way to prepare them one night," says this member from Eugene, Oregon.

1 cup all-purpose flour

1 teaspoon seasoning salt

Salt and pepper

8 boneless, skinless chicken breasts, thawed

12 tablespoons butter

4 cups sliced mushrooms

12 green onions, sliced

4 cloves garlic, minced

2 cups dry white wine

2 cups fat-free chicken broth

1/2 cup Dijon mustard

1/2 cup capers

**1.** On a plate or piece of waxed paper, mix together flour, seasoning salt, and salt and pepper to taste. Dust chicken with flour mixture, coating evenly.

**2.** Melt half of the butter in a skillet over medium heat. Add as many chicken breasts as will fit comfortably and brown on both sides until cooked thoroughly (about 15 minutes). Remove to plate and cover with foil. Cook remaining chicken.

**3.** In a skillet over medium heat, melt remaining butter. Add mushrooms, green onions and garlic and sauté until slightly soft (about 5 minutes). Add wine and chicken broth. Cook an additional 5 minutes. Stir in mustard and capers.

**4.** Place chicken breasts on a serving plate, top with mushroom-caper sauce and serve immediately. Makes 8 servings.

Costco Member
Debi White

## Splenda Asparagus with Sesame-Ginger Sauce

What would a spring dinner be without fresh asparagus, made delicious and lighter—only 60 calories per 4.3-ounce serving—thanks to Splenda, a no-calorie sweetener.

1 tablespoon soy sauce

1 tablespoon rice vinegar

1 tablespoon peanut oil

1 tablespoon water

1 tablespoon tahini (pureed sesame seeds)

1 teaspoon chopped fresh ginger

1/2 teaspoon chopped garlic

1 1/2 packets Splenda or 1 tablespoon Splenda Granular

Pinch red pepper flakes

48 medium-size asparagus spears, trimmed and peeled

Place everything but asparagus in food processor and combine thoroughly. Cut asparagus into 2-inch diagonal pieces. Fill a large skillet half-full of water, cover and bring to a boil. Add asparagus and simmer just until crisp-tender, 4-5 minutes. Drain well but do not rinse. Transfer to serving bowl. Pour sauce over hot asparagus and toss to coat. Serve warm or at room temperature. Makes 8 servings.

**Costco Member
Maureen Benoliel**

## Maureen Benoliel's Grandmother's Rice

This recipe was handed down by Costco employee Joel Benoliel's wife's grandmother, who in turn received it from her grand-mother, and so on. The family came from the Isle of Rhodes. This is but one of many examples of the Spanish influence on Sephardic Jewish cooking that have been preserved for well over 500 years. This particular recipe most likely reflects the Sephardic experience in Spain in the years before 1492.

2 cups pearl rice

2/3 cup olive oil

3 cups water

2 teaspoons salt

6 tablespoons tomato sauce

2 15-ounce cans garbanzo beans (chick peas)

**1.** Wash and drain the rice 3 times.

**2.** Put oil, water, salt and tomato sauce in a large saucepan and bring to a boil. Add rice and stir. Bring to a boil again. Lower heat to simmer, cover and continue cooking.

**3.** After 15 minutes, stir in the garbanzo beans. Continue cooking for another 15 minutes.

**4.** Leftovers can be refrigerated and reheated, and they're just as tasty the next day. Makes 8 servings.

### Sunkist Fresh Orange Whipped Cream

1/2 cup heavy whipping cream

2 tablespoons Sunkist fresh-squeezed orange juice

1 tablespoon chopped Sunkist fresh orange zest

1 tablespoon confectioners' sugar

Whip cream until soft peaks form. Stir in orange juice, zest and confectioners' sugar. Continue whipping until peaks are firm.

### Sunkist Citrus Mini-Tart with Fresh Orange Whipped Cream

Here's a decadent way to get a springtime shot of vitamin C!

1 cup Sunkist fresh-squeezed orange juice

1/4 cup brown sugar

8 3-inch puff pastry rounds, thawed if frozen

16 Sunkist fresh orange segments

8 Sunkist fresh pummelo segments*

8 tablespoons Sunkist Fresh Orange Whipped Cream

**1.** Preheat oven to 425°F.

**2.** In small saucepan, combine orange juice and brown sugar, stirring to dissolve sugar.

**3.** Heat to boiling and reduce mixture by one half to a syrupy consistency. Let cool to room temperature.

**4.** Brush 1 tablespoon of syrup on each pastry round.

**5.** Arrange 2 orange segments and 1 pummelo segment on each pastry.

**6.** Place on a cookie sheet and bake 10-15 minutes, or until lightly golden brown.

**7.** Top each tart with 1 tablespoon Sunkist Fresh Orange Whipped Cream. Makes 8 servings.

*Sunkist grapefruit can be substituted when pummelo is out of season.*

While some of the more conservative floral arrangers believe that certain conventions must be followed when designing flower arrangements, the latest inclination is to be much more laid-back and imaginative. Don't limit yourself to glass vases or clumps of daisies; look at your surroundings with new eyes.

The point of the arrangement is to offer a clue to the event. Is the occasion formal, themed or a buffet? A well-thought-out centerpiece will answer this question and many more. In essence, your arrangement becomes a feast for the eyes.

### Vegetable and Fruit Containers

- All sorts of containers can be made using different combinations of fruits and vegetables. For a single event, most kinds of produce can be used, but if you are seeking longevity, choose varieties that can survive out of the refrigerator or that have a thick skin.

- **Artichokes:** Use pliers to pull out the center leaves and thistles of an artichoke. Insert a small, empty can; add water and diminutive, whimsical flowers. (These artichoke containers are also the perfect size for votive candleholders. For a more elaborate presentation, hollow out 8 to 10 artichokes and use some for flowers and others for candles.)

- **Peppers:** Clean out peppers like jack-o'-lanterns, wrap in wet paper towels, and refrigerate until ready to be used as bright vases. To fill, hold each pepper over the sink and add water. Check for leaks before adding grower's bunches of flowers or herbs.

# It Has Been Arranged

*By Pat Volchok, Editorial Director*

- **Melons:** Poke three small holes in the top of a melon. Add water and a single daisy to each. To steady the round melon, make a small stand out of three twigs that are tied with raffia at the corners to form a triangle. Place the twig trivet on a table and position the melon inside.

### Large, Clear Vessels

- **Carrots and Beans:** Fill with a bottom layer of baby carrots, then a layer of uniformly cut green beans, followed by another layer of baby carrots. Add water and top with orange ranunculus, from the buttercup family. Just stunning!
- **Cranberries and Lemons:** Fill with layers of cranberries and sliced lemons, then add water and yellow and red roses. Or try unshelled nuts and sliced oranges or blueberries and sliced lemons.
- **Apples:** Fill with small apples, water and blooming apple branches.

### Food Cans and Jars

- **Green Beans:** Trim green beans to fit the height of a can. Using melted glue pillows, which can be purchased from a craft store, brush a 2-inch strip of glue around the outside of the can, covering thoroughly. Add the beans vertically and press them against the glue for just a few seconds, until they adhere. Continue until the can is covered and has been transformed into a green-bean vase. Add water, sweet peas and sage, and tie with bear grass, a dry grass available at crafts stores.
- **Asparagus:** This is a little trickier. An old glass pickle jar is a good container choice. Make sure all the asparagus are taller than the jar but not necessarily of uniform height. Place two rubber bands around the jar and carefully slide the asparagus in behind. The rubber bands will hold the asparagus in place. Cover the rubber bands with purple raffia and tie into bows. Add water and purple lilacs.
- **Savoy Cabbage:** Glue the leaves around a plastic floral container in overlapping layers. Start at the top of the container and work downward, layer upon layer, simulating the true positioning of cabbage leaves. Tie a beautiful ribbon around the leaves if you prefer a tighter look, add water and flowers, wrap with wet paper towels and refrigerate until ready to display.
- **Leeks:** These offer fabulous presentation when sliced in half lengthwise and glued vertically to a can, with the flat sides facing inward. Add water, tie with raffia and insert yellow flowers.

### Egg Vases

- Eggs make the most wonderful little vases, especially if you possess eggcups. Prick the top of an egg with a pin and carefully pick away the shell to make a hole about the size of a quarter. Drain (reserving the actual egg for a meal), add water and miniature garden flowers, and put one at each person's place using an eggcup or small terra-cotta flowerpot as the holder. The egg vases also can be crafted into name cards by writing guests' names on the shells with a wax pencil, staining the shells with tea, coffee or the juice of raspberries or blueberries and then filling with flowers. ∾

*Cabbage-Leaf Vase*

# Romantic
# Bridal
# Luncheon

*ife affords windows of pure happiness, one* of which is a wedding. Until the middle of the last century most brides were married at home, so whether you are the bride honoring your attendants or a friend honoring the bride, a romantic, classically elegant, at-home bridal luncheon is an appropriate and welcome bow to tradition.

The party should shout romance. Old-fashioned colors, ranging from creamy white to pale, feminine pink, work the best. Roses are a must and can be set in arrangements, candied for decorations, stuffed into napkins, added to gifts and tied with chiffon ribbons to the backs of chairs.

The meal itself is not to be overlooked. We've created a graceful luncheon with fruit smoothies, a luxurious spread, a delicate quiche, Champagne-poached salmon and a fruit tart, guaranteeing a party that will become a treasured memory for years to come.

## M E N U

# Decorating with Roses

*By Pat Volchok, Editorial Director*

There's nothing like roses and a bride. Here are some suggestions for decorating with this romantic flower for a bridal shower or, for that matter, any dreamy occasion.

### Candied Rose Blooms and Petals

Practice this technique on a few rose petals before attempting entire blooms. The roses must not have been sprayed with pesticides, so select from an environmentally green and clean yard, not from a florist. Pick full blooms, check for insects and clean thoroughly with water. Let dry. Using an artist's brush, paint all petals, including the underside, carefully with a thin layer of beaten egg white.* Work quickly. Holding the prepared rose over a piece of waxed paper, sprinkle evenly with superfine or confectioners' sugar. Carefully shake. Avoid touching up, because the sugared rose's appearance may turn clumpy. Let the blossoms dry on a wire rack before storing in tissue for up to one week. Do not refrigerate; the candied roses tend to weep just like chilled meringues.

- Scatter candied petals across the table like confetti.
- Place candied rose blooms on dessert platters.

### Pesticide-free rose petals can be:

- Laid on the bread-and-butter plate to hold pats of butter.
- Added to water in ice-cube trays and frozen to make rose-petal ice cubes.
- Placed on or around the dessert platter.
- Floated in water in a compote vase with buoyant votives.
- Made into rose-scented sugar by combining 2½ cups highly scented dried rose petals with ½ cup sugar and processing in a food blender until fine.

### Tie roses into other party elements:

- Select your rose and then purchase colored ribbon to match and tie around napkins or gift boxes.
- At the last moment, stick a rose in each person's favor or napkin.
- Tie roses to the back of everyone's chair.

And don't forget to serve blushing pink Rosé wine. ∾

*Note: While pesticide-free rose petals are edible, there are concerns about eating raw egg whites, so we strongly suggest that these be used for decoration only.*

## Arizona Smoothies

Arizona Smoothie* recently introduced smoothie concentrate and reports that it's sold in the juice aisle in bottles. The concentrate can be mixed with water and/or ice in a blender to create spectacular drinks. Each recipe serves 2-4.

*ARIZONA CRÈME SMOOTHIE*

*Blend the following until smooth:*
*12-ounce glassful of ice cubes*
*4 ounces Arizona Smoothie concentrate*
*2-ounce scoop of ice cream*

*ARIZONA NONFAT SMOOTHIE*

*Blend the following until smooth:*
*12-ounce glassful of ice cubes*
*4 ounces Arizona Smoothie concentrate*
*2 ounces nonfat yogurt*

*ARIZONA SMOOTHIE BLAST*

*Blend the following until smooth:*
*12-ounce glassful of ice cubes*
*4 ounces Arizona Smoothie concentrate*
*1 1/4 ounces light rum*

*ARIZONA SOUTH OF THE BORDER SMOOTHIE*

*Blend the following until smooth:*
*12-ounce glassful of ice cubes*
*4 ounces Arizona Smoothie concentrate*
*1 1/4 ounces tequila*

*Brands may vary by region; substitute a similar product.*

## Kirkland Signature
## Fruit & Nut Spread

This delectable creation is made with Kirkland Signature's new mix of banana chips, roasted non-pareil supreme almonds, dried cranberries, raisins, dried pineapple with mango and pineapple juice, wal-nuts, dried Utah cherries, extra-large Virginia peanuts and dried strawberries.

*8 ounces Kirkland Signature Fruit & Nut Medley*

*8 ounces cream cheese, softened*

In a food processor pulse Fruit & Nut Medley to a medium-fine grind. Stir into the cream cheese. Press into a heart-shaped container lined with plastic wrap. Refrigerate overnight. To present, unmold and decorate with edible rose petals. Serve with delicate crackers. Makes 12-18 servings.

## Michael Foods Better'n Eggs Quiche

Quiches are perfect party food, as they are sometimes better served at room temperature or even the next day. The added advantage with this recipe is the use of Michael Foods egg product, which is made of real egg whites and flavorings but without the fat or cholesterol usually associated with eggs.

*1 small zucchini, sliced*
*1 cup sliced mushrooms*
*1/2 cup chopped onion*
*1/2 cup diced red bell pepper*
*2 tablespoons olive oil*
*1 unbaked 9-inch piecrust*
*1/2 cup shredded Cheddar cheese*
*8 ounces (1 cup) Better'n Eggs**
*1/4 cup low-fat milk*

Preheat oven to 400°F. In nonstick skillet over medium heat, sauté zucchini, mushrooms, onion and pepper in olive oil until tender. Spoon mixture into piecrust. Sprinkle with cheese. Combine Better'n Eggs and milk in bowl. Pour over vegetables and cheese. Bake 30-35 minutes, or until a knife inserted near the center comes out clean. Let stand 5 minutes before serving. Makes 6-8 servings.

*Brands may vary by region; substitute a similar product.*

## Green Apple Slaw

2 green apples, cored and julienned

1 medium red onion, thinly sliced

2 medium Cubanelle sweet peppers, seeded and thinly sliced (or red bell pepper)

2 green onions, thinly sliced

2 small red or green jalapeño peppers, seeded and finely diced

2 tablespoons chopped fresh dill

1/4 cup olive oil

2 tablespoons lemon juice

Juice of 2 limes

Salt and black pepper

**1.** In a bowl combine the apple, red onion, Cubanelle pepper, green onion, jalapeños, dill, olive oil, lemon juice and lime juice. Gently mix, seasoning with salt and pepper to taste. Set aside.

**2.** Top each poached fillet of salmon with 2-3 tablespoons of slaw.

**3.** For an added touch, garnish each fillet with a teaspoon of salmon caviar and a sprig of fresh dill. Makes 8 servings.

**Note:** You can make the Green Apple Slaw up to 1 hour ahead of poaching the salmon.

## Napkins

Make rose-shaped napkins with green and colored napkins to match the centerpiece. Begin by stuffing a green napkin into a drinking glass with its corners dropping out to resemble petals. Fold the other colored napkin(s) into long 2-inch-wide strips. Starting at one end, roll up the individual strips into miniature sleeping bags, turn them so that the coils show, and stuff one into the center of the green napkin in each glass.

## Heritage Salmon's Champagne-Poached Salmon

Delicious boned and skinned salmon fillets take all the work out of preparing this stunning first course.

2 bottles Champagne

5 cups fish stock or water

2 teaspoons whole black peppercorns

2 teaspoons mustard seeds

4 medium shallots, sliced

6 sprigs fresh dill

1/4 cup lemon juice

4 teaspoons salt

8 4-ounce Kirkland Signature boneless, skinless salmon fillets*

**1.** Put the Champagne, fish stock, peppercorns, mustard seeds, shallots, dill, lemon juice and salt in a 3-inch-deep sauté pan, stirring to fully mix. Bring to a rolling boil over medium-high heat. Reduce heat to medium and simmer 5 minutes.

**2.** Carefully place salmon fillets, evenly spaced, in poaching liquid, making sure liquid covers salmon. If the tops of the fillets are exposed, spoon the hot liquid over them.

**3.** Cover and simmer 12-15 minutes, or until salmon is firm and just cooked through.

**4.** Gently remove salmon from poaching liquid and transfer to a serving platter. Makes 8 servings.

**Costco Tip:** Serve with fresh fruit salsa or Green Apple Slaw.

*Brands may vary by region; substitute a similar product.*

Costco Member
Kerry Comunale

## Kerry Comunale's Sherried Rice

Costco thanks this Redmond, Washington, member for sharing a recipe that everyone, including the newlyweds, will cherish long after the wedding cake is gone.

*1 medium onion, chopped*

*¹/₂ cup butter*

*2 cups rice*

*2 14.5-ounce cans chicken broth*

*¹/₂ cup dry sherry*

*1 cup grated Parmesan cheese*

*4 green onions, chopped*

**1.** Sauté onion in butter in a saucepan.

**2.** Stir in rice, chicken broth and sherry and bring to a boil. Reduce heat. Cover and simmer for 25 minutes.

**3.** When rice is done, sprinkle with Parmesan and green onions. Makes 8 servings.

### Gourmet Retailer *Magazine* says:

- *More engagements take place between Christmas Eve and Valentine's Day than at any other time of year.*
- *June is the most popular wedding month and then September. The least popular? January.*
- *For centuries, June has been the most practical month to get married. In the past, it was the time after planting and before harvesting; spring rains had ceased and the roads were passable once more. Today, it is the month of graduation.*

## Equal Peach-Berry Tart

If someone in the bridal party is worried about fitting into her dress, this dessert might come as a welcome relief. Imagine the same great taste as the traditional recipe, but with 31 percent fewer calories using Equal, a no-calorie tabletop sweetener.

*Pastry for single-crust 9-inch pie*

*5 cups sliced peaches (about 5 medium) or frozen peaches, thawed*

*1 cup raspberries or sliced strawberries*

*1 cup fresh or frozen blueberries, partially thawed*

*2 teaspoons lemon juice*

*3 tablespoons cornstarch*

*24 packets Equal*

*1 teaspoon grated lemon peel*

*¹/₄ teaspoon ground allspice*

**1.** Preheat oven to 425°F.

**2.** Roll pastry on floured surface into 12-inch circle; transfer to ungreased cookie sheet.

**3.** Toss peaches and berries with lemon juice in large bowl; combine cornstarch, Equal, lemon peel and allspice and sprinkle over fruit, tossing to coat.

**4.** Arrange fruit on pastry, leaving 2-inch border around edge. Bring edges of pastry toward center, overlapping as necessary.

**5.** Bake pie until pastry is golden and fruit is tender, 35- 40 minutes. Cool on wire rack. Makes 8 servings.

three most-listened-to tracks. Designate someone as DJ to create the lineup and keep the tracks spinning in surround sound. Your party will be jumping in no time as guests sing their selection of special requests!

### Create the Look

Simple touches go a long way toward spicing up your party. Perrier and Costco suggest setting up food and drink stations in different rooms. This creates a natural flow through your home and encourages mingling. To really get people talking, serve food in unexpected dishes, like salad in parfait glasses, drinks in shaving mugs, and so on.

Create arrangements that have that "fresh from the garden" look. Assemble flowers and garden clippings in containers or empty Perrier bottles in the center of your table. This saves money and displays your personal style.

Play with the light to create a festive atmosphere. Replace regular light bulbs with colorful ones. Place tea lights on mirrors to give a dancing bounced-light effect. If you're really feeling adventurous, have a glass-cutter remove the bottoms of empty Perrier bottles to cover tea lights, creating a subtle green glow.

### Serve an Original

So you've created a look that oozes style; now the burning question is what to serve your guests. Versatility is the name of the game. One of the most versatile entertainers is the original sparkle itself: bubbly Perrier. Completely natural and calorie-free, Perrier adds spirit to any cocktail and sophistication to any glass. Whether it's used as a mixer for the ultimate alcoholic or non-alcoholic libations or as a refreshing stand-alone, Perrier can lend originality and panache to any party. For instance, you can shake up a Perrier Sunset (4 ounces Perrier, 2 ounces orange juice, splash of Grenadine, and maraschino cherry garnish) or just pour Perrier over the rocks for a simple, exhilarating drink. ❧

# *Perrier's Suggestions for a Fun Evening Wedding Shower*

Perrier Sparkling Natural Mineral Water, whose water source is located in the town of Vergèze in the south of France near Nimes, offers these party tips for a lively, casual couples wedding shower.

### Set the Mood

Want a fun-loving wedding shower? Perrier suggests that you give it a festive theme like cool Kitchen & Karaoke. Tell friends to bring a kitchen appliance, selected from the gift registry, for the lucky couple and a special music CD. Have them place a sticker on the disc that lists their name and

# Wedding Gifts... the Costco Way

*Gifts are a token of love and appreciation. This is the time for giving enduring mementos that can be used over and over again. Today's newlyweds are combining formal tradition with personalized flair as they mix old and new, so it's little wonder that wedding-gift registries also reflect this trend.*

*Ninety-one percent of all newlyweds register for gifts* (Modern Bride), *with half of this number selecting everyday basics, 25 percent special-occasion tableware, 15 percent specialty appliances and 10 percent trend items.* (Gourmet Retailer)

*We suggest selecting gifts that reflect timeless tradition, are practical or have lasting meaning.*

## KitchenAid Stand Mixer

The KitchenAid mixer has been a fixture in the American kitchen since 1919, when the first model of a home stand mixer was described as "the best kitchen aid."

Still true to its name, this exceptional hands-free appliance now offers 10-speed control, ergonomically designed bowl and bowl-lift handles, rugged all-metal construction and:

**Burnished Flat Beater:** Specially designed to mix ingredients in every part of the bowl.

**Burnished Dough Hook:** Can knead even very large quantities of raised dough.

**Professional Wire Whip:** Incorporates optimal air into egg mixtures for fluffier meringues and soufflés; also whips cream and creates smooth icings.

## J. A. Henckels International, 12-piece Forged Knife Block Series

For more than 200 years, Henckels has been known for its superior-quality knives. This "just the thing for the newlyweds" classic set of fully forged, ergonomically designed knives includes two of the most frequently used knives in the kitchen—a 4-inch paring knife and an 8-inch chef's knife—plus 6-inch utility knife, 5-inch serrated utility knife, 8-inch carving knife, 8-inch bread knife and four steak knives. All knives feature full-tang, tightly bonded three-rivet handles and hot-dropped forged blades, and are hand honed for superb cutting performance, professional balance and reliable quality.

The set also includes the most popular and suitable storage system for fine knives, a slanted hardwood knife block, and a sharpening steel.

## Aroma Housewares Cool Touch Rice Cooker

Rice consumption in the United States has grown 250 percent in the last 25 years (www.preparedfoods.com), and we know of no bride or groom who wouldn't love to receive a Cool Touch Rice Cooker from Aroma Housewares. Its cool-touch exterior, sealed lid system, nonstick cooking pot for easy cleanup, 20-cup capacity and automatic "Keep Warm" setting ensure that rice is cooked to perfection each and every time. No stirring, turning or temperature adjustments are required.

*MARNEY AUSTIN'S AROMA RICE COOKER TIP*

This Phoenix member reports, "We purchased an Aroma rice cooker at Costco. While it does work great for rice, we decided to try it to steam Asian appetizers like dumplings. It works much better than a steamer because the appetizers stay warm for numerous courses."

# Sunbeam Appliances

The tradition of giving Sunbeam appliances to brides (and grooms) is as much in vogue today as it was when Sunbeam developed its first home appliance, the Princess electric iron, in 1910. Over the years, product innovations have included the governor-controlled food mixer, controlled-heat immersible frying pan and fully automatic radiant-controlled toaster. Here are just a few suggestions for making a wedding a "Sunbeam" affair:

## Mr. Coffee Programmable Coffeemaker

The Mr. Coffee 12-cup programmable coffeemaker has a sleek new design and offers features such as an adjustable-temperature warming plate, a 1- to 4-cup setting and water filtration. Plus, it includes a permanent filter—no paper filters needed.

## Osterizer 14-Speed Blender

This five-cup, dishwasher-safe, scratch-resistant glass jar blender features a powerful 450-watt motor and patented All-Metal Drive for extra durability. Blades include the PowerBlend ice crusher blade, which is designed to toss, catch and shatter ice as it falls to make perfectly crushed ice for drinks, and the milkshake blade, for frothy milkshakes.

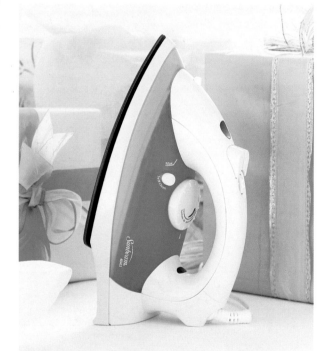

## Sunbeam Euro Press Iron

Sunbeam irons are known the world over for their sleek styling and attention to detail. The Euro Press Iron features a nonstick surface, spray mist and a powerful shot of steam for tough wrinkles. The vertical steam feature is perfect for hanging clothes and drapes, and the patented Motion Smart auto-off senses time, motion and location for safety.

## Kirkland Signature 18/10 Stainless Steel 13-piece Professional Italian Cookware

For newlyweds who are cooking purists and also appreciate the "feel" of strong, durable stainless steel, this 13-piece set is the ideal choice. Made in northern Italy, it features a quality stainless steel alloy made with 18 percent chromium and 10 percent nickel to maximize brilliance and durability. Designed in a stunning bell shape, the body features a patent-pending, multi-layer, extra thick (9 mm) base of aluminum, copper and steel. This technology provides exceptional heat conductivity for quick, even heat distribution that helps prevent food from burning even in the corners.

## Kirkland Signature Hard-Anodized Professional Roasting Pan and Rack

Costco also offers the Kirkland Signature Hard-Anodized Professional Roasting Pan. With all the same cooking and non-stick features of the hard-anodized cookware, the roaster has depth enough for lasagna and other oven-cooked foods and riveted cast aluminum handles designed extra wide for ease of potholder use.

An added bonus is the full-size, extra-sturdy wire roasting rack, which has a special nonstick coating for easy cleaning.

## *Kirkland Signature Cookware*

*Many young couples are clueless when it comes to selecting long-lasting, quality cookware. Costco comes to the rescue by offering private-label Kirkland Signature cookware in two sets of today's most popular fabrications as well as a perfect-for-the-holidays roasting pan.*

## Kirkland Signature Hard-Anodized 15-piece Professional Cookware

Manufactured with reinforced non-stick technology from DuPont, these Costco Kirkland Signature pots and pans are truly in a league of their own. Each piece is hard-anodized, which means it's twice as strong as stainless steel, with three times the wear. They also have an ultra-smooth exterior, plus riveted, sturdy stainless steel fittings for extra safety and commercial handles made of a thick hollow-core cast construction for a more comfortable grip.

This set is perfect for the bride or groom who enjoys pans that are easy to clean, durable, scratch-resistant, nonporous, nonreactive and non-stick.

**Costco Tip:** Add a few wooden spoons to the outside wrapping, as wooden or plastic utensils are recommended for maximum food release.

Cinco de
Mayo Fiesta

On May 5, 1862, *a ragtag army of Mexican villagers* from Puebla joined poorly equipped soldiers led by General Ignacio Zaragoza to prevent Emperor Napoleon III's mighty French army from marching on Mexico City, just 80 miles to the northwest. The victory at Puebla would come to be marked by a national holiday.

Each year, *cinco de mayo* commemorates this small group's contribution to history. The holiday symbolizes Mexican unity and national pride, and is increasingly celebrated in the United States in recognition of Mexican culture, food, music and customs.

While food is a primary focus of *cinco de mayo,* colorful touches such as bright red and yellow paper flowers, piñatas swaying from trees and music playing in the background add to the festivities.

*Viva la fiesta!*

## MENU

## Down Mexico Way

*A visit to colonial-style Puebla, Mexico, during* cinco de mayo *finds a re-enactment of the battle, fiestas and indigenous foods such as* mole poblano, *a chocolate-chile sauce poured over turkey or chicken;* chile en nogada, *meat-stuffed poblano chile peppers covered with walnut-pomegranate sauce; and* camotes, *a sweet-potato confection. A good souvenir is a piece of the lovely local blue-and-white glazed pottery called* azulejos.

Costco Member
Barbara Pullo

### Don Miguel Mexican Foods
## Guacamole Especial

Flautas, a Mexican favorite of warm, cigar-shaped, rolled tortillas stuffed with tender seasoned shredded beef or skinless chicken, are the perfect accompaniment to this avocado dip. *Muy bien!*

1 package Don Miguel Garlic Chicken
 or *Shredded Beef Flautas*

6 ripe avocados

1 medium onion, minced

2 tablespoons coarsely chopped cilantro

4 serrano chiles, or to taste,
 deveined and chopped

1/2 teaspoon salt, or to taste

Prepare flautas according to package instructions. Peel the avocados, place fruit in a bowl and mash with a fork. Add the remaining ingredients, reserving some onion and chile for garnish, and mix well. Serve immediately on one side of a platter of warmed flautas. Makes 3 cups.

## Barbara Pullo's Camarones Picantes

"These shrimp are even better the second day," says this Piermont, New York, Costco member.

1/4 cup white wine vinegar

1/4 teaspoon prepared horseradish

2 teaspoons prepared honey mustard

2 teaspoons tomato puree

1/2 teaspoon chili powder, or to taste

Salt, to taste

1 cup Kirkland Signature extra-virgin olive oil

1 dash Italian seasoning

1 pound frozen cooked shrimp, thawed, cleaned and deveined

4-5 plum tomatoes, sliced very thin

1 large sweet onion, sliced very thin

Combine the vinegar, horseradish, mustard, tomato puree, chili powder, salt, olive oil and Italian seasoning. Pour half of this mixture over the shrimp and refrigerate 5 hours. Pour the remaining sauce over the tomatoes and reserve. Put the onion slices in cold water so they will be crisp. At serving time, combine the shrimp, tomatoes and onions. Makes 8 servings.

## Nalley's South of the Border Quiche

1 1/2 cups flour

Pinch salt

1/2 cup margarine

1/4 cup cold water

30 ounces Nalley's Chili*

1 clove garlic, chopped

1 tablespoon chopped parsley

4 eggs, beaten

1/2 cup grated Cheddar cheese

Sour cream

Preheat oven to 375°F. Place flour and salt in bowl. Cut margarine into flour; stir in water. Turn onto floured surface and knead 5 times. Wrap and chill 30 minutes. Roll out and line 10-inch quiche dish. Fit foil over pastry and weight with dried beans. Bake 15 minutes; lift out foil and weights. Mix chili, garlic, parsley and eggs. Pour into pastry; top with cheese. Bake at 350°F 50 minutes, or until lightly browned. Slice and top with sour cream. Makes 8 servings.

*Brands may vary by region; substitute a similar product.*

## Farmer John Baja Bacon Bites

Specially cured and hardwood smoked, Farmer John Bacon adds a rich western flavor to this dish.

12 strips Farmer John Bacon, cut in half crosswise*

2 medium Fuji or Granny Smith apples, cored and peeled, cut in 3/4-inch slices

6 tablespoons packed brown sugar

1 teaspoon cinnamon

1 teaspoon chili powder

1/4 teaspoon cayenne pepper, or to taste

**1.** Cook bacon in skillet over medium heat until it just starts to brown but is still limp; drain.

**2.** Wrap each bacon piece around an apple slice. Secure with a toothpick.

**3.** In a small bowl, combine remaining ingredients and blend well. Dip both sides of each bacon bite in sugar, pressing into bacon.

**4.** Broil 4 inches from heat 2-3 minutes per side, or until bacon is browned, turning once. Makes 8 servings.

*Brands may vary by region; substitute a similar product.*

## Excel Corporation
### Tex-Mex Fillets

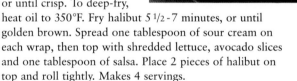

3/4 cup honey

1/4 cup balsamic vinegar

1 teaspoon condensed smoke-flavor seasoning

1 teaspoon chili seasoning

2 teaspoons salt

8 fillet steaks, about 8 ounces each

In a small bowl, combine honey, vinegar, condensed smoke-flavor seasoning, chili seasoning and salt. Place steaks in shallow non-metallic pan; brush marinade on fillets and reserve the remainder. Cover fillets and refrigerate 1 hour. Heat grill. Cook fillets 8-10 minutes per side for medium-rare, brushing occasionally with marinade. To serve, heat extra marinade and spoon over fillets. Makes 8 servings.

## Trident Seafoods
### PubHouse Halibut Santa Fe Wrap

8 pieces Trident PubHouse Halibut*

4 tablespoons sour cream

4 spinach wraps or flour tortillas

1/2 head lettuce, shredded

1 avocado, pitted, peeled and sliced

4 tablespoons salsa

Preheat oven to 425°F. Place halibut on baking sheet; cook 20-22 minutes, or until crisp. To deep-fry, heat oil to 350°F. Fry halibut 5 1/2 - 7 minutes, or until golden brown. Spread one tablespoon of sour cream on each wrap, then top with shredded lettuce, avocado slices and one tablespoon of salsa. Place 2 pieces of halibut on top and roll tightly. Makes 4 servings.

*Brands may vary by region; substitute a similar product.*

**Costco Member Shirley Kirchner**

## Prime Time Stuffed Peppers

8 Prime Time bell peppers
(red, yellow, orange or green)*

1 1/4 teaspoons salt, divided

1 teaspoon ground black pepper

3 cups cooked rice

1 15-ounce can black beans, drained and rinsed

1 11-ounce can corn, drained

1 medium onion, peeled and chopped

1 cup chopped walnuts

1 4-ounce can diced green chiles

1/2 teaspoon smoke-flavor seasoning

1/2 teaspoon ground cumin

1/2 cup (2 ounces) shredded Monterey Jack cheese
(or Jalapeño Pepper Jack)

Preheat oven to 350°F. Cut thin slice from one side of peppers; remove seeds and membranes; rinse. Cook peppers 5 minutes in boiling water to cover. Drain. Season insides with 1 teaspoon of the salt and the pepper. Combine rice, beans, corn, onion, walnuts, chiles, smoke-flavor seasoning, cumin and remaining salt in a medium bowl. Spoon 1 cup rice mixture into each pepper. Stand upright in 9-by-13-inch baking pan. Cover with foil and bake 20 minutes. Remove foil, sprinkle peppers with cheese and cook another 5 minutes, or until cheese has melted. Makes 8 servings.

*Brands may vary by region; substitute a similar product.*

## Shirley Kirchner's Sweet Potato Fries

This Lititz, Pennsylvania, member writes, "I could give you so many recipes, as I buy as much as possible from Costco." Our judges raved about Shirley's sweet potato fries. They are sure to liven up your *cinco de mayo* feast.

**1.** Preheat oven to 450°F.

**2.** Start by using 8-10 Costco Louisiana yams. Use one per person. Peel the potatoes and cut into french fry shapes. Place in a 1-gallon resealable plastic bag.

**3.** Add any herb you desire. Add chopped fresh garlic (2 cloves), grated Parmesan cheese (1/2-1 cup) and olive oil (1/2 cup). Season with salt and pepper. Shake the bag.

**4.** Place potatoes on a cookie sheet. Bake for approximately 25 minutes, or until soft inside and a little crisp on the outside. Makes 8-10 servings.

## Dare Foods Margarita Parfait

A light parfait made with cool-tasting lime and crunchy crackers is an excellent way to end the Fifth of May celebration.

40 Dare Cabaret Crackers*

1/4 cup sugar

1/2 cup butter, melted

4 8-ounce containers lime-flavored yogurt

2 tablespoons triple sec

2 tablespoons tequila

2 teaspoons grated lime zest, plus more for garnish

16 ounces whipped dessert topping

8-10 lime slices

**1.** Put crackers and sugar in food processor. While running, add melted butter and process until you have fine crumbs.

**2.** Mix yogurt with triple sec, tequila and lime zest. Fold in dessert topping until well incorporated.

**3.** In a parfait glass, add a spoon of yogurt filling and then top with a thick layer of cracker crumbs. Repeat until glass is full.

**4.** Sprinkle a pinch of lime zest on top. Garnish with a slice of lime. For fun, serve in a margarita glass with a salted rim. Makes 8-10 servings.

*Brands may vary by region; substitute a similar product.*

Costco Member
John Perea

## Norco Ranch Tutti-Frutti Meringue Round

1 cup plus
    3 tablespoons sugar

2 teaspoons cornstarch

1 teaspoon grated
    orange peel

4 Norco Ranch eggs,
    separated*

2 cups low-fat
    vanilla yogurt

1/2 teaspoon cream of tartar

4 cups assorted fresh fruit (whole blueberries, cherries, raspberries and/or grapes; sliced peaches, strawberries, apples, carambolas (starfruit) and/or peeled kiwi; and/or melon balls)

In medium saucepan, stir together 3 tablespoons sugar, cornstarch and orange peel. Add egg yolks and yogurt. Cook over medium heat, stirring constantly, until mixture boils and thickens. Cover and chill. Preheat oven to 225°F. In large mixing bowl at high speed, beat egg whites with cream of tartar until foamy. Add 1 cup sugar, 2 tablespoons at a time, beating constantly until whites stand in stiff peaks. With spoon, spread mixture in lined 12-inch pizza pan, forming a rim. Bake until firm, 1-1 1/2 hours. Turn off oven and let stand in oven 1 more hour. To serve, spread chilled custard over meringue shell and top with fruit. Makes 8 servings.

*Brands may vary by region; substitute a similar product.*

## John Perea's Bizochitos

This recipe came on stationery from Casa de los Pereas, and one taste told us that this family knows a thing or two about cooking.

2 cups lard

1 cup sugar

1 teaspoon
    crushed
    anise seed
    (or extract)

2 eggs

6 cups sifted flour

3 teaspoons baking powder

1/2 teaspoon salt

1/4 cup water (or wine)

Cinnamon sugar:
    1 teaspoon cinnamon in
    1/2 cup sugar

**1.** Preheat oven to 350°F.

**2.** Cream lard with hand thoroughly. Add sugar and anise seed.

**3.** Beat eggs and add to lard mixture, blending until light and fluffy.

**4.** Sift flour with baking powder and salt. Add to first mixture. Add water and knead until well mixed.

**5.** Roll 1/4 inch thick. Cut into fancy shapes.

**6.** Roll both sides of each cookie in cinnamon sugar.

**7.** Bake approximately 12 minutes, or until slightly browned. Makes 4-6 dozen.

# Personalized Piñatas and Mexican Crepe-Paper Flowers

*By Pat Volchok,*
*Editorial Director*

*Piñatas*— symbols or figures covered in paper with surprises hidden inside—may have originated in China. The custom of using a stick to break them open reached Europe in the 14th century.

In the early 16th century, Spanish missionaries to North America discovered that the Aztecs had a similar tradition. For many centuries, piñatas were part of religious occasions such as Lent or Christmas, but today they also are used for birthdays and other parties. They come in all shapes and sizes and are traditionally filled with candies and fruit. Coins, toys and party-themed mementos are modern additions.

To make a piñata, **1** blow up a balloon and cover it with three layers of newspaper mâché, making sure to leave a small gap at the knotted end so that the balloon can be removed later. Prop it on top of an empty tuna can and then drape a long, sturdy piece of string over the top and down the sides. Both ends should extend at least 2 feet beyond the balloon. Cut another equal-sized length of string and drape it over the first piece at right angles and down the sides.

Cover with another three or four layers of newspaper mâché. (Note: The more papier-mâché layers, the harder it will be to break, so take this into consideration. A piñata for a small child should have only two to three layers of mâché or it will never break.) **2** Let it dry for up to four days before popping the balloon and gently pulling it out through the hole. Put in candies, gum, small fruits, coins and even small toys. Close the hole with more newspaper mâché and let dry for

at least 24 hours. Cover with colored paper or paint and decorate with glitter, ribbons and crepe paper streamers. **3** Use as is, or attach cones or other odd-shaped cardboard pieces to form a rudimentary star, bunny ears or simple hands and feet.

Hang the piñata by the strings outside and let everyone have a turn at being blindfolded and trying to hit the piñata with a stick or bat. When the piñata breaks, the treats are up for grabs. (Note: If small children are playing, they can easily be pushed aside and end up with nothing, so always have a few extra goodie bags on hand.)

*Mexican crepe-paper* flowers come in all shapes and sizes. While the traditional approach is to fold squares of tissue paper or crepe paper into even accordion pleats and then tie and fan them, there is another method that provides an added touch of pizzazz.

Stack six to eight full sheets of brightly colored tissue or crepe paper on top of one another. On the top sheet only, create a template by drawing flat four- or six-petal flowers of different shapes and sizes (similar to the look of a flower cookie-cutter). Cover the entire sheet of paper. Using these patterns, carefully cut through all layers of paper at once. Each stack represents one flower.

Gather up a stack and poke a hole through the center of the flower. Run two pipe cleaners halfway through the hole and then slightly rotate each sheet of the flower. Pinch the paper to the pipe cleaners at the hole. Secure by twirling green florist tape around the flower and pipe cleaners. Frill the flower's edges and bend the inner pipe cleaners to resemble stamens. ∾

**Topps** *candy is the perfect piñata treat*

The Topps Company was founded in 1938 as a gum manufacturer. After World War II, the company redirected its efforts to the bubble gum business and introduced Bazooka, the "Atom Bubble Gum," a reflection of the mind-set in the postwar era.

Representing the gum was The Atom Bubble Boy, and he appeared in the original print ads. But he didn't really catch on, and within a couple of years, Bazooka Joe was created.

Today, major league ballplayers get free Bazooka in the dugouts, and recently a piece of discarded Bazooka from Luis Gonzalez of the Arizona Diamondbacks was auctioned on eBay.

We can't guarantee that your Bazooka gum will turn into a collector's item, but we can bet its appearance at cinco de mayo will have jaws moving. Besides Bazooka, The Topps Company offers a wide variety of specialty candy.

# Mother's Day:
# The Queen's Brunch

$\mathcal{M}$others the world over remind their children constantly that a good meal starts the day off right, so there's no better way to begin Mom's special day than with a brunch just for her.

The key words to remember—besides thank you—are awakening appetites, relaxed atmosphere and informal staging. Plan a menu that offers numerous choices and ease of preparation. Keep the atmosphere low-key, so the focus stays where it belongs, on Mom.

We've done our part by tailoring a menu that includes sweet buns, flavorful quiche, refreshing salad and decadent desserts. Now the rest is up to you.

## MENU

# Costco's Sue McConnaha Shares the Costco Muffin Story

Costco muffins—quick breads baked in a cup-shaped mold—are the perfect Mother's Day brunch assignment for those family members who don't know a pot holder from a plant stand.

Sue McConnaha, vice president of Costco bakery operations, whose stamp of approval has been on each bakery item since the department's inception in June 1987, reports, "The first Costco muffin was hand-dropped into a jumbo muffin tin designed to hold 15 extra-large muffins. The muffins were such an instant success that for the first year, some of Costco's current executive and senior vice presidents helped us hand-drop them into the pans each morning."

Since that time, Sue has overseen the growth of the Costco Bakery program, which now includes 286 bakeries, 715 ovens and 4,100 bakers. Costco's original muffin flavors were blueberry, banana nut, double chocolate chip, almond poppy, raisin bran and carrot. Four of the originals—blueberry, banana nut, double chocolate chip and almond poppy—are still in the family, along with the current additions of apple crumb, lemon-filled and corn.

Staying true to the formula, Costco muffins are baked fresh daily by Costco bakers and made with the best ingredients from around the world.

While it's hard not to eat the entire box of fresh muffins in one sitting, they can be frozen individually in plastic wrap and aluminum foil. To enjoy again, defrost overnight or place frozen muffins in a preheated 380°F oven for 15 minutes.

Costco muffins are available in packs of 12 in either a variety of flavors or just your single personal choice. While once considered only breakfast or teatime treats, muffins are now served with lunch or dinner and also work well for picnics, lunch boxes or traveling snacks.

Finally, as you sit down and enjoy a Costco muffin, think about this: It would take 11,333 days for one Costco oven, baking 360 muffins per cycle, to cook all of the muffins sold annually in Costco bakeries in the United States! ∾

Costco's Sue McConnaha has some creative ideas for using your muffins in other recipes:

• Place half of a banana nut muffin in a bowl, add a scoop of Kirkland Signature Vanilla Ice Cream and drizzle it with butterscotch topping and chopped walnuts.

• Chop up two double chocolate chip muffins and fold into your favorite brownie batter.

• Layer cubes of almond poppy muffin with fresh custard and whipped cream for a great parfait.

• Slice two blueberry muffins and use in your favorite bread pudding recipe.

• Slice the lemon-filled muffin in 1/2-inch slices and top with sliced fresh fruit.

## Minute Maid Orange-Pecan Sticky Buns

Minute Maid has taken all the guesswork out of making sticky buns by using premade frozen puff pastry. If you've never worked with this kind of dough, we suggest purchasing an extra box to practice with.

*2 cups Minute Maid Premium Orange Juice*

*1 1/2 cups chopped or whole pecans*

*1/2 cup raisins (optional)*

*1 teaspoon cinnamon*

*2 tablespoons unsalted butter, melted*

*1 box frozen puff pastry sheets, thawed*

*3/4 cup packed light brown sugar*

*3/4 cup light corn syrup*

**1.** Preheat oven to 375°F.

**2.** In a saucepan, bring orange juice to a boil; reduce heat to medium-high and cook for 25 minutes, or until juice is reduced by half.

**3.** Combine pecans with 1/2 cup reduced orange juice; set aside. If using raisins, combine with 2 tablespoons reduced orange juice; set aside.

**4.** Add cinnamon to melted butter. Remove 1 puff pastry sheet from package, open up to full size and brush with butter. If using raisins, drain and spread half over the sheet. Loosely roll the dough into a log and chill for 30 minutes. Repeat with the second sheet.

**5.** Scoop out pecans and divide among 2 greased 6-cup muffin pans. Divide brown sugar among the muffin cups. Pour 1 tablespoon corn syrup into each muffin cup. Cut each dough log into six buns and place one in each muffin cup, flattening slightly. Set muffin pans on a foil-lined baking sheet.

**6.** Bake 30-35 minutes, or until light golden brown. Remove from the oven and brush with reduced orange juice. Makes 12 muffins.

## Jimmy Dean Sausage and Egg Breakfast Pizza

Pizza for brunch, why not? Especially when the pizza is made with refrigerated crescent rolls, hash browns and Jimmy Dean, the No. 1 roll sausage brand in the country. This sausage makes any dish fit for a queen and easy enough for the king and court jesters to prepare.

*1 can refrigerated crescent rolls*

*1 pound Jimmy Dean Sausage, cooked, crumbled and drained*

*1 cup frozen hash brown potatoes, thawed*

*3 tablespoons each diced red, green and yellow bell pepper*

*1 cup grated sharp Cheddar cheese*

*5 eggs, beaten*

*1/4 cup milk*

*1/2 teaspoon salt*

*1/2 teaspoon ground black pepper*

*2 tablespoons grated Parmesan cheese*

**1.** Preheat oven to 375°F.

**2.** Separate crescent rolls into 8 triangles. Place in a circle in an ungreased 12-inch pizza pan with points toward the center. Press together to form a crust and seal perforations.

**3.** Sprinkle cooked sausage evenly over the crust. Top with potatoes and diced bell peppers. Sprinkle with Cheddar cheese.

**4.** Combine eggs, milk, salt and pepper. Pour over crust. Sprinkle with Parmesan.

**5.** Bake 25-30 minutes, or until the crust is browned and the eggs are set. Makes 8 servings.

## Switzerland Emmentaler
## Cheese and Onion Quiche

One of the most renowned cheeses of Switzerland is Emmentaler, which is handmade from cow's milk. This nutty-flavored cheese, with its round holes and natural light-colored rind, blends well with onions and fondues, or with fruit for dessert.

*7 ounces Switzerland Emmentaler Cheese*

*1 small onion*

*1 cup milk*

*1 tablespoon flour*

*3 ounces plain yogurt*

*Salt and pepper*

*1 9-inch single piecrust*

**1.** Preheat oven to 375°F.

**2.** Shred or cut cheese into small pieces. Cut onion into strips.

**3.** In a saucepan, mix milk and flour, heat rapidly and cook on low for 5 minutes. Mix in cheese, onion, yogurt and salt and pepper to taste. Pour into piecrust.

**4.** Bake 35-45 minutes, or until golden brown. Serve warm or at room temperature. Makes 8 servings.

## California Avocado and Ready Pac Spring Mix Salad

California avocados and baby leaf lettuces and greens are a fresh, natural and wholesome part of a healthy diet.

*1/4 cup + 2 tablespoons olive oil*

*3 tablespoons red wine vinegar*

*1 1/2 teaspoons grated lime peel*

*1 1/2 tablespoons fresh lime juice*

*2 tablespoons chopped fresh basil leaves*

*3/4 teaspoon dry mustard*

*1/2 teaspoon salt*

*1/2 teaspoon pepper*

*2-3 California avocados, peeled and sliced*

*1 16-ounce package Ready Pac Spring Mix (baby leaf lettuces and greens)*

*Shredded Parmesan cheese*

**1.** In a small bowl, whisk together oil, vinegar, lime peel and juice, basil, dry mustard, salt and pepper.

**2.** Arrange avocado slices on greens. Sprinkle salad with shredded Parmesan cheese to taste. Drizzle with dressing and enjoy. Makes 8 servings.

*Submitted on behalf of California Avocado Commission and Ready Pac Produce.*

## Melba Mallon's
## Apricot Bread Pudding

A recipe using stale croissants ... how brilliant! What's more, this Bridgewater, New Jersey, Costco member promises that bread pudding haters will love this recipe.

*1 cup orange-flavored liqueur*

*¹/4 cup freshly squeezed orange juice*

*5 cups heavy cream*

*6 large eggs*

*1 cup sugar*

*2 teaspoons vanilla extract*

*Zest of one orange*

*8 stale Costco Bakery croissants, cut into cubes*

*1 cup dried apricots, diced*

*¹/4 cup raisins*

*Confectioners' sugar for dusting (optional)*

*Vanilla ice cream*

**1.** Preheat oven to 350°F. Combine liqueur and orange juice in a saucepan, bring to a boil and simmer for a few minutes. Remove from heat and cool.

**2.** Using the whisk attachment of an electric mixer, blend the orange juice mixture with cream, eggs, sugar, vanilla and orange zest.

**3.** In another bowl, combine croissant pieces, diced apricots and raisins. Arrange in greased 9-by-13-inch glass baking pan and cover evenly with the custard. Let stand 15 minutes to soak up liquid.

**4.** Cover baking dish with foil and place in a water bath (put inside a larger pan and add hot water to the larger pan to come up about halfway). Bake 1 hour. Remove foil and bake one-half hour longer, or until pudding is firm and golden brown.

**5.** Serve warm with a dusting of confectioners' sugar and a generous scoop of ice cream on the side. Makes 8-10 servings.

Costco Member
Melba Mallon

## DFI/Gold Rush Cantaloupe–Cream Cheese Pie

*2 cups sugar*

*6 tablespoons cornstarch*

*4 egg yolks, beaten*

*4 cups milk*

*1 teaspoon vanilla extract*

*8 ounces cream cheese, softened*

*1¹/2 cups pureed DFI/Gold Rush cantaloupe, plus ¹/2 cantaloupe, thinly sliced*

*1 9-inch piecrust, baked*

Combine sugar, cornstarch and egg yolks in heavy saucepan. Gradually add milk while stirring over medium heat. Bring to rolling boil, being careful not to let custard stick to bottom of pan. Remove from heat and add vanilla and cream cheese, stirring until cream cheese melts. Add cantaloupe. Mix thoroughly, then pour into prepared crust. Chill 4 hours. To serve, lay thin slices of cantaloupe in pinwheel fashion on top of pie. Slice and serve with dollop of whipped cream if desired, and garnish with mint sprigs. Makes 8 servings.
*Recipe developed by Linda Carey and Pat Volchok.*

# Mother's Day Gifts...
## the Costco Way

*After the meal, a few gift suggestions for Mom*

*Bialetti Sauté Pans*

### Bialetti Sauce and Sauté Pans

With more than 60 years of experience in cookware, Bialetti's name is a guarantee of quality and durability for all its products. Bialetti has the simplicity of tradition but pursues modernity through constant aesthetic and practical innovation.

Whether you choose the deep 5.5-quart saucepan or the set of 8-, 10- and 12-inch sauté pans for Mom, all are made of heavy-duty aluminum for even heat distribution and have ergonomically designed handles that stay cool to the touch on a warm stove.

With DuPont Teflon applied in a three-coat spray process for toughness plus patented reinforcement against abrasions and scratches, the pieces are all perfectly balanced for excellent food release and easy cleaning.

Ideal for low-fat cooking, dishwasher safe and with lifetime warranties, Bialetti pans come in colors that add pizzazz to any kitchen—metallic green, blue or black.

So check out Mom's sauce or sauté pans, and if they are looking a little worn, surprise her with a Bialetti—it's sure to please.

*Bialetti Saucepan*

### Hamilton Beach Mix Smart
### 10-Speed Electronic Mixer

Our guess is that many moms still use the same hand mixer they received as a wedding present eons ago. If so, they will be astounded at the technological improvements that the leading mixer brand, Hamilton Beach, has achieved with its Mix Smart mixer. It is truly enlightening.

• Digital timer begins timing on a display screen when mixing starts, to prevent overbeating.
• Control pad displays each speed as you power up or down.
• Soft start speeds mixer up gradually to eliminate splatters.
• Microchip senses and adjusts power for optimal performance and to prevent mixer slowdown.

Included in the storage case is a whisk attachment, as well as traditional and wire beaters.

## Martex Bare Necessities Vellux Hotel Blanket

If you can't send Mom to a fine hotel for Mother's Day, why not give her a five-star accoutrement—a lightweight, soft-to-the-skin WestPoint Stevens Martex Vellux hotel blanket?

WestPoint Stevens, America's leading maker of linens and bath towels, notes that this blanket's "warmth without weight" concept provides all the best of a heavier blanket, with its tailored hem, double-needle stitching and all-nylon face on an insulating base, but without the cumbersome weight or dry-cleaning expense normally associated with quality blankets. It's also certain to look as fresh as the day it was purchased even after numerous launderings, and will not mat or pill.

P.S. These blankets make a great gift for grandmas, too!

## Cecil Saydah Kitchen Towel Set

Mom's kitchen can be inexpensively rejuvenated with an eight-pack kitchen towel set supplied by the Cecil Saydah Company, a 50-year-old Los Angeles-based manufacturer. These oversized 100 percent cotton terry and velour kitchen towels provide superior absorbency and durability while still being decorative.

Stand-outs generally include two printed towels, two printed accent border towels and four solid-color accent terry towels in blue, purple, yellow, sage and the hottest new kitchen color—red.

**Costco Tip:** Keep a supply of these towels on hand to use as "wrapping paper" for small kitchen accessory gifts, or divide up the eight-pack for numerous hostess gifts.

## Phoenix Down Corporation Throw

It's ideal if a Mother's Day gift can be both fashionable and functional. One such gift is Phoenix Down Corporation's popular throw.

Made especially for Costco at a full 58 by 74 inches so that it covers the whole body (traditional down throws are 50 by 58 inches), it's packed with 14 ounces of 500 fill power down, for surprisingly lightweight insulating warmth. The easy-care covering is made of soft, sueded, non-pilling lightweight polyester that comes in fashionable reversible colors, plaids and prints.

Cleaning is a breeze, as this down throw is made to be tossed in the washing machine on a cold, gentle cycle with like colors and then tumble dried on low. Professional dry cleaning is also an option.

This is the perfect gift for the mom whose life is split between home, sporting events, camping and curling up on the couch with a good book.

*Afternoon Tea Party*

"*At home*" teas were established during the 19th century in England. It was a time set aside by a hostess when she would be "at home" in the afternoon to greet guests. The tea was served not in the drawing room but rather at a buffet in the dining room, where light refreshments also would be provided. Tea soon became not just a drink but also a statement about the civilized world, in which ceremony and tradition were integral components.

A tea party is perfect for all ages, relatively easy to plan and prepare in advance, inexpensive and festive. The presentation can be well thought out or merely a jumble of plates of sweets next to trays of sandwiches. Mixed and matched china teacups and saucers, found rather reasonably priced in many thrift shops, are nice additions.

Of course, if Earl Grey is not your cup of tea, coffee and wine also can be served.

## MENU

## Quaker Glazed Honey Orange Oatmeal Muffins

Quaker Oatmeal and Tropicana Pure Premium orange juice both contain many nutrients that have been studied for their heart-healthy benefits. Quick and Old Fashioned Quaker Oats contain soluble fiber that may help reduce the risk of heart disease. Tropicana Pure Premium orange juice is a good source of potassium. So let your cravings get the better of you and indulge in an extra one or two of these muffins.

1 cup Quaker oats (quick or old-fashioned, uncooked)

2/3 cup low-fat buttermilk

1/2 cup plus 1 teaspoon Tropicana Pure
   Premium orange juice, divided

1/4 cup plus 2 tablespoons honey, divided

3 tablespoons vegetable oil

2 teaspoons grated orange peel, divided

1 egg, lightly beaten

1 1/4 cups all-purpose flour

1/4 cup wheat germ or oat bran

2 1/2 teaspoons baking powder

1/2 teaspoon baking soda

1/2 teaspoon salt

**1.** Heat oven to 400°F. Line 12 medium muffin cups with paper baking cups or spray bottoms only with cooking spray.

**2.** In large bowl, combine oats, buttermilk, 1/2 cup orange juice, 1/4 cup honey, oil and 1 1/2 teaspoons orange peel; stir well and let stand 10 minutes. Stir in egg until blended.

**3.** In medium bowl, combine flour, wheat germ, baking powder, baking soda and salt; mix well. Add to oat mixture all at once; stir just until dry ingredients are moistened. (Do not overmix.) Fill muffin cups almost full.

**4.** Bake 18-20 minutes, or until a toothpick inserted in center comes out with a few moist crumbs clinging to it. Cool muffins in pan on wire rack 5 minutes; remove from pan. Cool 10 minutes.

**5.** Stir together remaining 2 tablespoons honey, 1 teaspoon orange juice and 1/2 teaspoon orange peel in custard cup. Quickly dip tops of muffins into honey mixture, allowing excess to drip off. Serve warm. Makes 12 muffins.

**Costco Tip:** For small tea-party muffins, bake in mini muffin tins 10-12 minutes.

### Nancy's Petite Quiche Platter

Prebaked petite quiches made of a delicate flour-and-butter pastry and filled with milk, eggs, Swiss cheese, bacon, chives, onions and spinach are another excellent choice for teas, luncheons and even late-night snacks. Nancy's suggests rewarming the quiches in a conventional oven for a flakier crust or the microwave for a softer pastry. They also warn that overheating can cause dryness.

To add a little character to your presentation, try any of these Nancy's Petite Quiche garnishing tips:

- Cut slivers into a small piece of red bell pepper without cutting all the way through. Fan out the slivers and set across a celery leaf. Place garnish on top of and next to the quiches.
- For a festive look and a splash of color, sprinkle chopped red pepper and parsley around your plate of Petite Quiches.
- Line the bottom of your plate with a broad leaf. Example: Use a tea leaf or banana leaf and place quiches on the leaf for an Asian ambience. (These leaves can be found in Asian grocery stores.)

Costco Member
Barbara Boyd

## Barbara Boyd's Citrus Herb Wafers

"To achieve a dessert snack without dairy products or fat, I came up with this delightful wafer treat," says this Lake Tahoe, California, member.

1/2 cup light olive oil

1/2 cup sugar

1 large egg white

2 tablespoons minced fresh rosemary

2 tablespoons grated lemon or orange peel

1/2 teaspoon vanilla extract

1 1/4 cups all-purpose flour

**1.** Preheat oven to 350°F.

**2.** Beat olive oil and sugar in mixing bowl until creamy. Beat in egg white, rosemary, peel and vanilla. At low speed, mix in flour just until combined.

**3.** Shape dough into one 10-by-1 1/2-inch log. Wrap well in aluminum foil and refrigerate 1 hour.

**4.** Slice log into 1/4-inch-thick slices. Bake on ungreased cookie sheets until edges are lightly golden. Transfer to cooling racks. Makes approximately 24 wafers.

## Wilson Batiz Tomato, Mozzarella and Basil Tea Sandwiches

12 slices white bread, thinly sliced preferred

8 ounces mozzarella cheese, sliced in 1/4-inch-thick circles

1/4 cup mayonnaise

2-3 Wilson Batiz tomatoes, sliced in 1/4-inch-thick circles*

Salt and pepper to taste

Fresh basil sprigs

Using a circular cookie-cutter similar in size to the circumference of the tomatoes, cut out 24 circles of bread. (Freeze the leftovers for bread crumbs.) Use the cookie-cutter, if needed, to also cut the slices of mozzarella to fit the bread. Spread a thin layer of mayonnaise on each bread cutout, then top with a slice of tomato and a circle of mozzarella. Sprinkle lightly with salt and a touch of pepper. Top with a small cluster of basil leaves. Makes 24 petite sandwiches.

*Brands may vary by region; substitute a similar product.*
*Recipe developed by Pat Volchok.*

## Lindsay Olive Salad Finger Sandwiches

1 6-ounce can Lindsay small or medium ripe olives, drained, finely chopped†*

1/4 cup light mayonnaise

3 tablespoons pine nuts

1/8 teaspoon salt

Ground black pepper to taste

3 tablespoons chopped fresh basil

3 tablespoons chopped green onion

3 tablespoons chopped drained sun-dried tomatoes packed in oil

12 slices thin-sliced white bread

1/2 cup light cream cheese

Combine all ingredients except bread and cream cheese; mix well. Cover and chill at least 1 hour or up to 24 hours. Cut crusts from bread, forming 4-inch squares. Spread 6 slices of bread with olive mixture; smear cream cheese on other slices. Close sandwiches, pressing lightly. Cut into triangles or rectangles. Makes 24 sandwiches.

†*1 cup plus 2 tablespoons canned Lindsay chopped olives can be substituted.*
*Brands may vary by region; substitute a similar product.*

## Campbell's Savory Petite Meat Loaf Sandwiches

At first glance, meat loaf as a tea sandwich topping might not seem like a fit, but it's always fun to throw in an unexpected twist at any party, especially a party that can teeter precariously on the edge of being stuffy.

1 10 3/4-ounce can Campbell's Tomato Soup

1 1/2 pounds ground beef

1/2 cup dry bread crumbs

1 small onion, finely chopped

1 egg, beaten

1 tablespoon Worcestershire sauce

1/8 teaspoon pepper

Pepperidge Farm Sliced White Bread

1/2 cup mayonnaise

Thin slices of tomato

**1.** On the day before the party, preheat oven to 350°F.

**2.** Mix thoroughly 1/2 cup soup, ground beef, bread crumbs, onion, egg, Worcestershire and pepper. Shape firmly into an 8-by-4-inch loaf in a baking pan.

**3.** Bake 30 minutes. Pour off fat.

**4.** Spoon remaining soup over meat loaf. Bake 30 minutes longer, or until done. Remove from pan, drain and refrigerate overnight.

**5.** On the day of the party, remove crusts from bread, cut in heart shapes using a cookie-cutter and lightly smear with mayonnaise. Slice meat loaf as thin as possible, cut into hearts using a cookie-cutter one size smaller than the one used for the bread, and place on top of the mayonnaise. Top with a thin slice of tomato. Serve immediately. Makes 16-20 sandwiches.

### Campbell's Tomato Soup Suggestions

Campbell's Tomato Soup is good anytime. If you are feeling mellow and want a smooth, creamy texture, use milk. If your appetite calls for a more robust tomato flavor, just add water. Want something zesty? Mix in salsa and sprinkle cheese on top, or simply add croutons or a pat of butter—whatever your taste buds desire.

**Kirkland Signature** Coffee, roasted by **Sara Lee** Coffee & Tea, Iced Drink

Iced coffee is a great solution for the host or hostess who doesn't want to worry about serving warm coffee to a crowd.

Brew Kirkland Signature 100% Colombian or Decaf Arabica Coffee at double strength (to offset melting ice). Chill coffee, stored in a covered container to retain freshness. To serve, pour chilled coffee into a tall glass over ice. Add milk or cream and sugar to taste. Enjoy!

**Iced Coffee Cubes:** Using ice cubes made from coffee helps prevent iced coffee from becoming diluted.

Costco Member
Cynthia Colclasure

## Cynthia Colclasure's Delicious Microwave Caramels

A Costco member who lives in Connell, Washington, makes the best quick, easy and delicious caramels we've encountered. She writes, "My son loves these candies and requests them for every special occasion."

1 cup butter – no substitutes
2 1/4 cups packed light brown sugar
1 14-ounce can sweetened condensed milk
1 cup light corn syrup
1 teaspoon vanilla extract

**1.** Melt butter in a large microwave-safe bowl.

**2.** Add brown sugar, sweetened condensed milk and corn syrup. Stir well. Microwave on high 17-21 minutes, stirring every 3 minutes.

**3.** Add vanilla, mix well, and pour into buttered 9-by-13-inch pan. Cool until set. Cut into squares. Wrap in plastic or waxed paper. Makes 8-10 dozen 1-inch caramels.

## Kirkland Signature Cranberry Tea

Costco's private-label Kirkland Signature Cranberry Cocktail adds a pleasing blush to this tea drink.

8 cups water
24 whole cloves
4 short cinnamon sticks
1/4 cup sugar
8 tea bags
4 cups Kirkland Signature
    Cranberry Cocktail

Combine water, cloves, cinnamon and sugar in saucepan and bring to a boil. Remove cinnamon sticks, add tea bags and steep 3 minutes. Add cranberry cocktail and return to boil. Serve hot. Makes 16 teacup servings.

## Ghirardelli Tuxedo Brownies

1 20-ounce package Ghirardelli Brownie Mix
1/3 cup water
1/3 cup vegetable oil
3 eggs
16 ounces cream cheese, softened
2/3 cup sugar

Preheat oven to 325°F. Blend mix, water, oil and 1 egg until moistened. Spoon into lightly greased 9-by-13-inch pan. In a separate bowl, beat cream cheese and sugar on low speed until smooth. Add 2 eggs and beat until blended. Spread evenly over brownie batter. Bake 40-45 minutes. Cool, cut into 24 squares, and decorate with melted chocolate if desired. Store covered in the refrigerator.

**Kirkland Signature/ Delacre:** Belgian Chocolate Biscuit Assortment

Here's an easy way to add a little slice of European savoir faire to any occasion. Just offer Kirkland Signature Delacre chocolate covered biscuits.

The Delacre Company was established in Belgium in the 1870s by Charles Delacre and soon became recognized as a maker of fine chocolates. By 1890, the company had become renowned for their art in combining delicious Belgian chocolate with fine patissier's biscuits.

Today, Delacre offers more than 13 varieties of luscious biscuits covered in rich Belgian chocolate, and in keeping with tradition, they are all still made in Europe.

**Costco Tip:** These delectable biscuits are also nice gifts for business associates, hostesses, teachers, neighbors, or just as a special treat for you with a pot of tea.

*ea garden events were popular in* England long before the advent of "at home" teas. At these outdoor social occasions, members of fashionable society could, for an entry fee, stroll in beautifully manicured grounds while tea with bread and butter was served. Tea gardens soon became the talk of London.

You can create your own talk of the town by making a tabletop tea garden complete with grass inside your home. All that is needed is a little sense of adventure.

## Supplies

- Plywood, cut ½ inch narrower than all sides of your table's shape.
- Heavy-duty plastic cut to match your table's shape.
- Clean, partially dried pieces of rolled sod that have been cut to fit your tabletop. (This initial stage requires pre-planning, as rolled sod is very dirty. It must be hosed off, turned over occasionally and partially dried for two days to remove any excess mud and moisture and to make it lighter to carry into the house.)
- Coordinating ribbon, equaling the circumference of the cut-out plywood.
- Miniature spring or summer flowers and flowering bulbs. (This might be a good time to divide your perennials and use some of the clumps for the tabletop. You can replant them outside after the party.)
- Garden knife.

## Directions

- If you have table pads, lay them on your table.
- Lay the plastic on top of the pads.
- Place the plywood template on top of the plastic and then cover with the partially dried, pre-cut sod.
- Trim if necessary and stick any plastic that is visible back under the plywood.
- Wrap the entire edge of sod with the coordinating ribbon.
- Remove most of the excess dirt from your bulbs and flowers.
- Using your garden knife, dig holes in the sod and insert the flowers. (I like to make little clumps of assorted flowers down the table and between platters and trays.) The placement of the flowers should look natural, not planned. ✎

# Tea Garden Tablecloth

*By Pat Volchok, Editorial Director*

*Memorial Day*
*Family Reunion*

*A* family reunion is a living legacy. It provides a chance for members to appreciate the family as a unit, gives children a sense of belonging to an extended group, and renews family bonds through retelling stories and adventures, passing down advice and experiences, sharing food and just enjoying kinship.

The simplest reunion is a casual outdoor potluck in a family member's backyard or a nearby park. Red-and-white gingham tablecloths covering picnic tables, topped with milk pitchers full of old-fashioned flowers, are the most undemanding decorations.

Memorial Day is the occasion already set aside to remember those who have been lost to wars. What better time to gather the extended family and honor the past, embrace the present and welcome the future?

## MENU

## Kirkland Signature/Carando Spiral-Sliced Ham with Honey Sweet Potato Salsa

This Costco dual-brand spiral ham is smoked over real hickory chips, with no artificial smoke. No added ingredients are pumped into the meat, which has that rich, full "dry red" ham flavor in every bite. Already sliced with cuts to the bone, this product is easy to serve with little waste.

**1.** Heat oven to 325°F.

**2.** Remove all packaging materials, including the clear "button" on bone of ham.

**3.** Place ham in shallow roasting pan. Quarter and half hams should be cooked flat/face side down. Whole ham should be cooked fat side up. Cover with aluminum foil.

**4.** Bake approximately 8 minutes per pound, until heated through. Do not overcook!

**5.** A quality brown sugar glaze pack is included.

## Honey Sweet Potato Salsa

1/2 cup butter

2 pounds sweet potatoes or yams, peeled and diced

1/4 cup finely chopped yellow onion

1/2 cup pecan pieces, toasted

1/2 cup dried cranberries

1/2 cup honey

2 teaspoons cinnamon

1/4 teaspoon salt

**1.** Melt butter in skillet. Add sweet potatoes and onion; stir-fry over high heat until potatoes are tender.
**2.** Add remaining ingredients; heat through. Serve as an accompaniment to the sliced, glazed ham.
Makes 8 servings.

### Costco's Deli Party Trays

If time is short (when isn't it?) and the family list long, we suggest picking up a few of Costco's Deli Party Trays:

• Vegetable assortment – fresh carrots, broccoli, asparagus, and red and yellow bell peppers with peppercorn ranch dip

• 3 1/2 pounds of large precooked shrimp with cocktail sauce

• Turkey hye roller sandwiches with imported Swiss cheese, fresh lettuce and tomatoes, and real cranberry cream cheese

• Assorted meat-and-cheese platter, with the highest-quality sliced meats, cheeses and mustard

## General Mills Apple-Ricotta Brunch Biscuits

Why have just one kind of biscuit when two would be so much more fun? With just 15 minutes of prep time needed, not to mention oven-fresh flavor and convenience, these biscuits are crowd-perfect.

1 cup ricotta cheese

1/2 cup sugar

1 egg

1/4 cup sliced almonds

1/2 teaspoon cinnamon

1 can (1 pound 0.3 ounces) Pillsbury Grands! refrigerated buttermilk biscuits

1 small apple, cored, peeled and cut into eighths

**1.** Preheat oven to 375°F. Spray 8 jumbo muffin cups or 8 6-ounce custard cups with cooking spray.

**2.** Stir together ricotta, sugar and egg; beat 1 minute on high speed; set aside.

**3.** Stir together almonds and cinnamon; set aside.

**4.** Separate the dough into 8 biscuits. Press each biscuit into the bottom and sides of a muffin cup. Place 1 apple piece in each cup. Spoon 2 rounded tablespoonfuls of cheese mixture over each apple. Sprinkle almond mixture over each.

**5.** Bake 20-25 minutes, or until biscuits are deep golden brown and apples are crisp-tender. Remove from muffin cups and cool 15 minutes. Serve warm. Cover and refrigerate any remaining biscuits. Makes 8 biscuits.

## General Mills Cheese-Garlic Biscuits

Again, convenience with just a five-minute prep time and the backing of a trusted name. It's a combination that's hard to beat.

2 cups Original Bisquick

2/3 cup milk

1/2 cup (2 ounces) shredded Cheddar cheese

1/4 cup butter or margarine, melted

1/4 teaspoon garlic powder

**1.** Preheat oven to 450°F. Stir together Bisquick, milk and cheese until a soft dough forms; beat vigorously for 30 seconds.

**2.** Drop the dough by 10-12 spoonfuls onto an ungreased cookie sheet.

**3.** Bake 8-10 minutes, or until golden brown.

**4.** Stir together butter and garlic powder; brush over warm biscuits before removing them from the cookie sheet. Serve warm. Makes 10-12 biscuits.

Garden Tuna and Pasta Salad

Turkey Antipasto Salad

## ConAgra Foods Salad Trio

With $27 billion in sales, ConAgra Foods is one of the world's leading food companies. These salads will be remembered by all.

## ConAgra Foods Turkey Antipasto Salad

3 cups (12 ounces) bowtie pasta

3 cups chopped cooked Butterball Boneless Young Turkey Breast

3 tomatoes, cut into wedges

2 14-ounce cans quartered artichoke hearts, drained

1 6-ounce can whole pitted black olives, drained

9 pickled pepperoncini, seeded and cut into rings

3/4 cup red onion rings

3 tablespoons chopped fresh basil

1 1/2 teaspoons coarsely ground black pepper

1 cup Italian-style salad dressing

3 tablespoons shredded Parmesan cheese

**1.** Cook pasta according to package directions. Rinse under cold water; drain.

**2.** Combine pasta, turkey, tomatoes, artichoke hearts, olives, pepperoncini, onion, basil and pepper. Add 3/4 cup of the salad dressing; toss to combine. Chill.

**3.** Add the remaining salad dressing if needed. Sprinkle with Parmesan cheese and serve. Makes 12 servings.

## ConAgra Foods Garden Tuna and Pasta Salad

4 cups (16 ounces) mostaccioli pasta

1 28-ounce can Hunt's Whole Tomatoes No Salt Added, drained and coarsely chopped

2 cucumbers, peeled, seeded and coarsely chopped

1 12-ounce can Kirkland Signature/Bumble Bee Albacore Tuna, drained and flaked

3/4 cup shredded carrot

1/2 cup sliced green onion

1/2 cup chopped fresh basil

1 cup mayonnaise

1 teaspoon salt

1 teaspoon coarsely ground black pepper

**1.** Cook pasta according to package directions. Rinse under cold water; drain.

**2.** Combine all ingredients in a large bowl; toss to coat evenly. Chill. Makes 12 servings.

*Picnic German Potato Salad*

## ConAgra Foods Picnic German Potato Salad

*8 slices lean Armour Bacon, cut into 1-inch pieces*

*8 cups sliced small red potatoes*

*6 tablespoons mayonnaise*

*1/4 cup packed brown sugar*

*2 tablespoons grated red onion with juice*

*2 teaspoons Spicy Brown Gulden's Mustard*

*1/2 teaspoon coarsely ground black pepper*

*6 tablespoons cider vinegar*

*1/4 cup sliced green onion*

**1.** Cook bacon in nonstick skillet over medium heat until crisp. Drain on paper towel-lined plate. Crumble. Set aside.

**2.** Combine potatoes and water to cover in saucepan. Bring to boil over high heat. Cover. Reduce heat to low. Simmer 15-20 minutes, or until potatoes are tender. Drain.

**3.** Combine mayonnaise, brown sugar, red onion, mustard and pepper in medium bowl. Stir in vinegar. Add potatoes and half the crumbled bacon. Toss to combine. Garnish with remaining bacon and green onion. Makes 12 servings.

## Jane Klein-Shucklin's Hot Italian Sausage and Pepper Sandwiches

This Costco employee offers an old recipe she adapted from Tingalings and Dickee Dee's restaurants in Newark, New Jersey.

*2-3 baking potatoes, peeled and cut into large bite-size chunks*

*1 each green, red and yellow bell pepper, seeded, cut in strips*

*1 large onion, sliced thin*

*4 Italian sausages, hot or sweet*

*Olive oil*

*Salt, pepper and garlic salt*

*4 kosher hot dogs*

*8 soft French or sourdough rolls*

**1.** Preheat oven to 350°F.

**2.** Microwave or parboil the potatoes for a few minutes.

**3.** In a large baking dish, layer potatoes, peppers and onion with the sausages on top. Drizzle with olive oil so that there is a nice coating on the bottom of pan. Add salt, pepper and garlic salt to taste. Halfway through cooking time, stir the mixture and add hot dogs.

**4.** Bake 1 1/4 -1 1/2 hours. The vegetables, sausages and hot dogs should have a little bit of a roasted color.

**5.** Place hot dogs or sausages in rolls and add vegetables. Top with a squirt of mustard and a shake of salt. Makes 8 servings.

*Costco Employee*
*Jane Klein-Shucklin*

## Making Your Memorial Day Memorable

- Add a smile to your invitees' faces and set a spirited tone by enclosing small plastic ants with your invitation to the reunion picnic.

- It's best to plan a reunion near the family enclave so that tours can be included to sites such as houses where living relatives grew up, places where family members worked and cemeteries where they are buried.

- Remember to provide activities for children. This might be the perfect time to introduce them to sack and three-legged races, pass the orange and watermelon-seed-spitting contests. If prizes are given, make sure that by the end of the reunion every child is a winner, even if it means inventing rewards for extraordinary helper or great dishwasher.

Costco Member
Jody Wilson

## Bee Sweet Citrus Orange Cheesecake

1 cup graham cracker crumbs
1/3 cup firmly packed brown sugar
1/4 cup butter, melted
4 8-ounce packages cream cheese, softened
1 cup sugar
2 tablespoons flour
2 teaspoons vanilla extract
3 tablespoons Bee Sweet fresh orange juice
  (Bee Sweet lemons or limes may be substituted)*
3 teaspoons grated orange peel
4 eggs

Preheat oven to 325°F (300°F for dark nonstick pan). Mix graham cracker crumbs, brown sugar and butter; press in bottom of 9-inch springform pan. Bake 10 minutes. Mix cream cheese, sugar, flour and vanilla with electric mixer on medium speed until blended. Blend in orange juice and grated peel. Add eggs, beating thoroughly. Pour over crust. Bake 1 hour, or until center is almost set. Run knife around rim of pan to loosen cake. Cool before removing rim. Refrigerate 4 hours. Makes 12 servings.

*Brands may vary by region; substitute a similar product.

## Jody Wilson's Almond Joy Cake

We promise joy in Mudville with this Lake Arrowhead, California, member's decadent cake.

1 package devil's food cake mix
1 12-ounce can evaporated milk
2 1/2 cups sugar
25 large marshmallows
14 ounces flaked coconut
1/2 cup butter
2 cups semisweet chocolate chips
3 ounces slivered almonds, toasted

**1.** Prepare cake mix as directed for 9-by-13-inch pan.

**2.** In a saucepan, combine 1/2 can milk and 1 1/2 cups sugar. Bring mixture to rapid boil. Quickly remove from heat. Add marshmallows and stir until melted. Stir in coconut. Pour mixture over top of warm cake.

**3.** In a saucepan, combine remaining sugar and milk. Bring to a boil. Remove from heat. Add butter and chocolate chips. Stir until melted. Pour mixture over coconut-topped cake. Sprinkle with almonds.

**4.** Chill cake at least 2 hours before serving. Cake tastes best if baked the day before. Makes 12-14 servings.

# Family Tree Cookbook

*By Pat Volchok, Editorial Director*

This nation is a melting pot of peoples, and there is no better time than a family reunion to note the varied ancestral roots that make up a family. The compilation of heirloom recipes, handed down and enjoyed through the generations, is one way to document this celebration of family diversity.

The creation of a family-tree cookbook takes organization and tenacity. You can either ask relatives to prepare a favorite family dish and provide the recipe at the time of the reunion or ask everyone to send the recipe ahead of time and bring the dish to the event.

In the first scenario, you will have to compose the cookbook after the fact and devise a means of distribution, whereas the latter allows for delivery at the event and can act as a catalyst for conversation as well as providing a cherished memento. Either way, request a tried-and-true recipe that has some historical family significance, along with genealogy, anecdotes and period photos.

In keeping with the theme, the book's cover can be a line drawing of the family's genealogical tree, the introductory section a history of the family and each chapter a family branch of the tree.

If you plan to distribute the finished book at the reunion, keep in mind that you may need as much as a year to do a first-class job of gathering, testing, writing, proofing, printing and assembling a cookbook.

Be sure to give credit to all contributors by titling each recipe for the person who supplied it, e.g., Aunt Daisy's Cornbread, as shared by Mary Smith.

With the advent of e-mail, recipe collection is much easier, but before actual production, visit your local Costco Print & Copy Center to ask for printing and binding requirements, a time assessment and a price quote. Their free guidance at the beginning of the project can save you many hours of wasted work.

The Internet has a wealth of free information on creating your own cookbook, as well as sites that will do the job for a fee. A good starting point is www.bhg.com, where a Create-a-Cookbook interactive tools resource directory can be accessed free of charge.

Always keep the ultimate goal in mind. It doesn't matter whether the reunion cookbook is a photocopied handwritten document or a hardbound limited-edition masterpiece. What does matter is that it was created and that a family's history has been preserved for generations that follow. ❧

Summer Daze

# THE EASY-LIVIN' SEASON

# Summer Reflections

It's time to throw open the doors and windows—summer has arrived. The extraordinary nights of June, the wealth of products in July and the golden light of August become the perfect entertaining milieu. Activities are transformed into parties: gardening into a garden party, Father's Day into a grilling fantasy, berry festivals into Fourth of July specialties and beach-combing into a shore picnic. That's why an entertaining ambience, both indoors and out, replete with comfort, simplicity, relaxed informality and a wide variety of fresh seasonal foods, is of utmost importance.

Impressive tables can be created by just shifting pots of annuals from the deck, or foraging for additional greens such as blackberry vines, dried weed pods or pruned limbs to add to cut flowers.

Now is not the time to be stuck in the kitchen preparing for a party. The summer beckons all, even the cook.

## Summer Supplies

Party basics should be given a little pizzazz. Paper plates, napkins, and plastic utensils and cups can be presented in wicker baskets, clean flowerpots or even a new wheelbarrow. Wild patterns or splashy colors shout summer, whether indoors or out.

Picnic baskets are big in retro home-entertaining decor. From wicker to nylon, their versatility is unsurpassed. Used as carriers, they can be stocked with wineglasses, napkins, cheese boards, spreaders, cork pullers, plates and utensils. Placed on a table, they make fabulous centerpieces mounded with breads, fruits or drinks.

## Table Elegance

Extend the indoors outside by purchasing beautiful yet functional items that link the table to your surroundings. Accents might include wood, wicker, easy-to-launder tablecloths of sunny yellow or romantic midnight blue, and numerous flickering unscented votives.

Outdoor entertaining calls for serviceware that is unbreakable, unsmashable, dishwasher safe and of high quality.

Invest in extra folding tables and chairs, and remember that it's usually a long way from the kitchen to the picnic table, so gather numerous suitable platters, bowls and baskets.

## Floral Arrangements

Summer's floral decorating mantra must be: simplicity, simplicity, simplicity. Reproduce a farm-stand bouquet by using a water or juice pitcher and filling with a lovely mound of lacy flowers. To create the look, start with a few flower stems lightly gripped in one hand and build the bouquet by turning and adding a few flowers at a time on all sides. Trim off any leaves that will easily decay below the water line and cut the stems to stand a few inches above the pitcher. Or make a fresh flower topiary. Place a wide-mouthed glass jar inside a terra-cotta pot. Fill the jar with water and then stuff floral foam between the jar and pot to secure. Select flowers with sturdy stems, such as daisies or cosmos. Measure to determine how many stems can fit snugly into the jar. Tie a ribbon just under the clump's flower heads. Stuff the stem ends into the jar and cover its opening with dried floral moss. Check the water level daily.

## Costco's Summer Harvest

Set your guests' taste buds tingling with cool drinks, refreshing salads and grilled items...the Costco way.

Seedless Watermelons

Grapes

Peaches

Nectarines

Apricots

Bing Cherries

Rainier Cherries

Blueberries

Raspberries

Corn

Cantaloupes

Halibut

Copper River Salmon

Whole King and
  Coho Salmon

Salmon Milano with
  Basil Butter

Flank Steak with
  Portobello Mushrooms

Sliced Roast Beef, Ham
  and Turkey

Rotisserie Chicken

Cheeses such as
  Provolone, Muenster
  and Imported Swiss

Chicken Caesar Salad

Shrimp Tray with Cocktail Sauce

Greek Salad

Party Trays

Pork Back Ribs

Fresh Tomato and
  Mozzarella Salad

Cheesecakes

Key Lime Pie

Peach Pie

# Savoring the Season with David

**David Andrew
Costco Global
Wine Director**

## Summer

It's easy to think summer equals white wine equals Chardonnay. But stop and consider: Is it refreshing? Is it thirst-quenching? Do you want to go back for a second glass? Chardonnay is higher in alcohol and fuller-bodied than most other whites and, more often than not, oaked. This doesn't exactly add up to the perfect summer drink. Summer is the time to break the routine and try something new. Think cool, fresh, unoaked whites. Here are a few to consider:

Sauvignon Blanc: It has summer written all over it: bright, zesty and herbaceous, with flavors of lemongrass and gooseberry. The best are from Sancerre and Pouilly-Fumé in France and Marlborough in New Zealand.

White Bordeaux: Made from a blend of Sauvignon Blanc and Semillon, white Bordeaux is simply delicious. It's not as zesty as a straight Sauvignon Blanc but still fresh and creamy, making it an easy wine to serve with food without worrying

about any rules.

Vin de Pays de Côtes de Gascogne: From just south of Bordeaux, this is another fresh and lively summer sipper.

Riesling: This is a personal favorite when the sun shines. Try a Kabinett level from The Mosel-Saar-Ruwer in Germany. It has a gentle sweetness balanced by zingy acidity, and since it has very low alcohol (7-9%), you never tire of it. Australian and New Zealand Rieslings are also perfect for summer— drier than the German styles but with the same bright lime-juice acidity that can really make your mouth water.

Pinot Grigio: It's clean and usually pretty neutral, but that's not necessarily a bad thing. The popularity of Pinot Grigio is surging to new heights, probably because it goes with anything and people want a change from Chardonnay. The best are from regions in the north of Italy: Veneto, Trentino and Alto Adige.

Rosé: This is what everyone in Provence drinks in the summer. It's made from the same southern French grapes that they use for the reds: Grenache, Syrah, Cinsault, Mourvèdre—serious pink sippers to be served nice and cold. These are a great summer substitute for reds, but if you have to have red, put the heavy, super-ripe and tannic wines away for the summer and bring out the juicy, fruity ones. Beaujolais (you can even serve it chilled) fits the bill.

# *Progressive Garden Party*

*A progressive dinner party is an adventure in the making,* as guests are given the opportunity to visit and dine in several different homes within the same night.

The simplest approach is to divide the party among three or four houses that are within easy walking distance of one another. Let the mastermind of the party make the first selection between appetizer, salad, main course or dessert.

Setting a theme can add charm. For a progressive garden party, assign a different garden flower to each home. The host or hostess is then challenged to incorporate the flower into decorations, food, music and entertainment.

Select foods that can be partially prepared in advance, balance the drink offerings and be ready with easy-to-reach umbrellas and blankets, just in case.

## MENU

## Eileen Mintz's Sun-Dried Tomato and Basil Cheesecake Appetizer

"This is a real showstopper on any buffet table, and after it has been decorated with basil and sun-dried tomatoes, it looks glorious!" We agree with this dedicated Costco member from Mercer Island, Washington.

1 1/2 cups dark pumpernickel bread crumbs

3/4 cup unsalted butter

2 ounces Parmesan cheese, grated

3 8-ounce packages reduced-fat cream cheese

3 tablespoons chopped onion

1 32-ounce jar sun-dried tomatoes

1 tablespoon dried basil

5 large eggs

16 ounces low-fat sour cream

3 tablespoons pesto

Fresh basil leaves for garnish

**1.** Preheat oven to 350°F.

**2.** In a food processor, blend the bread, 1/2 cup softened butter and 3 tablespoons grated Parmesan cheese. Spray cooking oil in the bottom of a nonstick 9 1/2-inch spring-form pan. Cut a piece of parchment to fit the bottom of the pan. Press crumb mixture into pan, going up 1/4 inch on sides. Refrigerate.

**3.** Beat the cream cheese until smooth in a sturdy electric mixer. Add chopped onion, 1/4 cup grated Parmesan cheese, 1/4 cup melted and cooled butter, 1 tablespoon oil and herbs from the tomato jar, and the basil. Add eggs, 7 tablespoons chopped sun-dried tomatoes and sour cream, blending until smooth.

**4.** Pour a third of the filling into the refrigerated crust. Add a layer of about 15 coarsely chopped sun-dried tomatoes, followed by another third of the filling. Add a thin layer of pesto (don't go too close to the edge with this) and remaining third of filling.

**5.** Bake 50-60 minutes on second-to-lowest rack of oven, placing a foil sheet underneath to catch drippings. When set in center, turn off oven and let the cheesecake sit 20 more minutes. Cool and refrigerate for a day.

**6.** Remove sides of pan and place cheesecake on a serving platter. Garnish with fresh basil leaves and pieces of sun-dried tomato. Enjoy with crackers or rustic breads. Makes 30-plus servings.

*Costco Member Eileen Mintz*

## Carlene Canton's Pesto Pizza

This Seattle member says that her pizza recipe is quick and flexible enough to be used as an hors d'oeuvre, side dish or main dish.

Dough for one homemade pizza crust or
    1 tube prepared pizza dough

3-4 tablespoons pesto

16-ounce jar artichoke hearts, drained and chopped

1 pound mushrooms, chopped

1 cup grated mozzarella cheese

1 cup grated Cheddar cheese

Pizza seasoning, or mixture of Italian spices

**1.** Roll out pizza dough on pizza stone or cookie sheet.

**2.** Spread pesto over uncooked dough. Sprinkle chopped artichokes and mushrooms over pesto. Top with grated cheese and pizza seasoning or Italian spices.

**3.** Bake according to pizza dough directions, about 15-20 minutes, until crust is browned and cheese has melted. Makes 12 servings.

**Note:** 1 cup diced cooked chicken can be added as a topping.

*Costco Member Carlene Canton*

## High Liner Honey-Broiled Scallops

*3/8 cup lime juice*

*2 tablespoons vegetable oil*

*2 tablespoons honey*

*2 tablespoons soy sauce*

*1/2 teaspoon ground ginger*

*2 pounds High Liner sea scallops, thawed\**

*1/4 cup toasted sesame seeds (optional)*

Combine lime juice, oil, honey, soy sauce and ginger. Add scallops and toss to coat. Cover and refrigerate 1 hour. Preheat broiler. Remove scallops from marinade (save marinade), thread on 8 skewers and place in shallow baking pan. Broil 4-6 inches from heat 4-5 minutes. Turn, baste with marinade and cook 4-5 minutes longer. Roll in sesame seeds to evenly coat. Makes 8 servings.

*\*Brands may vary by region; substitute a similar product.*

## Mastronardi's Sunset Salad with Vinaigrette

From the family kitchen of Mastronardi Produce comes this very lively salad.

*2 romaine lettuce hearts*

*1 radicchio lettuce heart*

*2 Sunset beefsteak tomatoes, cut into sections\**

*1 Sunset seedless cucumber, chopped\**

*1 each Sunset red, yellow and orange bell pepper, cored, seeded and sliced\**

*1 medium red onion, sliced*

*3 tablespoons minced shallots*

*1/4 cup red wine vinegar*

*1/4 cup extra-virgin olive oil*

*1 tablespoon honey*

*2 tablespoons chopped fresh dill*

*Freshly ground black pepper and salt*

**1.** Tear romaine and radicchio into bite-sized pieces and place in a salad bowl. Top with tomatoes, cucumber, bell peppers and red onion.

**2.** In a bowl, whisk together the shallots, vinegar, olive oil, honey, dill and black pepper and salt to taste. Add dressing to salad and toss. Makes 12 servings.

*\*Brands may vary by region; substitute a similar product.*

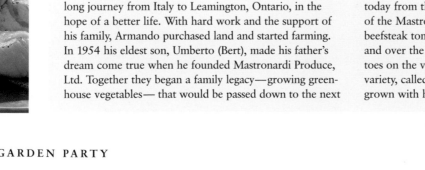

### The Mastronardi Story

In 1925, Armando Mastronardi and his family made the long journey from Italy to Leamington, Ontario, in the hope of a better life. With hard work and the support of his family, Armando purchased land and started farming. In 1954 his eldest son, Umberto (Bert), made his father's dream come true when he founded Mastronardi Produce, Ltd. Together they began a family legacy—growing greenhouse vegetables— that would be passed down to the next two generations. The family atmosphere is still present today from the farm to the shipping floor; everyone is part of the Mastronardi family. European seedless cucumbers and beefsteak tomatoes were the first vegetables to be grown, and over the years the line has expanded to include tomatoes on the vine, sweet bell peppers and the latest tomato variety, called Campari. Each product is like the first crops, grown with hard work, family support and love.

## Kirkland Signature/Swift Pork Loin Rib Chops

Pork is now the most popular meat in the world and it's no wonder, with hogs 50 percent leaner than they were 25 years ago. All fresh pork cuts except ribs and bacon currently are considered healthy dietary choices. High-temperature cooking is no longer required (unless it's ground pork). The government suggests cooking fresh pork to an internal temperature of 160°F for medium to 170°F for well-done.

*1/2 cup vegetable oil*

*1 12-ounce can beer*

*3 tablespoons brown sugar*

*2 tablespoons soy sauce*

*1/2 teaspoon salt*

*1/2 teaspoon ground pepper*

*1/4 teaspoon dried sage*

*8 Kirkland Signature/Swift pork loin rib chops*

**1.** Combine oil, beer, brown sugar, soy sauce, salt, pepper and sage. Add meat and marinate 15 minutes.

**2.** Grill meat over medium heat, turning often. Cook until chops reach an internal temperature of 160°F (about 4-6 minutes per side, depending on thickness). Makes 8 servings.

### Swift and Costco Meat Tips

- Plan 6 to 8 ounces of raw meat per individual serving.
- Always preheat your grill. This prevents flare-ups that can lead to charring.
- Spray your grill with cooking spray to prevent meat from sticking.
- Always use a meat thermometer.
- Always let cooked steaks or roasts rest before slicing, covered with cloth.
- When cooking a roast, start with a preheated oven that is 50 to 75 degrees hotter than your roasting temperature. Place roast in oven for 10 minutes and then lower temperature for the duration of roasting. This promotes caramelization, resulting in a pleasing appearance and great taste.

### Freezing

- Rewrap fresh raw meat in freezer wrap.
- Freeze quickly.
- Spread meat out in the freezer so it freezes evenly.

### Rain Forest Aquaculture Tilapia Parmesan Sauté

1/2 cup grated
    Parmesan cheese
2 teaspoons garlic powder
1/4 cup dried parsley flakes
2 tablespoons olive oil
1/4 cup butter†
2 tablespoons lemon juice
8-12 Rain Forest
    Tilapia fillets*

Mix Parmesan, garlic powder and parsley flakes. Heat a large sauté pan and add olive oil, butter and lemon. Sauté fillets on medium-high heat 2-3 minutes per side, or until white and flaky. Sprinkle cheese mixture on fillets and sauté for another minute on each side. Makes 8 servings.

*\*Brands may vary by region; substitute a similar product.*
*†May be replaced with olive oil as needed.*

### Mountain Stream Grilled Teriyaki Tilapia

2 tablespoons dry mustard
1/2 cup soy sauce
1/2 cup dry sherry
1 cup chicken broth
2 tablespoons sugar
4 teaspoons cornstarch dissolved in
    2 tablespoons water
8 8-ounce Mountain Stream Tilapia fillets*
2 tablespoons oil
1/2 cup chopped parsley

Mix mustard with just enough hot water to make a paste; set aside. Combine soy sauce, sherry, chicken broth and sugar in a saucepan and simmer over low heat. Add cornstarch and cook, stirring constantly, until mixture thickens. Set aside. Preheat barbecue to medium-high. Coat fish with oil, place in a grilling basket and brush with about 4 tablespoons of glaze. Grill skinned side down 6-8 minutes, basting with glaze. Mix remaining glaze with mustard and spoon a little onto each fish. Garnish with parsley.
Makes 8 servings.

*\*Brands may vary by region; substitute a similar product.*

### RioMar Baked Tilapia

2 pounds 2- to 3-ounce RioMar tilapia fillets *
1 tablespoon oil
1 tablespoon butter
1 lemon, juiced
Salt and pepper to taste
2 cups canned black-eyed peas, rinsed
1/4 pound chorizo (cooked),
    cut in 1/2-inch slices
1 cup chicken broth
1 tablespoon butter
1/2 cup grated Parmesan cheese

Preheat oven to 350°F. Layer tilapia in baking dish, sprinkle with oil, dot with butter, sprinkle with lemon juice, and add salt and pepper. Bake 8-11 minutes, or until just opaque. Combine peas, chorizo, chicken broth and butter in a saucepan, bring to boil, and simmer 4-6 minutes. Add Parmesan. Serve tilapia over peas. Makes 8 servings.

*\*Brands may vary by region; substitute a similar product.*

### Flav-R-Pac Vegetable Medleys

Lovely Flav-R-Pac* vegetables should be simply sauced.

- A quick glaze of olive oil, Dijon mustard, minced garlic, salt and pepper lends a tasty zing to vegetable blends.

- Add a splash of soy sauce, orange marmalade and minced fresh ginger while stir-frying.

- Toss pesto, a spritz of lemon juice, fresh shaved Parmesan cheese and pine nuts into steamed or sautéed vegetables.

- Try lemon zest-thyme, mango-lime or basil butter.

*\*Brands may vary by region; substitute a similar product.*

## D'Orazio Stuffed Shells with Sauce

This simple sauce is perfect with pasta. For dinner, try it with D'Orazio Stuffed Shells* and follow the baking directions on the package.

1/2 cup chopped onion

2 cloves garlic, finely chopped

1 tablespoon olive oil

1 28-ounce can plum tomatoes, undrained and chopped

1 cup peeled, seeded and diced fresh tomatoes

1/4 cup chopped fresh basil

1 tablespoon dried oregano, crushed

In large skillet, cook onion and garlic in oil until tender. Stir in canned tomatoes; bring to a boil. Add remaining ingredients. Reduce heat to medium-low and cook, uncovered, until sauce thickens (about 1 hour). Makes enough sauce for 1 pound of pasta.

*Brands may vary by region; substitute a similar product.*

## Domex Marketing Fresh Cherries Jubilee

This easy but elegant dessert creates grand finale fireworks when warmed brandy is poured over the sweet cherry and orange juice base and then ignited. When the flames die down, the sauce is ladled over scoops of rich vanilla ice cream. Dark cherries offer the most dramatic color contrast.

1/2 cup sugar

1 tablespoon cornstarch

1/4 cup each water and orange juice

3 cups pitted Domex Northwest fresh sweet cherries*

1/2 teaspoon grated orange peel

1/4 cup brandy, optional

1 quart vanilla ice cream

Combine sugar and cornstarch in a saucepan. Blend in water and orange juice. Bring to a boil over medium-high heat and cook, stirring, until thickened and smooth. Add cherries and orange peel; return to boil and simmer 10 minutes. Gently heat brandy, pour over sauce and flame, if desired. Serve over ice cream. Recipe can be halved. Makes about 8 servings.

*Brands may vary by region; substitute a similar product.*

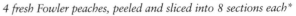
FROM THE MEMBER'S KITCHEN

Costco Member
Linda Carey

## Linda Carey's Dutch Cake with Fowler Peaches

Costco member Linda Carey, of Seattle, shares a recipe from her private files using delicious Fowler peaches.

2 cups prepared biscuit mix

3 tablespoons sugar

3/4 cup milk

1 egg, slightly beaten

2 tablespoons butter, melted

4 fresh Fowler peaches, peeled and sliced into 8 sections each*

1/4 cup sugar

2 teaspoons cinnamon

1 tablespoon prepared biscuit mix

2 tablespoons butter, melted

Preheat oven to 350°F. Combine first 5 ingredients; spread in greased 8-inch round cake pan. Place peaches on batter in a pinwheel design. Combine remaining ingredients and sprinkle on peaches. Bake approximately 40 minutes, or until golden brown. Serve with heavy cream or whipped cream with melted raspberry jam drizzled on top. Makes 12 servings.

*Brands may vary by region; substitute a similar product.*

# Dining Out-of-Doors

*By Pat Volchok,*
*Editorial Director*

There is nothing more pleasurable than dining in the open air, within walls built of vines, under a canopy of twinkling stars. It can, however, be spoiled by uncomfortable, dirty outdoor furniture, poor lighting and lack of preparation for the weather.

Select outdoor furniture that matches your needs. Wood options include timeless and classic teak, with its natural resistance to decay, insects and weather corrosion; less expensive pine, which must be a premium kiln-dried, pressure-treated grade to withstand weather; and beautiful western cedar, with its simple rustic charm.

Metal outdoor furnishings include cast aluminum with 100 percent rustproof finishes, hammered wrought iron and substantial cast iron.

There's a very fine line between the beauty of twilight and the pitch black of night. Lighting is essential. Unscented candles are the easiest and usually the least expensive. They add a wonderful warm glow, transport easily and can adapt to various locations. Numerous tea candles strategically and safely placed in the garden have an added benefit of drawing insects away from you and the food.

If your outdoor entertaining area is electrically wired, be sure to purchase waterproof fixtures that harmonize with your decor. Think about adding strings of economical, festive miniature outdoor patio lights.

Weather can be a challenge. You might want to consider investing in a portable patio heater, outdoor movable wood stove or patio umbrella.

If you take half as much time with your outdoor entertaining area as you do with your garden, we guarantee a delicious outcome. ∾

# Father's Day: King for an Hour

*F*ather's Day is supposed to be celebrated for an entire day, but in reality good ol' Dad is lucky if he gets a special hour crammed in between all the Sunday chores. Keeping this in mind, we've created a simple Father's Day feast that's guaranteed to please even the most exhausted "king."

Design a royal outdoor food court using portable tables placed end to end, attach ribbon streamers to trees and decorate a chair as his highness's throne. For fun and practicality, cover the "kingly" banquet table with colorful, washable king-size flat sheets and napkins made of coordinated hand or wash towels.

Serve Dad's favorites: grilled chicken, pasta and a gooey dessert. Conclude the festivities early so that Dad still has enough daylight left to mow the lawn and take out the garbage.

## M E N U

## Pat Volchok's Grilled Trout Appetizer

Whole trout make a wonderful appetizer.

*¹/₂ cup soy sauce*

*2 teaspoons chopped fresh rosemary*

*¹/₄ cup honey*

*2 tablespoons lemon juice*

*3 Clear Springs Foods whole trout*

Combine soy sauce, rosemary, honey and lemon juice. Marinate trout in refrigerator about 1 hour. Grill over medium-high coals about 5 minutes per side, basting occasionally, until it flakes easily. Serve with crusty bread. Makes 12 servings, depending on size of fish.

### Clear Springs Foods
*Trout-Boning Technique*

*To bone whole trout after cooking:*

**1.** *Cut along entire length of backbone, steadying trout with fork.*

**2.** *Leaving cut fillet with head on plate, flip top portion of trout over onto plate.*

**3.** *Lift away bone structure and tail from top fillet. Remove head from bottom fillet.*

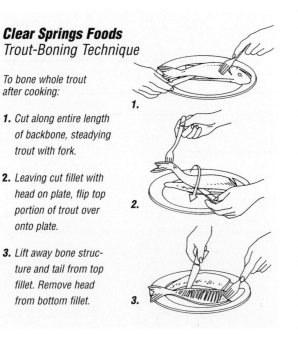

**1.**

**2.**

**3.**

### Handle with Care ... Costco's Charlie Winters' Meat Tips and Barbecue Sauce

*He's been in the meat business for more than 35 years and with Costco's fresh meat department since its inception in June 1987. So if there's one person who knows his Costco meats, it's Charlie Winters, vice president of fresh meat operations. The program, which originally offered just a small selection of deli and meat products, has been so successful that Costco is now one of the largest buyers of fresh meat in any category in the United States.*

*Charlie says, "The program, then as now, focuses on the basic Costco tenet of safe, quality products representing exemplary value to members. We've taken the extra steps necessary with our fresh meat program to guarantee the finest for our members, even though taking the easy way out would have been so much simpler. Doing what's best is the only way we'll do business."*

*When asked to discuss the basics of home meat-handling, he doesn't mince words.*

- *Cross-contamination of fresh meat is the most likely cause of food-borne illness, so remember the 4 C's of food safety: clean, cook and combat cross-contamination by separating raw meat, poultry and seafood from other foods in your shopping cart, in the refrigerator and on cutting surfaces.*
- *Use zipper-lock bags to stop cross-contamination in the refrigerator.*
- *Always wash hands, cutting boards, dishes and utensils with hot, soapy water after they come in contact with raw meat, poultry, seafood, eggs and unwashed produce.*

*He is also pleased to share some Costco meat information.*

- *Costco grinds extra-lean ground beef at only 12 percent fat.*
- *Costco's lamb loins and pork chops are individually trimmed.*
- *The vacuum-packaged (oxygen removed) meats at Costco are identical to those wrapped in the traditional manner. They stay fresher.*
- *Costco is now the largest purchaser of fresh boneless pork loins in the country.*

### Charlie Winters' Favorite Barbecue Sauce

*10 ounces pre-made barbecue sauce*

*1 ounce apple cider vinegar*

*5 tablespoons brown sugar*

*1 tablespoon Dijon mustard*

*Pinch of red pepper flakes*

*Combine all ingredients and mix well. This is especially good poured over ribs and marinated in the refrigerator for 24 hours. Grill or cook at low heat until the meat reaches an internal temperature of 165°F. Makes 6 servings.*

## Tanimura & Antle Smoked Gouda and Turkey Cobb Salad

Any father who likes to share some of his wisdom on Father's Day (to a captive audience) will appreciate the words of George Tanimura, lettuce grower and cofounder of Tanimura & Antle: "If you work hard and try hard, you've got just as much chance as anyone else."

*Half of 3-pound bag SaladTime Garden Salad\**

*2 cups chopped smoked turkey*

*1 cup shredded smoked Gouda cheese*

*2 6-ounce packages garlic-and-onion croutons*

*1/2 cup bacon bits*

*1/2 cup sunflower kernels*

*2 hard-boiled eggs, peeled and diced*

*4 green onions, sliced*

*2 ripe avocados, peeled and diced*

*2 tomatoes, diced*

*16 ounces ranch dressing*

**1.** Combine all ingredients in a medium bowl and mix well, adding dressing to taste.

**2.** Serve immediately or refrigerate briefly before serving. Makes 8 servings.

*\*Brands may vary by region; substitute a similar product.*

## Foster Farms Grilled Chicken Pizzas

Begin with Kirkland Signature boneless chicken breasts,*
brushed with olive oil, salt and pepper, and grilled until just
cooked through. Slice or chop and set aside.

Mix and match the ingredients below with grilled chicken
on a premade pizza crust to create your own individual
pizza. Suggestions: olive oil, artichoke hearts, garlic and
mozzarella. Or basil, garlic, tomatoes, tomato sauce,
mozzarella and Parmesan.

| SEASONINGS (CHOOSE 1 OR MORE) | VEGETABLES (CHOOSE 2-3) |
|---|---|
| basil | tomatoes, diced |
| oregano | garlic, minced |
| rosemary | onions, sliced |
| cilantro | peppers, sautéed or grilled |
| red pepper flakes | mushrooms, sliced |
| | artichoke hearts, sliced |
| | asparagus, sliced |
| | zucchini, sliced |
| | sun-dried tomatoes, chopped |

| SAUCES (CHOOSE 1) | CHEESES |
|---|---|
| olive oil | mozzarella |
| tomato | Parmesan |
| pesto | feta |

**1.** Adjust grill so that all heat is on the perimeter, keeping
the center of the grill the coolest. Do not put pizzas over
direct heat.

**2.** Grill top of the pizza crust 3 minutes. Slide off the grill,
turn over (grill marks should be facing up) and cover with
your choice of toppings, seasonings and cheese.

**3.** Return to grill, close the lid and cook about 8-10
minutes, or until bottom has grill marks and is crisp but
not burned. Watch closely!

**4.** Slide off the grill, cut into slices and serve. Season with
additional salt and pepper and chili flakes, if desired.

*Brands may vary by region; substitute a similar product.*
*Recipe created by Deborah Fabricant for Foster Farms.*

## Foster Farms Grilled Chicken Pouches

Begin with Kirkland Signature chicken breasts,* one per serving. Mix and match your choice of vegetables and seasonings. For example: sweet onions, peppers, oregano and olive oil. Or mushrooms, onions and barbecue sauce.

| VEGETABLES | oregano |
|---|---|
| tomatoes, diced | rosemary |
| sweet onions, sliced | cilantro |
| asparagus, sliced | thyme |
| mushrooms, sliced | SAUCES |
| bell peppers, sliced | olive oil |
| fresh corn, cut off cob | butter |
| zucchini, chopped | barbecue |
| HERBS AND SEASONINGS | teriyaki |
| basil | Worcestershire |

**1.** Cut parchment paper into 12-by-15-inch squares and place one per person on a flat surface.

**2.** Place a chicken breast on parchment paper and let each person top with vegetables, herbs and seasonings. Drizzle with 1-2 tablespoons of preferred sauce. Dust with salt and pepper.

**3.** Form into pouch and tie with kitchen twine.

**4.** Place pouches on a medium-hot grill and cook with lid closed for 20 minutes. Present on plates, cut open and enjoy.

*Brands may vary by region; substitute a similar product.*

*Recipe created by Deborah Fabricant for Foster Farms.*

### Pouch Prep

*Make things easier on yourself by using these simple time-saving tips.*

- *Prep ingredients in advance: grate cheese, chop vegetables and herbs.*
- *Cut parchment paper into squares.*
- *Put all ingredients in individual serving bowls and display them on a table. People can mix and match their choice of toppings.*

### Foster Farms
### Chicken-Grilling Food-Safety Tips

A cost-effective way to feed the family, entertain friends and save energy, grilling chicken is a leisurely process to be savored and enjoyed. The key to perfectly grilled chicken is low temperature, at least 6 inches from the heat, and adequate cooking time. Here are some of Foster Farms' favorite grilling tips:

- Thaw chicken in the refrigerator or microwave oven, never on the kitchen counter or picnic table.
- Keep uncooked chicken in the refrigerator or cooler until it's time to grill.
- Serve chicken from the grill on a clean platter, never on the dish used to hold raw chicken before cooking, unless the dish has been washed thoroughly with soap and water.
- Wash hands, kitchen counter, cutting boards, knives and other utensils with hot, soapy water after each contact with raw poultry.
- Chicken should be well-done, never medium or rare. The most accurate way to tell when chicken is properly cooked is with a meat thermometer. The internal temperature should reach 180°F for whole chicken or parts with bones; boneless parts should be cooked until the internal temperature is 160°F. Chicken is done if juices run clear when it is pierced with a fork. When in doubt, cut the chicken with a knife to be sure the center is no longer pink.

## Stemilt Growers Spicy Sweet and Sour Fresh Cherry Sauce

Cherries add color, flavor and intriguing aromas to otherwise ordinary dishes. This lovely summer sauce complements grilled chicken.

6 cups pitted Stemilt fresh sweet cherries

1 cup each *water and dry white wine*

1/2 cup chopped sweet onion

1/4 cup each *honey and lemon juice*

1 large clove garlic, minced

2 teaspoons grated lemon peel

1/2 teaspoon crushed red pepper flakes

1 teaspoon salt

Combine all ingredients in heavy saucepan; bring to boil. Reduce heat and simmer, uncovered, 30 minutes, or until mixture thickens; stir frequently. Makes about 3 cups.

**Costco Tip:** This sauce is also good with fish or pork.

## Barilla America Peppers Penne

With its tubular shape, penne is perfect for thicker sauces, and the short pieces are easy for children to manage.

1 pound Barilla Penne Pasta*

1 tablespoon olive oil

1 each *red, green and yellow bell pepper, cored, seeded and cut into strips*

1 26-ounce jar Barilla Marinara Pasta Sauce*

2 tablespoons grated Parmesan cheese

Cook pasta according to package directions. Drain. Meanwhile, add olive oil to large skillet. Sauté peppers over medium heat 1 minute. Reduce heat; stir in pasta sauce. Heat 5 minutes. Pour sauce over pasta. Sprinkle with Parmesan cheese. Makes 6-8 servings.

*Brands may vary by region; substitute a similar product.*

## Lee Brands Roasted Asparagus

Roasting creates a caramelized crust on vegetables that is truly magical.

1-1 1/2 pounds Lee Brands asparagus, trimmed*

1/2 pound mushrooms, thickly sliced

1/2 large red onion, sliced

1 tablespoon oil

1/2 teaspoon salt

1/2 teaspoon pepper

Heat oven to 425°F. Line a baking sheet with foil. Gently toss all ingredients in a large bowl until coated with oil. Spread evenly on baking sheet. Roast 20-25 minutes, stirring once, until veggies are slightly charred and tender. Makes 6 servings.

**Costco Tip:** The mushrooms will exude liquid as they roast, but it will evaporate as they continue to cook.

*Brands may vary by region; substitute a similar product.*

## Fordel Honey Macadamia Nut Fruit Skewers

Kabobs are back in fashion, so why not create a skewered fruit salad for a change of pace?

*3/4 cup toasted and coarsely chopped macadamia nuts*

*2 tablespoons butter*

*1/2 cup honey*

*1 Fordel cantaloupe, with flesh cut into small chunks**

*1 Fordel honeydew melon, with flesh cut into small chunks**

*1/4 Fordel watermelon, with flesh cut into small chunks**

*32 9-inch skewers*

*2 lemons, cut in wedges*

Spread the nuts in a jelly-roll pan. In a small saucepan, heat the butter and honey. Spear a mixture of the fruits on the skewers, brush with the warm honey and roll in the nuts. Place on a platter and squeeze a few wedges of lemon over the fruit. Makes 8 servings.

*Brands may vary by region; substitute a similar product.*

*Recipe developed by Pat Volchok.*

## Martinelli's Nonalcoholic Passion Punch

Toast Dad with this exceptionally tasty drink.

*5 bottles (25.4 ounces) Martinelli's Sparkling Cider**

*1 quart orange juice*

*1 quart cranberry juice cocktail*

*Grated rind of 1 orange*

*4 cups sliced strawberries (or other fresh berries)*

Combine cider and juices in a punch bowl with 3 trays of ice cubes. Sprinkle with orange peel and float berries for decoration and color. Makes 18-24 servings.

*Brands may vary by region; substitute a similar product.*

## Nestlé Candy Shop Pizza

What could be more fun than a pizza crust made out of refrigerated chocolate chip cookie dough and topped with peanut butter and chopped Nestlé Crunch, Butterfinger, Baby Ruth or 100 Grand? Oh boy, is Dad gonna be happy today!

*1 18-ounce package Nestlé Toll House Refrigerated Chocolate Chip Cookie Dough**

*1 cup Nestlé Toll House Semi-Sweet Chocolate Morsels*

*1/2 cup creamy or chunky peanut butter*

*1 cup coarsely chopped assorted candy bars: Nestlé Crunch, Butterfinger, Baby Ruth and/or 100 Grand*

**1.** Preheat oven to 325°F. Grease a baking sheet or pizza pan.

**2.** Place dough scored side down on baking sheet. Mold to desired shape.

**3.** Bake 30-35 minutes, or until golden brown.

**4.** Immediately sprinkle morsels over hot crust; drop peanut butter by spoonfuls onto morsels. Let stand 5 minutes, or until morsels are shiny. Gently spread chocolate and peanut butter evenly over cookie crust.

**5.** Sprinkle chopped candy bars in a single layer over pizza. Cut into wedges; serve warm or at room temperature. Makes 12 servings.

*Brands may vary by region; substitute a similar product.*

# Grand Old Fourth

*I*ohn Adams, this country's second president and an originator of the Declaration of Independence, prophesied our nation's annual independence day celebration when he wrote to his wife that this day "will be the most memorable epic in the history of America, to be celebrated by succeeding generations as the great anniversary festival."

Now, more than ever, it is the day on which we pause to cheer our nation's independence, accomplishments and aspirations. It is a time of community, reflection and flag-waving.

Not surprisingly, we build upon our nation's time-honored patriotic themes for our Grand Old Fourth celebration. Tables decorated with old-fashioned gingham cloth, watermelon pots filled with red, white and blue flowers, firecracker favors, grilled salmon, cherry salad and flags galore salute the strength of our country's past, present and future.

### Douglas Perfect Peach Daiquiri

Juicy peaches, fireworks and the sound of laughter—
it's hard to imagine a better Fourth.

*4 cups sliced ripe Douglas Fruit Washington peaches*

*1 cup rum*

*1/3 cup brown sugar*

*1/3 cup sweetened key lime juice*

*2+ cups ice*

*1/2 pint cream, whipped*

Put peaches, rum, brown sugar and lime juice in a blender.
Top with ice. Blend 3 minutes. Add more ice as space
allows and reblend for desired consistency. Pour into clear
glasses and top with whipped cream. Garnish with a peach
sliver and serve with a straw. Makes 6-8 servings.

### Pillsbury Flaky Croissants*

Make sure you
have fresh, flaky,
buttery croissants,
available in Costco
Bakeries by the
dozen, for the
Fourth. Did you
know they can be
frozen and still
retain their original flavor and texture? To freeze, wrap
each croissant in stretch wrap and then in aluminum foil.
Before serving, heat your oven to 375°F. Place croissants
on a baking sheet and bake 12 minutes.

*\*Brands may vary by region; substitute a similar product.*

### Costco's Apple & Eve Ruby Red Vinaigrette

Ruby Red Grapefruit juice comes from "Rio Reds," a native
grapefruit found only in the Rio Grande River Valley of
Texas. It is naturally sweet, loaded with 130 percent of your
daily vitamin C requirement and made without any artificial
flavors or preservatives.

*1/2 cup Apple & Eve Ruby Red Cocktail*

*4 teaspoons fresh lime juice*

*1/2 teaspoon finely grated peeled fresh ginger*

*2 tablespoons vegetable oil*

*Salt and pepper to taste*

Whisk together all ingredients.

*COSTCO SUGGESTS FOR THE SALAD:*

*1 pink or red grapefruit, peeled, pith removed*

*1 white grapefruit, peeled, pith removed*

*2 firm-ripe avocados, pitted and peeled*

*1 teaspoon fresh lime juice*

*Salt and pepper*

*4 cups baby spinach (4 ounces)*

*1/2 cup pine nuts, lightly toasted and coarsely chopped*

Cut grapefruit segments away from membranes. Halve
enough segments to measure 3 cups. Cut avocados
lengthwise into 1/4-inch-thick slices. Drizzle with lime
juice and season with salt and pepper. Toss together
spinach, grapefruit and half of vinaigrette with salt and
pepper to taste. Arrange on plates and top with avocado.
Spoon remaining vinaigrette over salad and sprinkle with
nuts. Cooked shrimp may be added. Makes 8 servings.

## BC Hot House Marinated Campari Tomato Salad

Here's a terrific summertime recipe that's perfect for any barbecue, picnic or get-together. It's easy to prepare, and with BC Hot House Campari Tomatoes, Sweet Bell Peppers and Long English Cucumbers, it will taste as good as it looks. Enjoy!

1¹/4 cups white wine vinegar

¹/4 cup balsamic vinegar

¹/2 teaspoon salt

¹/4 cup finely chopped shallots

2 tablespoons finely chopped chives

2 tablespoons fresh lemon juice

¹/4 teaspoon ground white pepper

2¹/2 tablespoons extra-virgin olive oil

1 bag BC Hot House Campari Tomatoes on the Vine
    (2 pounds), quartered vertically*

2 yellow tomatoes (if available),
    cut horizontally into ¹/2-inch slices

4 BC Hot House Sweet Bell Peppers
    (assorted colors will provide a great presentation!),
    cored, seeded and cut in ¹/2-inch slices*

1 BC Hot House Long English Cucumber,
    cut in ¹/2-inch slices*

**1.** To prepare the marinade, combine vinegars and salt in a large bowl; stir until salt is completely dissolved. Add shallots, chives, lemon juice and white pepper; mix well. Slowly whisk in oil until well blended.

**2.** Add tomatoes and peppers to marinade; toss well. Cover and let stand at room temperature 2-3 hours.

**3.** Add cucumber and mix before serving.

**4.** To serve, remove any remaining marinade (you can save it for later if you like) and place salad in a large bowl or serving plate. Makes 8 servings.

*Brands may vary by region; substitute a similar product.*

### The Natural Way

BC Hot House produce is hand picked and greenhouse grown. These nutrient-rich vegetables are grown hydroponically, not in soil. The growers combine the latest technology with traditional indoor growing techniques to create the ideal growing environment. The need for pesticides is drastically reduced by using ladybugs and other "good bugs" to do Mother Nature's work, including bumblebees for efficient pollination. BC Hot House produce is packed with vitamins, minerals and disease-fighting antioxidants—in a natural way. The result is nutritionally superior vegetables grown in the great indoors.

**Marine Harvest,** *the largest farmer of first-class salmon in the world, shares these diverse recipes from its private collection. There's surely one among them to fit your Grand Old Fourth party—it's up to you to decide which one.*

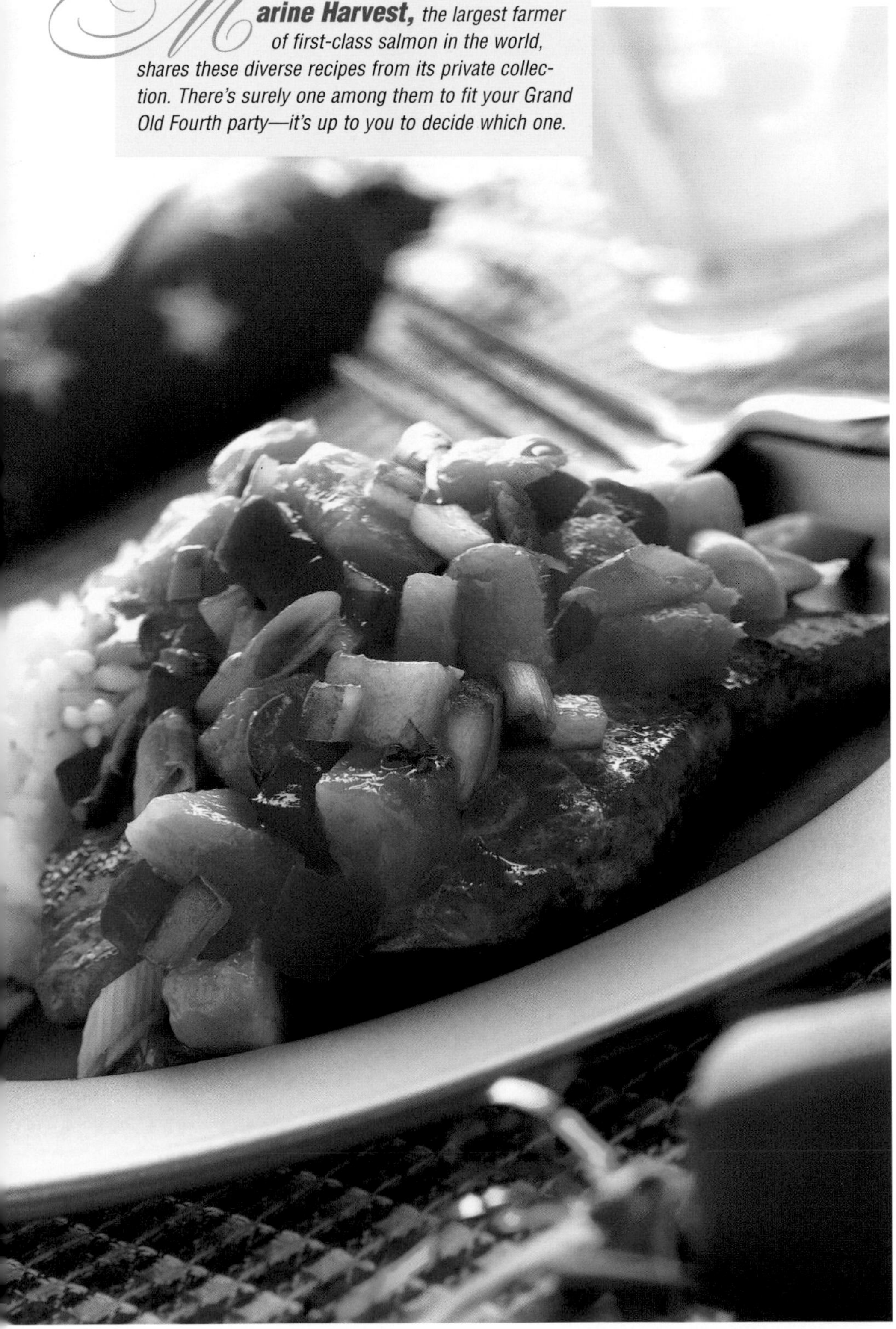

## **Marine Harvest** Tropical Grilled Salmon

*2 ripe mangoes*
*2 cups sake*
*1 cup light soy sauce*
*1/4 cup toasted sesame oil*
*1/4 cup honey*
*4 teaspoons grated fresh ginger*
*4 cloves garlic, peeled*
*4 green onions, trimmed and sliced*
*1 teaspoon chili oil (or to taste)*
*8 Marine Harvest Atlantic salmon fillets, about 6 ounces each*

**1.** Peel and remove flesh from mangoes. Place all ingredients but salmon in a food processor and blend until smooth.

**2.** Spread generously over fish and marinate in refrigerator 1 hour or on the counter 20 minutes.

**3.** Place salmon on heated fish-and-vegetable grill and cook approximately 5 minutes on each side, or until it flakes easily with a fork. Serve with Mango and Peach Salsa. Makes 8 servings.

## Mango and Peach Salsa

*2 mangoes, pits removed and finely diced*
*2 peaches, peeled, pits removed and finely diced*
*2 tomatoes, diced and drained*
*6 scallions, finely chopped*
*4 teaspoons finely chopped fresh ginger*
*1/2 cup chopped fresh cilantro*
*1/2 cup chopped red onion*
*2 serrano or jalapeño peppers, seeded and finely chopped*
*2 tablespoons balsamic vinegar*

Toss all ingredients together gently. This salsa can be made up to 2 days in advance and refrigerated to maximize flavor. Serve as an accompaniment to cooked salmon, jasmine rice and a steamed green vegetable. Makes 8 servings.

## Marine Harvest Grilled Salmon Teriyaki

*1 cup soy sauce*

*1/2 cup dry sherry*

*1/4 cup brown sugar*

*1/4 cup honey*

*1/4 cup light oil (canola or safflower)*

*8 cloves garlic, minced*

*2 tablespoons minced fresh ginger*

*8 Marine Harvest Atlantic salmon fillets,
    about 6 ounces each*

**1.** Whisk together soy sauce, sherry, brown sugar, honey, oil, garlic and ginger. Pour over salmon and marinate 1/2 hour on the counter or 1 hour in the refrigerator.

**2.** Heat grill while salmon is marinating. Place salmon on fish-and-vegetable grill, making sure that all pieces are evenly arranged. Cook approximately 5 minutes on each side, or until salmon flakes apart evenly with a fork. Makes 8 servings.

## Marine Harvest Poached Atlantic Salmon

*3 cups dry white wine or water*

*3 cups clam juice*

*4 lemon wedges*

*8 fresh dill sprigs*

*24 peppercorns*

*8 Marine Harvest Atlantic salmon fillets,
    about 6 ounces each*

**1.** Combine the wine, clam juice, lemon wedges, dill and peppercorns in a shallow pan and bring to a gentle boil.

**2.** Drop the salmon into the gently boiling liquid, making sure it is fully submerged. Cook until the salmon easily flakes with a fork. Remove immediately from the liquid and let cool for a few seconds. Pat the fish dry.

**3.** Serve salmon with a dollop of vegetable dip or mayonnaise mixed with fresh lemon juice. Garnish with fresh parsley. This recipe tastes great hot or cold and takes only minutes to prepare. Makes 8 servings.

GRAND OLD FOURTH

## Suzanne Huening

Suzanne Huening of Royal Oak, Michigan, has streamlined salmon preparation!

"I wanted to submit one of my favorite recipe tips—so easy and so gourmet! We serve Vidalia onion vinaigrette as a sauce on salmon—either fresh or frozen. It enhances the flavor of the salmon and tastes like I fussed making a homemade sauce."

## Dennis Anderson

Dennis Anderson of Danville, California, cooks salmon the Pacific way.

*1 salmon fillet*
*1/4 cup chopped fresh dill or 2 tablespoons dried dill*
*1/2 stick butter, melted*
*1 each lemon, lime and red onion, thinly sliced*

Preheat a covered gas grill or use a pot grill with soaked wood chips for smoky flavor. Sprinkle with dill. Drizzle with butter and cover the salmon with alternating slices of lemon, lime and red onion. Cook on covered grill for about 20 minutes; do not turn and do not overcook.

## Ronnie Sklarin

Ronnie Sklarin of Albuquerque wanted to share this longtime family favorite.

*2 pounds salmon fillet*
*16 ounces plain nonfat yogurt*
*2 tablespoons low-fat mayonnaise*
*1 pound green seedless grapes, thinly sliced*
*2 cucumbers, peeled and shredded*

Grill or bake salmon. Combine yogurt and mayonnaise well. Add grapes and cucumber. Pour over salmon. Makes 4-6 servings.

## Donna Holt

Donna Holt of Chowchilla, California, remembers her mom's salmon patties, which were made from canned salmon. Now she makes them using Costco's frozen salmon.

Crumble up grilled salmon to equal 2 cups. Add 1/4 cup bread crumbs, 1 or 2 eggs, 1/2 onion, chopped, and salt and pepper. Mix together into a rolled ball and smush into patties. Fry in about 6 tablespoons hot oil. Drain on paper towel. Drizzle with olive oil and seasonings to taste. Makes 6 patties.

# A Costco Salmon Love Affair

We received nearly 1,800 recipes from our members in just 60 days, and it soon became perfectly clear that many cooks love Costco Kirkland Signature salmon.

Costco Member
Imelda Trinidad

## Imelda Trinidad's **Monterey Pasta** Pesto Salmon

Monterey Pasta Company, founded in 1989, has more than 65 gourmet products that are always fresh, are manufactured with only the highest-quality ingredients and use no preservatives or artificial colors. Imelda, a Costco member from Los Angeles, has created a perfect pesto and salmon combination.

*Salmon fillet*

*Salt and pepper*

*8-10 ounces Monterey Pasta Company*
   *Pesto Sauce or Roasted Garlic Pesto Sauce*

*Pine nuts, chopped (optional)*

Preheat oven to 350°F. Wash the salmon in running water and pat dry. Place in a rectangular glass baking dish. Season the salmon with a dash of salt and pepper. Spread the pesto sauce generously over both sides of the fish. Add pine nuts if desired. Bake 20 minutes, or until salmon is barely opaque in center. Makes 8 servings.

## Michaelene Hearn

Michaelene Hearn of Clarkston, Michigan, reports, "I love Costco salmon!" Just cook the salmon fillet and add this sauce at the end and for dipping.

*1 cup butter*

*6 tablespoons soy sauce*

*4 tablespoons ketchup*

*2 tablespoons Worcestershire sauce*

*4 cloves garlic, crushed*

*2 tablespoons Dijon mustard*

Combine all ingredients in a small saucepan. Heat gently but thoroughly. Do not burn.

### Holtzinger Fruit Cherry and Hazelnut Salad

Sweet, juicy Washington-grown cherries at the peak of freshness are the perfect red ingredient on this oh so red, white and blue day.

2 pounds fresh sweet Holtzinger cherries, pitted and sliced*

12 cups mixed lettuces, cleaned and dried

1 1/2 cups crumbled Gorgonzola cheese

1 cup chopped toasted hazelnuts

2/3 cup vinaigrette

In a large bowl, combine cherries, lettuce, cheese and hazelnuts. Just before serving, drizzle salad with vinaigrette and toss gently. Makes 8-12 servings.

**Costco Tip:** Serve this salad in disposable cups so that guests can mingle and munch at the same time.

*Brands may vary by region; substitute a similar product.*

### Kirkland Signature/Bumble Bee Bayside Waldorf Salad

Let the fireworks begin!

12 ounces small shell pasta, cooked and drained

1 1/2 cups red grapes, halved

1 1/2 cups apple chunks

3/4 cup diced celery

3/4 cup walnut pieces

3/4 cup mayonnaise or bottled Italian dressing

3 6-ounce cans Kirkland Signature/Bumble Bee Albacore Tuna, drained

Lettuce leaves to line bowl or for individual plates

In a bowl, mix pasta, grapes, apple, celery, walnuts and mayonnaise. Add tuna and toss to combine. Spoon into lettuce leaves. Makes 8-12 servings.

**Costco Tip:** Keep this salad cool at all times; to serve it outdoors, we suggest using Italian dressing.

### Holtzinger Fruit Apple Snackin' Dips

These dips pair well with crisp, sweet Washington apple varieties, including Braeburn, Fuji, Gala, Red Delicious, Golden Delicious and Granny Smith.*

**Pacific Rim**
Combine 1/4 cup peanut butter, 1 teaspoon minced green onion, 1/2 teaspoon soy sauce, 1/4 teaspoon sesame oil and dash hot red pepper sauce.

**Chutney**
Combine 1/4 cup peanut butter, 1 1/2 tablespoons chutney and 2 teaspoons minced green onion.

**Tex-Mex**
Combine 1/4 cup peanut butter, 2 teaspoons chopped green chilies and 2 teaspoons chopped fresh cilantro.

*Brands may vary by region; substitute a similar product.*

## Dorothy Reid's Sticky Toffee Pudding

If you'd like to catch the "Sticky Toffee Pudding wave," try this recipe from a Costco member in Aberdeen, Scotland.

6 ounces dates, pitted and chopped

1 teaspoon baking soda

6 tablespoons butter, softened

6 ounces fine sugar

2 eggs

6 ounces self-rising flour

1/2 teaspoon vanilla extract

SAUCE:

7 ounces brown sugar

3/8 cup heavy cream

4 1/2 ounces butter

1/2 teaspoon vanilla extract

Preheat oven to 350°F. Grease a 7-inch loose-bottom cake tin. In a saucepan, pour 1 cup water over dates and bring to a boil. Remove from heat, add soda and let stand. In a separate bowl, cream butter and sugar, then add eggs, one at a time. Beat well. Carefully fold in the flour. Stir in dates with their liquid and vanilla extract. Pour into pan and bake 30-40 minutes. Combine sauce ingredients in a saucepan. Bring to a boil and simmer 3 minutes. Pour a little sauce over pudding and return to oven to soak until bubbling. Serve with extra sauce and chopped nuts. Makes 12 servings.

## CMI Cherry-Apple Crisp

It's always fun to tie in the colors of a holiday with the food being served.

12 cups sliced peeled CMI apples, preferably McIntosh*

2 cups pitted CMI cherries*

2/3 cup butter

1 cup packed brown sugar

2 cups old-fashioned oatmeal

2 teaspoons cinnamon

1 teaspoon nutmeg

2/3 cup flour

**1.** Preheat oven to 375°F.

**2.** Spread apples and cherries in a greased 9-by-13-inch pan.

**3.** Melt butter; add brown sugar, oatmeal, cinnamon, nutmeg and flour. Sprinkle over apples and cherries.

**4.** Bake 30 minutes, or until topping is nicely browned. Makes 12 servings.

*Brands may vary by region; substitute a similar product.*

### Freezing CMI cherries is as simple as 1-2-3

**1.** Rinse firm, ripe cherries in cold water; drain thoroughly.

**2.** Pack cherries in plastic freezer bags or freezer-proof containers. Remove excess air; fasten or cover tightly.

**3.** Freeze.

**Costco Tip:** If you want cherries that are not stuck together, place them on a cookie sheet to freeze and then transfer to baggies for longer storage.

Costco Member
Dorothy Reid

## Kirkland Signature/Hansen's Fruit Juice Creamsicles

Popsicles were invented accidentally in 1905 by 11-year-old Frank Epperson when he left a container of soda and a stirrer outside overnight and discovered them frozen together in the morning. This flavored ice on a stick takes on a nutritional dimension when made with Kirkland Signature 100 percent real fruit juice, which has no preservatives, additional sugar, or artificial colors or flavorings. This is a great recipe for kids.

2 boxes Kirkland Signature/Hansen's Tropical Fruit Punch

1 banana, diced

1 cup lime-flavored yogurt

1/4 cup grated coconut

2 tablespoons honey

1/2 teaspoon chopped fresh ginger

Combine all ingredients in blender and puree. Pour into eight 3-ounce plastic cups. Insert a popsicle stick in the center of each cup and freeze until firm. Makes 8 servings.

# Colorful
## Decorations

By Pat Volchok,
Editorial Director

There is always a nostalgic longing for past Fourth of Julys that were full of parades, fireworks shows, lazy afternoons and watermelon seed-spitting contests. Rather than just reminiscing, why not take these fond memories and re-create an old-fashioned Fourth in your own backyard?

Start by finding an old bike in the garage or junk shop. Give it a good cleaning, add a basket full of red, white and blue flowers, wind crepe-paper streamers through the spokes, attach an American flag to the back of the seat and place it at your front door as a celebratory welcome sign.

### Tissue Firecracker Favors

*Replicate the rather larger firecrackers of yesteryear by creating a tissue firecracker favor for each guest.*

#### Supplies per firecracker:

*3 1/2-inch length of 1 1/2-inch-wide cardboard tube*

*7 1/2-by-7 1/2-inch square of red tissue paper*

*Double-sided tape*

*Star stickers*

*1 piece of black shoestring licorice*

*Candies*

*Finely shredded Mylar stuffing, in patriotic colors*

*8-inch piece of blue ribbon*

#### Directions

*Place the tube on the tissue paper, leaving 1 inch of tissue at one end and 3 inches at the other. Roll the paper around the tube to cover, and attach with double-sided tape. Press the bottom 1 inch of tissue across the tube opening to close and secure the bottom with tape.*

*Cover with star stickers. Insert the licorice stick into the other end of the tube, making sure it extends out of the top by about 5 inches, stuff with candies and top with shredded Mylar. Tie closed with the blue ribbon, decorate with more stars, and make sure some of the shredded Mylar and the licorice firecracker wick stick out of the top. Stand one upright at every person's plate, looking just like a days-gone-by firecracker.*

Cover outdoor tables in flimsy time-honored muslin with hems randomly gathered and secured with safety pins that are covered in flag-colored streamer ribbons. For an extra festive note, add bunches of red, white and blue flowers tied with ribbon.

Compose watermelon centerpieces. In the kitchen or out on the grass, lay whole watermelons on their sides to find the balance point and then carve a large oval out of each top. Scoop out the seeds and flesh and save for eating and a seed-spitting contest. Fill the melons with soil and plant with red geraniums, white alyssum and blue cornflowers and perhaps some American flags. Water and place the containers on the tables. After a few days, the watermelons will begin to deteriorate, at which time transplant the flowers into the ground.

Tie red-and-white-checkered tea towels like kerchiefs around bottles of wine and beer, and place votive candles in small terra-cotta pots. Festoon bushes, flowerpots, fences and trellises with different-sized American flags.

If spitting watermelon seeds doesn't hold a lot of appeal, perhaps a flowerpot-decorating station might be more to your liking. Purchase numerous terra-cotta pots in all shapes and sizes, acrylic paints in patriotic red, white and blue, and disposable watercolor brushes. Provide aprons and towels, and ask everyone to paint a Fourth of July flowerpot. Once dry, put them on the tables as additional decorations and fill with nuts and candy. Later, send your guests home with their own Fourth of July keepsake flowerpots.

By the end of the day, your Fourth of July celebration will be affectionately referred to as a grand old-fashioned event, too. ∾

# Birthday Cheer

*A wonderful birthday party is often the best gift of all.* That is why this kind of occasion should be casual in nature, need little advance preparation and have simple decorations. The focus must be on the person, not the party.

Add good cheer with bowls of pretzels and crackers, fun drinks, bright flowers in vases, and perhaps a few helium balloons anchored to chairs. A luscious-looking birthday cake, complete with candles, graces the center of the table.

All that is left to do is scoop out the ice cream.

## MENU

## Sara Moulton's Tonnato-Stuffed Eggs

*6 eggs*

*¹/4 cup mayonnaise*

*3-ounce can tuna, drained*

*5 anchovy fillets, coarsely chopped*

*1 tablespoon capers, drained*

*1 tablespoon fresh lemon juice*

*1 tablespoon extra-virgin olive oil*

*Salt and freshly ground black pepper to taste*

*Celery leaves and Niçoise olives, for garnish*

Place eggs in a large saucepan and pour in enough cold water to cover by 1 inch. Bring to a boil over high heat. Remove from heat, cover and set aside for 15 minutes. Cool completely in ice water and peel. Cut the eggs in half lengthwise and remove the yolks. Sieve yolks, add mayonnaise and stir until smooth. Combine tuna, anchovies, capers, lemon juice and olive oil in a food processor. Process until smooth. Stir into yolks and season with salt and pepper. Fill whites with the yolk mixture. Garnish. Keep chilled until ready to serve. Makes 12 stuffed eggs.

*Sara Moulton, Gourmet magazine's executive chef, a Food Network celebrity host and author of Sara Moulton Cooks at Home (November 2002), shares one of her favorites.*

## Sorrento/Precious Spicy Cheese Crostini

Waylay hunger pains with this tasty delectable.

*1 baguette*

*2 cups shredded Sorrento/Precious Mozzarella Cheese*

*¹/2 cup chunky salsa (hot or mild)*

*¹/4 teaspoon garlic powder*

*1 dash hot pepper sauce (optional)*

Preheat oven to 400°F. Cut baguette into ¹/4-inch slices; place on foil-lined baking sheet. Bake 5-8 minutes, or until lightly browned. Combine remaining ingredients and blend well. Spread about 2 teaspoons of cheese mixture on each bread slice. Continue baking 5-6 minutes, or until cheese has melted. Makes about 3 dozen.

## Babé Farms Greek Salad

Chef Rick Manson, of Chef Ricks in Orcutt, California, shares his Babé Farms recipe.

*1-pound bag Babé Farms Continental Salad Blend\**

*1 basket Babé Farms Yellow or Red Teardrop Tomatoes, cut in half\**

*¹/2 each red and green bell pepper, cored, seeded and diced*

*¹/2 small red onion, diced*

*1 cucumber, peeled and diced*

*³/4 cup olive oil*

*2 tablespoons fresh lemon juice*

*2 tablespoons red wine vinegar*

*1 teaspoon minced garlic*

*1 teaspoon fennel seeds*

*3 tablespoons roughly chopped fresh oregano*

*Salt and pepper to taste*

*¹/2 cup Kalamata olives*

*¹/2 cup feta cheese, crumbled*

Place salad blend, tomatoes, bell peppers, onion and cucumber in a bowl. Combine oil, lemon juice, vinegar, garlic, fennel, oregano, and salt and pepper. Add dressing to taste. Sprinkle with olives and feta. Makes 12 servings.

*\*Brands may vary by region; substitute a similar product.*

## IBP/Tyson Beef Top Loin Steaks (New York) and Mushroom Kabobs

Is there any aroma more tantalizing than that of the backyard grill covered with thick, juicy steaks? Steaks are always a treat, especially on a birthday.

*6 large cloves garlic, minced*

*5 teaspoons lemon pepper*

*1 tablespoon dried oregano*

*2 pounds medium mushrooms*

*1 large red onion, cut into 1-inch pieces*

*1/4 cup olive oil*

*12 lemon wedges*

*4 boneless beef top loin steaks (New York), cut 1 inch thick (about 2 1/2 pounds)*

*1/2 cup crumbled feta cheese (optional)*

**1.** Blend rub ingredients: garlic, lemon pepper and oregano. Combine mushrooms, onion, oil and 2 teaspoons of rub in medium bowl. Thread mushrooms and onions onto 12 12-inch metal skewers. Finish with a lemon wedge.

**2.** Press remaining rub onto steaks. Grill steaks over medium coals, uncovered, 15-18 minutes for medium-rare to medium, turning occasionally. Grill kabobs 6-8 minutes, or until mushrooms are tender, turning occasionally.

**3.** Remove vegetables from skewers; toss with cheese. Carve steaks. Makes 8 servings.

### IBP and Tyson Foods

IBP started providing beef for consumers in the early 1960s, and is now part of the Tyson Foods family. No matter what the occasion, Tyson Foods chicken, beef and pork products become the main attraction of a meal that brings family and friends together.

## Grower Direct Romaine Salad with Bing Cherries

*2 heads Grower Direct romaine lettuce, chopped\**

*1 cup crumbled feta cheese*

*1/2 cup diced green onion, some green included*

*2 11-ounce cans mandarin oranges, drained*

*2 cups 1/2-inch cubes smoked turkey*

*1 1/3 cups California Bing cherries, halved and pitted*

*2/3 cup extra-virgin olive oil*

*1/4 cup balsamic vinegar*

*2 tablespoons stone-ground mustard*

*2 teaspoons honey*

*1/2 teaspoon salt*

*Freshly ground pepper to taste*

Combine first 6 ingredients in a large bowl. Whisk together oil, vinegar, mustard, honey, salt and pepper. Drizzle vinaigrette over salad and toss. Makes 8 servings.

*\*Brands may vary by region; substitute a similar product.*

### King Pak Twice-Baked Potatoes

A perpetual favorite, baking potatoes are low in moisture and high in starch.

8 large, uniform King Pak baking potatoes
8 tablespoons butter
Salt and pepper
1 cup hot milk
Cheddar cheese, shredded
Parsley, chopped

Preheat oven to 400°F. Wash and gently scrub potatoes with brush. Bake 45-60 minutes, or until tender. Cut off top third of each potato, scoop out insides and mash. Add butter, salt and pepper to taste, and milk. Beat until fluffy. Fill shells with mashed potatoes and top with cheese and parsley. Reduce oven to 375°F and bake 12-15 minutes. Makes 8 servings.

### Seald Sweet Florida Citrus Grilled Steak

If you're looking for something a little more fruity-sweet, we suggest this marinade.

3 tablespoons ground thyme
3 tablespoons garlic powder
3 tablespoons onion powder
3 tablespoons paprika
2 teaspoons dry mustard
2 teaspoons brown sugar
1 tablespoon Worcestershire sauce
3 Seald Sweet Florida grapefruits, peeled and sectioned
8 New York strip steaks
1/4 cup Florida grapefruit juice

Mix dry ingredients together in a small bowl. Spread Worcestershire sauce over grapefruit and steaks. Rub the spice mix over the steaks. Grill, using 1/4 cup grapefruit juice to baste. Makes 8 servings.

### Mott's Apple Sauce Scalloped Potatoes

Here's another way to serve potatoes, this time by adding apple sauce and Cheddar cheese.

1 tablespoon butter
2 tablespoons flour
3/4 cup skim milk
1 cup Mott's Apple Sauce
1 1/2 cups (about 4 ounces) grated extra-sharp Cheddar cheese
1 teaspoon salt
1/2 teaspoon ground black pepper
1 pound (about 4 medium) baking potatoes, peeled, cut into 1/8-inch rounds
1/4 cup Italian-style bread crumbs

Preheat oven to 350°F. In saucepan, melt butter over low heat and whisk in flour. Continue whisking 2 minutes and then add milk and applesauce. Whisking, bring sauce to boil and simmer until thickened, about 3 minutes. Remove from heat and add cheese, salt and pepper, stirring until melted. In greased 8-by-8-inch baking dish, add potatoes and sauce in alternating layers, beginning with potatoes. Sprinkle with bread crumbs and bake, uncovered, until potatoes are tender and top is golden brown, about 1 hour. Makes 8 servings.

Costco Employee
Pennie Clark Ianniciello

## Pennie Clark Ianniciello's Mom's Cake

"My mom's cake is the best," wrote this Costco employee. What more can we say?

1 teaspoon baking soda

1 cup sliced pitted dates (cut in thirds)

1 cup hot water

1/2 cup butter

1/2 cup solid vegetable shortening

1 cup sugar

1 3/4 cups flour

2 eggs

2 tablespoons cocoa

1 teaspoon vanilla extract

1 1/2 cups chocolate chips

1/2 cup chopped nuts (preferably walnuts)

**1.** Preheat oven to 350°F.

**2.** Add baking soda to dates. Pour hot water over them and soak 5 minutes, or until soft.

**3.** Cream butter/shortening and add sugar. Combine dates, flour, eggs, cocoa and vanilla with butter mixture. Stir in 1/2 cup chocolate chips.

**4.** Pour into a greased 9-by-13-inch pan. Sprinkle with the remaining chocolate chips and nuts.

**5.** Bake 40 minutes, or until a toothpick inserted in the center comes out clean. Frost hot cake with a thin glaze of confectioners' sugar or frosting. Makes 12 servings.

### Costco Cakes

You say you need a cake for 48 of your closest friends? That's not a problem at Costco. Just special-order a half sheet cake from your Costco bakery. It is the best value around and will serve at least 48 party guests. The cake selections are white, chocolate and carrot, and they're all rich, moist and full of flavor. Add 2 pounds of your favorite mousse filling: chocolate, apricot, vanilla cheesecake or strawberry, and then one of five different frostings: white or chocolate, light rich chocolate, white whipped icing or real cream cheese icing.

For the final touch, each cake is finished with a handmade three-dimensional design by a skilled decorator, complete with your personalized inscription. It's up to you to provide the candles.

# Cook's
# Time-Out

We all have those days, weeks or months when preparing a good-tasting meal is just out of the question. Whether it is because of a lack of time or a shortage of ideas, you are not alone. A vast percentage of Americans don't get around to deciding what they are serving until right before the evening meal.

This is where Costco steps up to the table with phenomenal mealtime options, including packaged entrées, ready-to-eat foods, precut and cleaned salad mixes, vegetables, meats and cheeses, frozen entrées, and much more.

You might want to photocopy this section and keep it near at hand so that when the mood strikes, you'll be ready to have Costco do the cooking.

## M E N U

# Lunch

## Bear Creek and Sea Watch International
## Hearty Clam Chowder

Here's an easy way to change creamy potato soup into clam chowder.

2 tablespoons butter

1 cup freshly chopped celery

2 cups water

3 pints half-and-half

2 2/3 cups Bear Creek Country Kitchens
    Creamy Potato Soup Mix (dry)

1 cup Sea Watch Chopped Clams, plus 1/3 cup clam juice*

Salt and pepper

In a 2-quart saucepan add butter and celery to water and bring to a rolling boil. Whisk in half-and-half and return to boil. Whisk in soup mix and clams with juice. Reduce heat to medium and simmer, uncovered, 15 minutes, stirring occasionally. For heartier flavor, add more clams and juice. Add salt and pepper to taste. Makes 6-8 servings.

*Brands may vary by region; substitute a similar product.*

## Chicken of the Sea
## Smoked Gouda
## Tuna Melt

If you prepare this spread early in the day and then microwave and refrigerate the bacon, the only dirty dish will be the grilling skillet.

1 8-ounce package cream
    cheese, softened

1/2 pound smoked Gouda
    cheese, grated

2 6-ounce cans
    Chicken of the Sea
    Premium Albacore Tuna
    in water, drained*

8 slices bread

Sliced tomatoes

8 slices bacon, cooked crisp

Butter

In food processor, blend cream cheese and Gouda. Stir tuna and cheese mixture together. Spread tuna on 4 slices of bread. Top with tomato, bacon and second slice of bread. Butter outside of bread. Grill until golden brown on both sides. Makes 4 servings.

*Brands may vary by region; substitute a similar product.*

## Member Tips

### Carmelita Downey's Bear Creek Soup with Salmon

"Here's my recipe for an awesome salmon chowder, a great way to use that skinny tail end on those beautiful sides of Costco salmon," wrote this Babylon, New York, Costco member.

1 quart water

1 1/3 cups Bear Creek Creamy
    Potato Soup Mix (dry)

1 14 3/4-ounce can
    cream-style corn

Tail end section of salmon
    fillet, cut in 1/2-inch cubes

Dash (or few) hot sauce

1. Bring water to a boil.
   Whisk in soup mix and
   reduce heat to medium.
   Simmer 10 minutes.

2. Add remaining ingredients
   and continue cooking
   until salmon pieces are
   cooked, 3-5 minutes.
   Makes 4-8 servings.

### Terri Franklin's Corn and Cheddar Broccoli Chowder

Here's another quick-and-easy fix for unexpected company from a Sacramento, California, Costco member.

2 medium potatoes

15-ounce can corn

Bear Creek Cheddar
    Broccoli Soup Mix (dry)

Salt and pepper

Bacon bits (optional)

1. Peel and cut potatoes into
   soup-size pieces. Bring to
   a boil in 2 cups water and

cook until tender. While
potatoes are cooking, heat
corn. Drain and reserve
liquid from both potatoes
and corn. Cover potatoes
and corn to keep warm.

2. Add enough warm water
   to the reserved potato and
   corn liquid to measure
   8 cups, and put in a large
   saucepan. Shake the Bear
   Creek can well and measure
   2 2/3 cups of soup mix.
   Whisk into the warm water.
   Cook, uncovered, on
   medium heat 10 minutes,
   stirring occasionally.

3. Add cooked potatoes and
   corn to soup. Add salt and
   pepper to taste. Garnish
   with bacon bits and serve
   with bread. Makes 8 servings.

### Mary Scheer's Tips for Bear Creek Soup

This Billings, Montana, Costco member says that with her tip, you'll never have to eat potato soup the same way twice.

Here are some of the ingredients she recommends adding to Bear Creek potato soup: cheese, cooked bacon, cooked ham, green chilies, pureed homemade vegetable soup and dehydrated vegetables.

At the end of her e-mail she added, "Thank you, Costco, for being in Billings for us."

And we thank you, too.

## Pocket Meals Stuffed Sandwich with Italian or Fresh Tomato-Yogurt Salad

A Pocket Meals Sandwich goes nicely with a small, crisp salad. Here are two salad dressings that work well with this lunch.

### ITALIAN SALAD DRESSING

1½ cups bottled Italian dressing

2 tablespoons grated Parmesan cheese

2 tablespoons sugar

1 large raw egg or 2 tablespoons mayonnaise

¼ cup oil

Combine dressing, Parmesan, sugar and egg in blender at high speed 30 seconds, or until smooth. Pour into a double boiler and add oil. Whisk over gently boiling water until it begins to thicken and egg is cooked. Chill several hours before serving.

### FRESH TOMATO-YOGURT DRESSING

2 Roma tomatoes, peeled and chopped

2 tablespoons each red wine vinegar and lemon juice

¼ cup each extra-light olive oil and plain nonfat yogurt

½ teaspoon each dry mustard, oregano and basil

Dash each of cayenne, garlic powder and salt

Combine tomatoes, vinegar and lemon juice in blender at high speed. Add other ingredients, blending again at medium speed. Chill overnight before serving.

## Pierre Foods Chicken Sandwiches

These Pierre Flame Broiled Chicken Sandwiches* also make a satisfying dinner offering when accompanied by a small green salad or fresh fruit. Thaw sandwiches, add toppings and heat according to package directions.

**Sicilian-Style:** Add ¼ cup marinara sauce, ½ cup roasted vegetables and sliced mozzarella cheese.

**Chicken Santa Fe:** Add ¼ cup salsa and 1 slice Monterey Jack cheese to the chicken, and serve with black beans and rice.

**Caesar Chicken:** Add ¼ cup Caesar salad dressing, 1 slice romaine lettuce and 1 slice tomato.

**BLT Chicken:** Add 2 strips cooked bacon, 1 slice lettuce and 1 slice tomato, and serve with mayonnaise or ranch dressing.

*Brands may vary by region; substitute a similar product.

### Lunch Hour?

A true lunch hour is now considered a luxury—the average American finishes the day's second meal in a rapid 24 minutes. This compressed eating time necessitates foods that are convenient, diverse and less filling. A 1999 American Dairy Association and National Cheese Institute survey indicates that the favorite foods for lunchtime are cheese, fruit, salad and chicken.

### Cheese Statistic

Americans' top five lunchtime cheeses:
Cheddar (45%)
Swiss (38%)
American (33%)
Monterey Jack (10%)
Provolone (9%)

### Sandwich Tips

Sometimes all it takes to spice up lunch is a change in presentation. When preparing sandwiches, use a variety of breads and spreads, such as bagels, pita bread, muffins, grainy mustards, relishes, yogurt mixed with garlic and cucumbers, and chutneys. Spread your filling out to the edge of a sandwich, so that the first bite is as good as the last.

# Dinner

### Hormel/Stagg Classic Ranchero Chili Pie

Plan ahead for one of those nights when cooking is just out of the question by baking and then freezing this pie. Reheat at 375°F for 10 to 15 minutes.

1 19-ounce can Hormel/Stagg Classic Chili
1 9-inch piecrust, baked
1 cup sour cream
1 2 1/4-ounce can chopped olives, drained
3/4 cup crushed tortilla chips
1 cup shredded Cheddar cheese
2 tablespoons chopped green onions

Preheat oven to 425°F. Pour chili into piecrust. In a bowl, mix sour cream, olives and tortilla chips. Spread over chili. Sprinkle cheese over filling. Bake 10-15 minutes. Sprinkle top with green onions. Makes 6 servings.

### El Monterey Burrito Cacerola

No one will ever guess that this dish was prepared in less than 10 minutes.

3 cups instant rice
3/4 cup chunky salsa
1/2 cup water
8 El Monterey Shredded Beef & Cheese Burritos, frozen*
4 ounces diced green chiles (half of small can)
8 ounces shredded Cheddar cheese
3 ounces canned sliced olives, drained

Preheat oven to 350°F. In a 9-by-13-inch baking pan, combine rice, salsa and water. Spread mixture evenly to cover bottom of pan. Arrange burritos side by side over rice mixture. Spread chiles evenly over burritos, sprinkle with shredded cheese, and garnish with sliced olives. Cover and bake 45-50 minutes, or until hot and bubbling. Makes 8 servings.

*Brands may vary by region; substitute a similar product.*

### Rich-SeaPak Popcorn Shrimp Pita Envelopes

Rich-SeaPak credits television chef Frank Terranova for the creation of this tasty, easy Greek-style dinner or lunch sandwich.

2 cups shredded romaine lettuce
1 red onion, julienned
1 red bell pepper, cored, seeded and julienned
1 cup diced mango
1 cup plain low-fat yogurt
2 tablespoons lime juice
1 tablespoon chopped fresh mint
1 cucumber, peeled, seeded and chopped
1 1/2 pounds SeaPak Popcorn Shrimp
4 pieces pita bread, cut in half

Preheat oven to 400°F. Combine lettuce, onion, pepper and mango. Set aside. Combine yogurt, lime juice, mint and cucumber. Chill. Prepare shrimp according to package directions. Heat pita bread in oven 15-20 seconds. Quickly add shrimp to the lettuce mixture and drizzle with yogurt dressing. Stuff into pita bread halves and serve immediately. Makes 8 servings.

### Fish House Foods Solution for Unexpected Company

Costco's Stuffed Salmon is the perfect answer for unplanned dinner guests. The stuffing, a combination of cheese, rice, shrimp, imitation crabmeat and seasonings, enhances the flavor of the salmon and keeps it moist.

To serve, simply preheat the oven to 350°F, place the oven-ready package on a cookie sheet, and bake for approximately 15 minutes, or until the fish flakes easily. Broiling or barbecuing also are suggested cooking methods.

## Schwan's Pizza Story and Topping Tips

Marvin Schwan began Schwan's Home Service in 1952 with one 1946 Dodge panel van and 14 gallons of ice cream. He took his ice cream to homes, and the route delivery system was born.

Since then the company has expanded greatly. Frozen pizza was added to the delivery trucks in 1965. Today, Schwan's is the world leader in frozen pizza production. Their pizza brands include Tony's, Red Baron and Freschetta.

So, plan a quick party the easy way—just heat up a pizza and serve.

### Costco Tip:

To add a little extra pizzazz to a pizza party, we suggest adding toppings to 3 out of 4 equal sections of each pizza and then letting people select their favorites. For example, you might add cooked shrimp, fresh garlic and a drizzle of olive oil to one section, extra cooked ham and sautéed mushrooms to another, and then perhaps banana, ham and pineapple to the other. As for the last section, leave it alone for the purists in the crowd.

## Countryside Baking Old World Fruit Rugala à la Mode

Rugala, pronounced rug-gala, is a rolled pastry made of paper-thin dough that was created by the royal chef for the king of Hungary in 1522. Countryside Baking has taken all the hassle out of this delicacy, which makes it an ideal dessert for unexpected guests.

All you have to do is remove four pieces of apple cinnamon or raspberry walnut rugala* per serving from the package and reheat for 4 minutes at 350°F.

Arrange the 4 warmed pieces of rugala around the outside of a dessert plate and place a large scoop of vanilla ice cream in the center.

Sprinkle the dessert with cinnamon or drizzle with your favorite ice cream topping.

*Brands may vary by region; substitute a similar product.*

## Member Tips

### Marlene Wright's Ravioli Lasagna Tip

This Costco member from Tucson, Arizona, sent in a quick-and-easy recipe. You can put it together in the morning before work, she reports, and then pop it in the oven as soon as you get home.

26-ounce jar pasta sauce

1/2 bag of four-cheese ravioli (about 18 pieces), unthawed

10-ounce box chopped frozen spinach, thawed and squeezed dry

8 ounces ricotta or cottage cheese

8-ounce bag shredded mozzarella

1. Heat oven to 350°F. Coat a 9-by-13-inch pan with cooking spray.
2. Spread 1/3 of pasta sauce evenly in the bottom of the pan. Arrange three rows of ravioli, overlapping the edges slightly, to cover the bottom of the pan.
3. Mix spinach and ricotta and spread over ravioli. Top with 1/2 of the mozzarella. Cover with another layer of ravioli and the remaining sauce and mozzarella.
4. Cover with foil and bake 30 minutes. Uncover and bake 15 more minutes, or until bubbly. Remove from oven and let sit 10 minutes. Serve with salad and bread sticks. Makes 8 servings.

### Conard Eyre's Oooooo La La Lasagna

Given the name and a note saying that no one will ever know how simple this dish is, we just had to share this Volcano, Hawaii, member's secret.

1 package (double casserole) frozen eggplant lasagna, partially defrosted

1 roasted chicken, boned and cut into 1-inch pieces

3 cups marinated artichoke hearts, quartered

4-5 cups grated mozzarella

1. Preheat oven to 350°F. Lightly oil a 4-inch-deep casserole dish that conforms to the size of the partially defrosted lasagna.
2. Place 1 lasagna in the bottom of the casserole. Sprinkle with 2 cups or more chicken, then half of the artichoke hearts and half of the cheese. Place the other lasagna on top of this mixture, and repeat the layering process. Make sure your casserole is completely covered with cheese.
3. Cover dish with foil. Bake 45 minutes, or until hot and bubbly. Serve with green salad and crusty bread. Makes 12 servings.

## Costco's Deli Delight

Costco's Deli offers a smorgasbord of freshly prepared ready-made meals and products.

- Rotisserie chicken and baby back ribs
- Take-N-Bake pizza (18 inches, 4-4 1/2 pounds)
- Chicken enchiladas
- Stuffed salmon
- Salmon Milano with basil pesto butter
- Chicken Caesar salads and more
- Luncheon-perfect hye rollers (turkey, Swiss cheese and cranberry dressing)
- Party platters of assorted meats and cheeses or vegetables
- Chicken strips
- Sliced turkey breasts
- Imported Swiss, Emmental, Muenster, Cheddar and provolone cheeses
- Sliced roast beef
- Black Forest and honey-baked hams, whole and sliced

What's more, your taste buds will never get bored, because new food selections are always showing up.

## Patty Andersen's Chicken Stock

*We can't think of a more heavenly place for a Costco warehouse than Paradise Valley, Arizona, and we are sure this member agrees.*

"I wanted to share with you what I've been doing with the tasty and economical cooked rotisserie chicken you sell. After a hard day's shopping at Costco, I bring it home for dinner the first night. (Yeah, I don't have to cook that night!) The next night, I shred what is left off the bone and make chicken salad or enchiladas.

Then I make chicken stock: throw the carcass in a pot, cover with water and add whatever is on hand, such as onions, carrots, celery, leeks (no need to peel—just throw it in). Bring to a boil and simmer until bedtime. You can put the whole thing, pot and all, in the fridge, and strain it the next morning. You could make chicken soup at this point. Whatever you choose to do, you'll have the best-tasting chicken stock in the world to do it with! Talk about a no-brainer!

If you choose to, you can make some super-concentrated stock. In the morning, bring it back up to a boil and continue to simmer, and it cooks down to a most flavorful chicken gelatin glace. I seal it with my Food Saver Vac 1050 (another Costco purchase) and it will keep for months in the freezer! All that with a $5 chicken!"

Makes cents to us.

## Lisa Jakob's Chicken Stretch

*Lisa Jakob of Albuquerque doesn't mince words when talking about Costco's rotisserie chicken.*

"I *love* your rotisserie chicken. I buy 2 or 3 at a time. Once I get them home, I cut them up and freeze the drumsticks for school lunches and after-school snacks. I debone the rest and freeze the white meat and dark meat in separate freezer bags for later use in chicken enchiladas, quiches, chicken salad, etc. I always buy an extra one for that night's dinner! Thanks for making my life so much easier. No more disinfecting my kitchen counters after raw chicken, and I'm always prepared to make a wonderful meal for my family and friends!"

## Emma Dueck's Slow-Cooker Stock

*"We buy your roasted chicken each week and enjoy them so much," reports this Costco member from Dana Point, California.*

"I save the bones and skin from 2 Costco rotisserie chickens and put them into an electric slow-cooker overnight, filled to the top with water, and cook them on low. The next morning, I strain the broth and let it cool in the refrigerator. After it jells, I measure out 2 cups and put that into a freezer baggie and after folding it over, put it in the freezer. That way, I have 3 or 4 bags, 2 cups each, of pure low-fat, low-sodium chicken broth that can be used in place of water for soups, rice, pasta, etc. We get double duty from a $4.99 chicken, plus having 3 meals for 2 people. Thank you, Costco."

# A Costco Rotisserie Chicken Love Affair

**Here is just a smattering of the dozens of recipes we received for Costco's Kirkland Signature Rotisserie Chicken.**

## Martha Ruiz's Quick Chicken Flautas

*Friends and family of this Salida, California, member will now know the trick behind her famous chicken flautas.*

"I always purchase the rotisserie chicken, corn tortillas and guacamole from Costco. First I cut up the chicken and shred in smaller pieces. I have my oil already at 400°F on the stove. I warm up the tortillas in the microwave and then put the Costco shredded chicken in the tortillas and roll them up and fry them about 1 minute, until brown on both sides. Then I remove them and put them on a rack. I add the guacamole and salsa and serve. This is everyone's favorite, and no one knows how I get my flautas to taste the way they do. Thank you, Costco."

## Sara Bulow's Costco Chicken Soup

*"My husband loves to pick up one of your delicious rotisserie chickens at least once a week," says this Superior, Colorado, member. "Our family of seven makes quick work of it, but I don't toss out the leftovers. The next day I put the leftovers to work making a scrumptious chicken soup that leaves our house smelling like Grandma's."*

1 rotisserie chicken carcass
   (include the drippings in the bottom of the pan)
4 cups water
1/2 onion, chopped
2 garlic cloves, quartered
15 baby carrots, sliced
2 stalks celery, sliced
1/2 cup rice or 1 cup noodles

Combine carcass, water, onion and garlic in pot and bring to a boil. Cover and simmer 1 hour, or until the remaining chicken falls from the bones. Strain. Return the meat to the soup. Add carrots, celery and rice or noodles and simmer until tender. Add salt or bouillon to taste. For a thicker soup, whisk in a can of cream of chicken soup after all the other ingredients are ready. Use the leftovers to create another soup.

221

### Cuisinart Kitchen-Friendly Products

*The name says it all: cuisine art, or the ability to prepare beautiful food. If there was ever a company that helps a cook create gorgeous fare in short order, it is Cuisinart.*

### Cuisinart Grind & Brew Programmable Coffee Maker

What could be better than having a cup of coffee waiting for you? With this remarkable coffeemaker, up to 10 cups of coffee-bar quality can be made at one time, and all you have to do is pour whole beans into the grinder, add water, set the number of cups and walk away. The water temperature can even be personalized to your exact preference.

With its self-clean setting and time-to-clean monitor, maintenance worries are all but eliminated.

### Waring Health Juice Extractor with 32-Ounce Stainless Steel Juice Collector

Ideal for today's fast and healthy lifestyles, this brushed stainless steel, contemporary-look Waring juicer, with its extra-wide feed tube (3½ inches) and high-speed motor, requires less preparation of fruits and vegetables and extracts more juice from less produce. There is no processing mess, cleanup is quick and easy, and the drinks are delicious. Good nutrition has never been quicker or easier.

### Cuisinart Five-Speed Duet Blender/ Food Processor

Imagine a machine that performs the duties of both a premium blender and a food processor. The SmartPower Duet makes kitchen chores easy with its three-cup work bowl, reversible slicing/shredding disc, stainless steel food processor and blender blades, 40-ounce glass blender jar and 350 watts of ice-crushing power for smooth frozen drinks.

## Cuisinart Custom Prep 11 Food Processor

When it was introduced at the National Housewares Exposition in Chicago (1973), the Cuisinart food processor revolutionized the way people prepared food. Over the years, Cuisinart has improved the processor motor, increased the work-bowl capacity and added high-performance features.

Today, Cuisinart's Custom Prep 11 (11-cup) Food Processor, with its uncompromising quality and ability to speed meal preparation by acting as both a processor and mixer, can not only shorten the time spent in the kitchen but also make it a pleasure.

This easy-to-use appliance with its revolutionary motor of alternating speeds kneads, slices, shreds, chips, mixes and purees. Included is an extra 11-cup work bowl, spatula, how-to video, stainless steel dough blade that kneads up to 2 1/2 pounds of dough in seconds, stainless steel chopping/ mixing blade, and stainless steel slicing and shredding discs. What's more, the parts are dishwasher safe.

### Helpful Tips:

• The Supreme Wide Mouth Feed Tube is two and a half times the size of any other food processor's feed tube.

• Never try to process dough that is too stiff to knead by hand.

• The Custom Prep 11 is backed by a 10-year warranty, the longest in the industry.

## Wearever 14-Piece Aluminum Cookware Collection

Wearever is the best choice for those who want to toss all their dirty cookware in the dishwasher at the end of a meal. Wearever, which has nearly 100 years of experience, is so confident about its cookware that it is the first in the industry to offer a lifetime guarantee.

This nonstick surface features the NeverStick, NeverScratch promise that there will be no sticking or scratching under normal conditions, even using metal utensils.

This set is made with a porcelain exterior that's both chip and scratch resistant and can be used on gas, electric and glass-top surfaces or in the oven up to 350°F.

It also features silicone soft-grip, stay-cool, ergonomically designed, riveted handles, as well as see-through glass lids and anti-warp disc-bottom pans for even cooking.

An added bonus is the stainless steel steamer insert for cooking vegetables and reheating food.

### Costco Tips:

• Great for low-fat cooking and made in the U.S.A.

• Soak in warm soapy water to remove tough spots where the food is sticking.

*Summer Beach Blast, at the Shore or in the City*

*T*he heat wave arrives and the asphalt seems to be melting. While some are lucky enough to escape to the shore, others will make do by staying home and enduring. In either case, it's a perfect time to gather friends and family and have a blast of a party.

Keep things simple and organized. For those going to the beach, these fundamentals are imperative for beach-combing and enjoying the scene. For those staying home, it makes the heat more manageable, with preparations done in the cool of the evening.

Take advantage of your surroundings, either real or imagined, by decorating with shells, driftwood, rocks and sand, always being mindful of local marine and plant-life regulations.

So grab the marshmallows and skewers and have a ball!

# *Picnic Packin'...*
# *the Costco Way*

*By Pat Volchok,*
*Editorial Director*

Be prepared. The best picnic spot might still be damp, so take two vinyl tablecloths and spread one vinyl side down to inhibit moisture. Add a blanket on top for sitting. Use the other one as a tablecloth. Just remember to anchor the corners with rocks and never food containers; someone invariably will pick up a container, and a gust of wind will blow the untethered cloth up and over the food, sand and all.

Fill plastic jugs three-quarters full of drinking water, lemonade or ice tea, and freeze. They will slowly thaw in the car and still be chilled when it's time to eat.

Make sure food is well wrapped to keep it tasting fresh and to give fragile items extra cushioning in hard plastic containers.

Basic tools might include: pocketknife with corkscrew, blanket, knives, forks, glasses, plates, premoistened towelettes, plastic bag for garbage, extra-large resealable storage bags for beachcombers, salt and pepper, beach towels, two vinyl tablecloths, serving utensils, cutting board, paper towels, firewood, propane starter and skewers.

Freeze wet sponges and place them in resealable plastic bags to use as additional coolants in the ice chest and then as cleanup tools after the picnic. ❧

SUMMER BEACH BLAST, AT THE SHORE OR IN THE CITY

# At the shore...

## Coca-Cola Barbecue Sauce

Take the worry out of your playtime at the beach by grilling your foods at home and transporting them to your seaside party in a cooler. Napkins are a must!

1 cup Coca-Cola

1/2 cup butter or margarine

2 cups Worcestershire sauce

1 1/4 cups ketchup

4 teaspoons sugar

1 tablespoon salt

1 tablespoon pepper

Combine all ingredients in a large saucepan. Bring to a boil over medium heat, then reduce heat and simmer 30 minutes, stirring frequently. Brush sauce onto meat or chicken as you grill. Makes 4 1/2-5 cups.

## Snapple Marinated Chicken Wings

If you'd like to give your picnic a little kick, these spicy chicken wings will do the trick. This marinade was created by Snapple using their all-natural (except diets) beverages containing no preservatives, no artificial flavorings and no chemical dyes, just for Costco members.

24 chicken wings

16 ounces Snapple Lemon Tea

4 teaspoons cornstarch

1/2 cup hot sauce

Cut slits in the wings. Soak overnight in Lemon Tea. When ready to cook, preheat oven to 450°F. Mix cornstarch into a smooth paste with 8 ounces warm water. Add to the hot sauce. Pour mixture on the wings and blend well. Place wings in a pan and bake 30 minutes, or until thoroughly cooked.

## Sun World Pecan Chicken Salad

There are those who like salads and those who prefer sandwiches, so why not make everyone happy by preparing this one dish, filled with juicy grapes, and offering sliced rolls on the side? Just remember to keep the salad iced in a cooler until ready to serve.

2 cups 1/2-inch cubes cooked chicken

1 1/2 cups halved seedless Sun World red, green or black grapes

1/2 cup diced celery

1 cup toasted and coarsely chopped pecans

2 tablespoons chopped fresh basil

1/2 cup thinly sliced green onions

1 cup mayonnaise

1/4 teaspoon salt

1/4 teaspoon ground black pepper

1 tablespoon fresh lemon juice

12 slices bread or 6 rolls

Lettuce

Combine chicken, grapes, celery, pecans, basil, onions, mayonnaise, salt, pepper and lemon juice and mix well. Makes 6 servings.

## Sunny Cove and Kirschenman
### Ginger Honey Fruit Salad

Beach salads should be prepared at home, stored
in plastic bags in the cooler and tossed with dressing
at the last second.

*¹/₂ cup plain yogurt or mayonnaise*

*¹/₄ cup honey*

*8 cups sliced Sunny Cove and Kirschenman watermelon,
    grapes, oranges and peaches*

*¹/₄-¹/₂ cup diced candied ginger*

*¹/₂ cup chopped walnuts*

Combine yogurt or mayonnaise with honey. Refrigerate
sauce and prepared fruit until ready to serve. Carefully
blend fruit and sauce. Top with candied ginger and
chopped walnuts. Makes 8-12 servings.

*Recipes provided by Pat Volchok.*

## Sunny Cove and Kirschenman
### Red and White Potato Salad

*12 small Sunny Cove and Kirschenman red potatoes*

*12 small Sunny Cove and Kirschenman white potatoes*

*2 teaspoons Dijon mustard*

*1 clove garlic*

*¹/₂ cup fresh lemon juice*

*1 cup olive oil*

*Salt and pepper*

*1 red onion, julienned*

*2 each red, yellow and orange peppers,
    cored, seeded and julienned*

Boil potatoes in salted water until barely done, about 15-20
minutes. Cool and then cut into quarters. Store in refrigerator
until ready to use. Place mustard, garlic and lemon juice in a
food processor. With motor running, slowly drizzle in olive oil
to emulsify. Add salt and pepper to taste. Store dressing in a jar
in the refrigerator. To serve, shake dressing to blend and combine with potatoes, onion and peppers. Makes 8-12 servings.

Ginger Honey Fruit Salad

Red and White Potato Salad

Costco Member
Nancy Colavito

## Nancy Colavito's **Delano Farms** and **Four Star Fruits** Grape Ambrosia

The letter from this Whippany, New Jersey, Costco member read, "This great summer dessert goes a long way. It's cool and refreshing and can be made the night before."

1 box instant vanilla pudding

1 20-ounce can crushed pineapple, juice drained and reserved

16 ounces sour cream

8 ounces frozen whipped dessert topping

3 6.1-ounce cans mandarin oranges, drained

1 cup halved seedless Delano Farms/
   Four Star Fruits green grapes

8 ounces (1 cup) mini marshmallows

1/4 cup shredded coconut

Mix pudding and pineapple juice with a whisk. Add sour cream and whipped topping. Add fruit, marshmallows and coconut. Mix well. Cover and refrigerate. Makes 8 servings.

## Brown & Haley Almond Roca Buttercrunch Quick-and-Easy Cookies

We doubt if even a little sand will stop these cookies from being devoured.

1 cup butter, softened

3/4 cup sugar

3/4 cup firmly packed
   brown sugar

1 teaspoon vanilla extract

2 eggs

2 1/4 cups unsifted flour

1 teaspoon baking soda

1 teaspoon salt

1 cup semisweet
   chocolate chips

1 cup milk chocolate chips

1 cup crushed Almond
   Roca Buttercrunch

Preheat oven to 375°F. Cream butter, sugar, brown sugar and vanilla together until smooth. Beat and add eggs. Mix flour, baking soda and salt together. Add gradually to butter mixture. Stir in chocolate chips. Stir in Almond Roca. Drop batter by well-rounded teaspoonfuls onto greased cookie sheet. Bake 8-10 minutes, or until slightly brown on the bottom. Makes 6 dozen.

## Jolly Time Rocky Road Peanut Butter Popcorn Bars

Here's how to guarantee a jolly time at the beach or at home:

3 quarts popped Jolly Time Pop Corn*

1/2 cup raisins

1 cup light corn syrup

1 tablespoon butter or margarine

1/2 cup peanut butter chips

1/3 cup chunky or creamy peanut butter

3/4 cup miniature marshmallows

1/2 cup peanuts

1/2 cup semi-sweet chocolate chips

1 teaspoon vegetable shortening

Place popped popcorn and raisins in large bowl. In saucepan, heat corn syrup and butter to a boil over medium heat; boil 3 minutes. Remove from heat. Stir in peanut butter chips and peanut butter until smooth. Pour over popcorn, tossing gently to coat. Press into buttered 9-inch square baking pan. Sprinkle with marshmallows and peanuts, pressing lightly. Melt chocolate chips and shortening over very low heat. Drizzle over top. Cool several hours. Makes 36 bars.

*Brands may vary by region; substitute a similar product.

# In the city...

## Pacific Seafood Oyster Stew

If you can't visit the shore, then why not bring a little of the shore to your party? Serve with oyster crackers.

2 tablespoons butter
1-2 celery stalks, chopped
1 bunch green onions, chopped
1 32-ounce jar Pacific Seafood SeaRock Shucked Oysters
6 cups cream or half-and-half
Salt and pepper
1/2 cup diced red bell pepper

**1.** In a medium-sized saucepan, melt butter over medium heat and add the celery and green onions. Sauté until translucent.
**2.** Add oysters with their liquor and sauté until plump; don't overcook.
**3.** Add the cream and cook until hot, being careful not to burn.
**4.** Season to taste with salt and pepper (add garlic powder for a little zing).
**5.** Serve in a large bowl, garnished with the diced red pepper.
**6.** Add a pat of butter for richer flavor. Makes 6-8 servings.
**Note:** To reduce fat content, sauté celery and onions in 1 tablespoon olive oil. Use nonfat milk or nonfat half-and-half instead of cream.

## Kingsburg Apple Asian Pear and Pluot Salsa

Asian pears are crisp and juicy like apples but have a distinctive texture. Pluots are a complex hybrid fruit that blends the delicious flavors of plums and apricots.

2 Kingsburg Asian pears, cored and finely diced
3 Dinosaur Brand Pluots, finely diced
1 medium red onion, finely chopped
1/2-1 jalapeño pepper, seeded and finely chopped
1/4 cup chopped cilantro
Juice of one lime
Salt to taste

Combine ingredients in a medium bowl and serve with toasted baguette slices, tortilla chips or grilled fish. Makes 6 servings.

## Metz Fresh Spinach Salad

1 1/4 cups olive oil
7 tablespoons red wine vinegar
2 1/2 teaspoons salt
1/4 teaspoon pepper
3/4 teaspoon paprika
1 teaspoon sugar
1 teaspoon creamy horseradish
3 tablespoons chili sauce
1 teaspoon prepared mustard
1/4 teaspoon minced garlic
1/2 bag Metz Fresh packaged spinach leaves (approx. 10 cups, or 1 1/4 pounds)*
8 ounces sliced mushrooms
10 slices bacon, cooked and crumbled
4 medium tomatoes, quartered or sliced

Combine oil, vinegar, salt, pepper, paprika, sugar, horseradish, chili sauce, mustard and garlic. Blend well and chill overnight. Before serving, toss spinach, mushrooms, bacon and tomatoes with dressing to taste. Makes 10-12 servings.
*Brands may vary by region; substitute a similar product.*

## Greenstripe Grape Tomato, Pasta and Chicken Salad

8 ounces bowtie pasta
8 ounces Greenstripe grape tomatoes (1/4 of 2-pound container)*
1 garlic clove, finely chopped
1/3 of a sweet red onion, sliced thin
2 handfuls of baby spinach
8 ounces diced grilled chicken
1/2 cup sliced pitted black olives
2 ounces red wine vinegar
6 ounces extra-virgin olive oil
Salt, pepper and chopped fresh basil to taste

Cook pasta according to package directions and drain. Combine all ingredients in a large bowl and toss. Allow to stand at room temperature 10 minutes. Serve with grilled sliced Italian or French bread. Makes 4-6 servings.
*Brands may vary by region; substitute a similar product.*

## McCormick's Broccoli Salad

1/4 *pound bacon*

4 *cups broccoli florets*

1/2 *cup chopped red onion*

1 *cup raisins*

3/8 *cup white wine vinegar*

1/4 *cup sugar*

2 *cups mayonnaise*

1 1/2 *cups McCormick Salad Toppins*

**1.** Cook bacon over medium heat until evenly brown. Drain, crumble and set aside.

**2.** In a large bowl, combine the broccoli, onion and raisins.

**3.** In a medium bowl, whisk together the vinegar, sugar and mayonnaise. Pour over broccoli mixture and toss until well mixed. Refrigerate at least 2 hours.

**4.** Before serving, toss salad with crumbled bacon and McCormick Salad Toppins. Makes 8 servings.

## McCormick's Strawberries and Sweet Vanilla

8 *cups fresh strawberries*

1/2 *cup granulated sugar*

2 *tablespoons McCormick Vanilla Extract*

**1.** Wash and slice strawberries.

**2.** In a large bowl combine strawberries, sugar and vanilla extract. Mix well and refrigerate at least 2 hours before serving. Makes 8 servings.

## McCormick's Cajun Aioli for Steak or Chicken

It's summer in the city, and the living is easy with McCormick spices and seasonings. And just think, staying in town means there'll be no beach sand to clean up or coolers to unpack.

1 *cup mayonnaise*

2 *tablespoons McCormick Cajun Seasoning or McCormick Bayou Cajun Seasoning*

2 *tablespoons orange juice*

8 *rib-eye steaks*

**1.** In a large bowl, combine mayonnaise, McCormick Cajun Seasoning and orange juice.

**2.** Brush on both sides of steak before grilling. Grill over a medium-high grill 5-6 minutes per side.

**3.** Can substitute boneless, skinless chicken breasts for rib-eye steaks. Makes 8 servings.

# Rainy Day Beach Party

By Pat Volchok,
*Editorial Director*

If the weather has turned sour or you just can't get to the beach, there's no need to despair. You can easily bring the ambience of the beach into your own home with just a few fun decorations.

You may recall the Spring Afternoon "At Home" Tea Party (page 166), where a sod tablecloth was suggested. Surprisingly, this rather inexpensive clump of grass also can be transformed into a wonderful beachscape.

This time you must start your process about a month ahead by purchasing enough sod to either act as a runner down the center of your table or cover your fireplace hearth area. As before, begin by measuring the space and cutting a piece of plywood to fit the desired area. Staple durable black plastic sheeting to both sides. Note: The plywood from the At Home Tea Party tabletop can be reused.

Unroll the sod outside, cut it to fit the plywood template and start hosing it off. Continue cleaning for two or three days, until most of the mud has been washed away. Then, move the plastic-covered plywood to the garage or unfinished basement and lay the grass on top. Do not water or let rain fall on the sod. Over the next few weeks, the grass will at first begin to grow and then eventually turn dry and brown. What remains is something that looks remarkably like beach grass.

Carefully transfer your new grass to your chosen spot in the house and decorate with shells, rocks, driftwood, collectibles from past beach excursions and perhaps even some sand.

To create a simpler beachscape, make a quick trip to a nursery for a selection of ornamental grasses and white sand. Protect the area to be covered with thick plastic or plywood. Mound sand in dune shapes and strategically place clumps of grasses and shells.

If no fireplace is available or you just can't stand the thought of a fire, marshmallows can be carefully "toasted" in a microwave. Place four to six large marshmallows an equal distance apart on a microwave-safe plate. Cook in the microwave for a minute or two, until they begin to brown. They must be carefully watched at all times, as the pillows of fluff get quite large and can burn quickly. Use potholders to remove the plate and place it on a heat-resistant surface until the marshmallows are completely cool. While they may not look as beautiful as those toasted at the beach, the cooked flavor is similar to that of their fire-toasted cousins.

Use shipwreck bottles as placecards. Fans can create an offshore breeze, but only if they face away from the sand. Play soothing ocean music in the background. In lieu of Frisbee, play a few hands of Fish.

Who knows, everyone may have such a good time that the real beach won't even be missed. ✎

# All-American
# Labor Day
# Sampler

*W*e asked our members, *via* The Costco Connection magazine, to send in recipes or tips using Costco products. The sophistication and breadth of knowledge shown by those who participated was outstanding.

Candy Barnhart, of Hollywood, California, submitted a party so Costco-esque that we had to include it. She wrote, "Our All-American Buffet was created more than a year ago, but it seems especially appropriate these days. Separate food stations allow us to feature the best of America's regional favorites. Everything can be found at Costco and is easily prepared."

Sounds like a Costco all-American winner to us.

Costco Member
Candy Barnhart

# All-American Labor Day Sampler Decorations and Party Suggestions

*By Costco Member Candy Barnhart and Pat Volchok, Editorial Director*

For the All-American Labor Day Sampler, Costco member Candy Barnhart suggests having tablecloths at each station made out of inexpensive paper maps representing that specific region of the country. For example, a map of the East Coast covers the eastern region table; just purchase a number of appropriate maps, steam-iron until limp and drape over the table. Candy uses four helium balloons and writes a region's name on each one. They are then attached to the tables so that guests know where to wander for specific cuisines. Additional balloons in state colors can be anchored to the table using cans that are covered with colorful tissue or newspapers from the area.

Create regional arrangements for the four tables using state flags and flowers or the fruits derived from the flowers. For example, the southern table arrangement, depending on the season, could use Alabama's state flower, the camellia; Florida oranges to represent the state's flower, the orange blossom; or Kentucky's goldenrod, plus miniature southern state flags on long sticks randomly poking out of the arrangements. State flag and flower information and products can be found on many e-commerce Web sites.

Party favors can be as simple as handing out boxes for leftovers and letting guests select their favorite regional flavors to take home. ❧

We tapped one of the water masters, Talking Rain, for drink ideas. These drinks are suggested for a Pacific-style bar, but we're sure that no one will mind if they're served at the Atlantic bar, too.

## All-American Labor Day Drink Stations

Besides presenting four grand food offerings to guests, Candy prepares two beverage stations, decorated as the Atlantic and the Pacific, situated at each end of the party area.

### Atlantic Beverage Station

Soft drinks and libations of the Atlantic coast—for example, cranberry juice, the state drink of Massachusetts, or tomato juice for Ohio—are offered, and the table is decorated with fishnet and glass floats.

### Pacific Beverage Station

Soft drinks and libations of the Pacific coast such as those shown here are offered, and the table is decorated with tropical flowers.

## Talking Rain Ginger Sparkler

Talking Rain Sparkling Water is pure, natural spring water, enhanced with only the purest carbonation and 100 percent natural fruit extracts and oils to create a uniquely refreshing beverage with the taste of the great outdoors. And it contains no sodium, sugar, calories, caffeine, artificial additives or artificial sweeteners.

8 ounces grated fresh ginger

Zest and juice of 4 limes

4 cloves (optional)

2 cups brown sugar

Talking Rain Lemon-Lime Sparkling Water*

**1.** Add first 4 ingredients to 1 quart of boiling water. Reduce heat and simmer on low 5 minutes, stirring to dissolve sugar. Strain and chill.

**2.** To serve, add 1 part ginger mixture to 1 part Lemon-Lime Sparkling Water. Adjust to taste. Makes 8 servings.

*Brands may vary by region; substitute a similar product.

## Vita Passion Crush

1 large pineapple, peeled and cut into chunks (or substitute 16 ounces canned or frozen)

Juice of 1 lemon

1 20-ounce bottle VitaRain Passion Peach*

1 banana

Sugar or honey (optional)

Blend all ingredients until smooth. Serve over cracked ice. Makes 4 servings.

## Kiwi–Key Lime Virgin Margarita

2 ripe kiwis, halved and scooped

Juice of 1 lime

1 16.9-ounce bottle Diet Ice Botanical Key Lime*

Blend fruit with lime juice and Key Lime drink until smooth. Serve immediately. Makes 4 servings.

## Costco suggests:

**FROM THE MEMBER'S KITCHEN**

### Richard Roberts' Tomato-Mozzarella-Prosciutto Salad

This Longwood, Florida, Costco member's salad is stunning.

6 tablespoons Kirkland Signature balsamic vinegar

4 teaspoons minced garlic

Salt, if desired

Freshly ground black pepper

1 cup Kirkland Signature extra-virgin olive oil

1/4 cup chopped fresh basil

6-8 medium ripe tomatoes

8 ounces mozzarella

1 pound prosciutto panino

3/4 cup pine nuts

**1.** Combine vinegar, garlic, salt and pepper. Whisk in olive oil and basil. Set aside in refrigerator.

**2.** Cut tomatoes, mozzarella and prosciutto into 16 slices (1/8 to 1/4 inch).

**3.** Toast pine nuts in a small skillet or in toaster oven until golden; cool.

**4.** Remove vinaigrette from refrigerator and let warm to nearly room temperature.

**5.** Starting with the tomato, layer slices of tomato, mozzarella and prosciutto with 2 slices of each on small plates.

**6.** When ready to serve, drizzle with vinaigrette and sprinkle with toasted pine nuts. Can be served as an appetizer or salad course with Italian bread. Makes 8 servings.

Costco Member
Richard Roberts

**FROM THE MEMBER'S KITCHEN**

Costco Member
Melitta McGuire

### Melitta McGuire's Fisherman's Stew

This Vancouver, Washington, member doesn't live in the East, but her stew fits the theme.

1 tablespoon olive oil

1 medium onion, chopped (about 1 1/3 cups)

3 cloves garlic, finely chopped

1 medium bulb fennel, chopped (about 1 1/2-2 cups)

2 14 1/2-ounce cans chopped Italian peeled tomatoes

5 cups water

4 chicken bouillon cubes, crushed

1 tablespoon lemon juice

1 teaspoon crushed dried basil

Dash of cayenne pepper

2 ounces small shell pasta (1/2 cup), uncooked

1 pound shelled raw tiger prawns

1 pound large scallops

1 pound cod, cubed

9-ounce package frozen artichoke hearts, quartered

In a large kettle, heat the oil over medium-low heat. Add onion and garlic. Cook slowly about 10 minutes, until soft and brown. Add fennel and cook slowly about 5 more minutes. Add tomatoes, water, bouillon cubes, lemon juice, dried basil and cayenne. Bring to boil. Reduce heat, cover and simmer 10-15 minutes. Add pasta and simmer 10 minutes, stirring now and then. Add prawns, scallops, cod and artichoke hearts. Simmer until just done, about 10 minutes. Makes 6-8 generous servings.

## New York Style Sausage Stuffed Bread

New York Style Sausage Company is proud of its tradition of high-quality lean sausage, made fresh daily with no preservatives or MSG.

2 1-pound loaves frozen dough

2 pounds New York Style Italian Sausage—
    Hot, Mild, Garlic Basil, Turkey or Bratwurst*

1 10-ounce box frozen spinach, thawed and squeezed dry

4 ounces sharp Cheddar cheese, shredded

4 ounces Monterey Jack cheese, shredded

1/2 cup grated Parmesan cheese

1 tablespoon chopped parsley

1 egg, beaten

1 egg white

**1.** Thaw frozen bread dough completely.

**2.** Preheat oven to 325°F.

**3.** Remove sausage from casing and brown in frying pan; drain and set aside until cool.

**4.** Combine sausage, spinach, cheeses and parsley in a large bowl, add beaten egg and mix thoroughly.

**5.** Roll dough on a floured board into a rectangular shape approximately 1/2 inch thick. Spread filling evenly over dough to within 1/2 inch of edges and roll up tightly, folding in the ends.

**6.** Beat egg white with 1 tablespoon water and brush dough. Place on greased baking sheet and bake 45 minutes, or until golden brown. Perfect for picnics and sporting events! Makes 12 servings.

*Brands may vary by region; substitute a similar product.*

### Boursin *Party Dip*

*This cheese is 100 percent natural and certified kosher.*

4 ounces Boursin Cheese*

1 tablespoon sour cream

1 teaspoon Dijon mustard

1 tablespoon chopped
    fresh chives

1 tablespoon capers,
    drained (optional)

Freshly cut vegetables

*Combine Boursin and sour cream until smooth. Stir in mustard, chives and capers. Cover and refrigerate. Serve with vegetables.*

*Brands may vary by region; substitute a similar product.*

239

**Costco suggests:**

## Chandler's Crabhouse "Seattle Style" Seafood Cioppino

Schwartz Brothers Restaurants, headquartered in Bellevue, Washington, was founded in 1970 by Bill and John Schwartz. Their restaurants include Chandler's Crabhouse and Fresh Fish Market in Seattle and Yokohama, Japan, Daniel's Broiler at South Lake Union and at Leschi Marina in Seattle, and in Bellevue, and Spazzo Mediterranean Grill and Tapas Bar in Bellevue. All of the restaurants are repeat winners of such prestigious honors as the Zagat Award of Excellence.

While this recipe is not strictly speaking from this region, you'd be hard-pressed to find a better seafood soup.

*Celebrity CHEF*
**DAN THIESSEN**

*Dan Thiessen, Chandler's Crabhouse executive chef, graduated from New York's Culinary Institute of America and has used his talents to craft menus that feature the finest products of the Pacific Northwest.*

## Cioppino Base

1/2 cup canola oil

12 ounces onions, julienned

4 ounces celery, julienned

8 ounces fennel, julienned

8 ounces red bell pepper, julienned

8 ounces green bell pepper, julienned

2 ounces minced garlic

1 fresh thyme sprig

1 tablespoon whole celery seeds

1 teaspoon red pepper flakes

1/2 tablespoon fennel seeds, ground

1 1/2 cups red wine vinegar

2 ounces tomato paste

24 ounces plum tomatoes, peeled and chopped

1 1/2 quarts fish stock

4 tablespoons salt

Warm oil in heavy-bottomed pot over medium heat. Add vegetables and cook until slightly soft. Add spices and cook for 1 minute. Deglaze pan with wine. Add tomato paste and cook 5 minutes. Add tomatoes, stock and seasoning. Bring to a boil, reduce heat and simmer 5 minutes. The base can be used immediately or cooled for later use.

## Cioppino Entrée

1/4 cup canola oil

3 fresh Dungeness crabs, cleaned and cracked

2 pounds sea scallops

2 pounds Manila clams

2 pounds Penn Cove mussels

2 pounds 71/90-count prawns

2 pounds halibut and/or salmon, diced

2 cups dry sherry

Cioppino Base Recipe

1/4 cup kosher salt

2 tablespoons black pepper

12 ounces butter

36 pieces grilled focaccia

Heat oil in soup pot and add all seafood. Sear for 2 minutes and deglaze with sherry. Add Cioppino Base and seasonings and simmer until crab has reached 160°F. Stir in butter and adjust seasonings as needed. Garnish with grilled focaccia. Makes 12 servings.

## Delta Pride Grilled Catfish with Fresh Salsa

Catfish, with its mild taste and lean, firm flesh, is catching on across the country. Delta Pride's fish are raised in clay-bottom ponds filled with pure water from deep aquifers and fed a grain-based, high-protein diet to ensure good flavor and a light, even texture. Delta Pride is the only catfish processor in the country with full-time USDA inspectors.

6 medium yellow and/or red tomatoes, chopped

1/2 cup chopped onion

1/4 cup sliced red onion (optional)

4 medium jalapeño peppers, seeded and chopped

6 tablespoons white wine vinegar

2 teaspoons salt

8 Delta Pride U.S. Farm-Raised Catfish fillets

1 teaspoon garlic salt

1 teaspoon ground black pepper

2 teaspoons cayenne pepper, or to taste

**1.** Prepare a grill or preheat the broiler.

**2.** Place tomatoes, onion, jalapeños, vinegar and salt in a medium bowl and stir well. Let stand at room temperature about 30 minutes before serving. Store leftovers in the refrigerator.

**3.** Sprinkle catfish fillets with garlic salt, black pepper and cayenne. Place fillets on an oiled grill rack or broiler pan rack. Grill or broil about 4 inches from heat source about 5 minutes on each side, or until fish flakes easily when tested with a fork. Place fillets on serving plates and top with fresh salsa. Makes 8 servings.

*Recipe provided by the Catfish Institute.*

## Reynolds Baby Back Barbecue Rib Packets

Reynolds Wrap Aluminum Foil takes the mess out of grilling.

6 pounds baby back pork ribs

4 sheets (18 by 24 inches each) Reynolds Wrap
   Heavy Duty Aluminum Foil

2 tablespoons packed brown sugar

2 tablespoons paprika

4 teaspoons garlic powder

1 tablespoon ground pepper

1 cup water

3 cups barbecue sauce

**1.** Preheat grill to medium or oven to 450°F.

**2.** Center one-fourth of ribs in single layer on each sheet of foil. Combine brown sugar and seasonings; rub on ribs.

**3.** Bring up foil sides. Double-fold top and one end to seal packet. Add 1/4 cup water. Double-fold remaining end, leaving room for heat circulation. Repeat to make 4 packets.

**4.** Grill 45-60 minutes in covered grill. Remove foil; place ribs on grill. Or bake 45-60 minutes on a broiler pan in oven.

**5.** Brush ribs with sauce. Either continue grilling or broil 4-5 inches from broiler, 10-15 minutes, brushing with sauce and turning every 5 minutes. Makes 10 servings.

**Reynolds Kitchen Tip:** While the ribs are cooking, prepare your favorite vegetables and keep them warm by using a Reynolds Foodservice packaging steam table pan. These foil steam table pans, available in full or half size, can go from cooking to transport to storage to freezer to reheating, all in one, which makes for fewer dishes and less mess to clean up.

## Candy suggests:

- Rotisserie chicken cut into bite-size pieces; or roast whole chickens after generously oiling and evenly dusting with a seasoning salt.
- Assorted bell peppers cut into strips (if not available, use fresh celery and carrot strips)
- Ranch dressing as a dip
- Stuffed green olives and black olives
- Tortilla chips and salsa
- Gazpacho can be presented in a hollowed-out watermelon half. Cut the melon flesh into chunks and serve it on the tropical fruit plate. (Candy notes, "Watermelon isn't tropical, but it works well and I haven't had any complaints.")

### Candy's Salsa Spread:

Spread 8 ounces cream cheese in a dish and top with 2 cups salsa. Use chips to scoop salsa and cream cheese together. The softer the cheese, the easier it is to scoop.

## Costco suggests:

### Kirkland Signature/Tyson Apricot-Honey Labor Day Chicken Dijon

Tyson is a proud partner with the Share Our Strength organization, one of the nation's largest hunger-relief agencies. Over a three-year period, Tyson committed to donate $10 million of support, including 6.5 million pounds of chicken, which will provide 32.5 million meals.

1¹/₃ cups honey mustard or Dijon mustard

³/₄ cup apricot preserves

4 teaspoons ground ginger

8 Tyson Boneless, Skinless Chicken Breasts*

**1.** In a small mixing bowl, blend together mustard, apricot preserves and ginger. Pour half of the mixture into a separate bowl. (Half will be used to marinate the chicken and the other half to drizzle over the finished chicken.)

**2.** Rinse chicken with cold water and then place in one of the bowls with the mustard mixture. Cover and refrigerate for a minimum of two hours.

**3.** Place chicken on a preheated grill about 6 inches from heat source. Grill 6-8 minutes on each side, or until chicken is done. To ensure that the chicken has been properly cooked, insert an instant-read thermometer into the thickest part. Internal temperature should read 170°F.

**4.** Drizzle sauce from second bowl over chicken just before serving. Makes 8 servings.

*Food Safety Note: Do not baste the chicken with the sauce that it was marinated in.*

*\*Brands may vary by region; substitute a similar product.*

## Bill Beeh's Lamb Mango Tango

The first time this Bellevue, Washington, Costco member made this recipe was for a special sunset patio dinner with his wife and mother-in-law. His salsa made the meal.

2 ripe mangoes

2 ripe papayas

2 medium cucumbers

16 fresh mint leaves, chopped

2 limes (zest and juice)

1/2 cup sugar

2 cups olive oil

Juice of 4 lemons, plus 4 lemons cut in quarters

24 garlic cloves, roughly chopped

1 cup fresh rosemary

Ground black pepper

4 racks of lamb

Salt

**1.** Peel mangoes and remove seeds. Cut papayas in half and remove seeds. Peel cucumbers, cut in half and scoop out seeds. Chop mangoes, papayas and cucumbers into 1/4-inch cubes. Place in mixing bowl with mint.

**2.** Add lime zest and juice, and sugar to taste. (It should taste sweet and tart.) Mix. Refrigerate, covered, 12-24 hours.

**3.** Combine olive oil, lemon juice and quarters, garlic, rosemary and pepper to taste in a 1-gallon resealable plastic bag.

**4.** Place lamb in plastic bag with marinade. Marinate in refrigerator 12-24 hours, turning every 3-4 hours.

**5.** Remove lamb from marinade, reserving marinade. Salt and pepper lamb on both sides.

**6.** Grill lamb over medium-hot coals 8-10 minutes each side, or until medium-rare. Let lamb rest 10 minutes.

**7.** Place marinade in saucepan and bring to a boil. Reduce volume by 50 percent. Strain.

**8.** Slice lamb between ribs (4 ribs per serving). Pour reduced marinade over lamb. Serve with a generous side of salsa and fresh asparagus. Makes 8 servings.

Costco Member
Bill Beeh

## The Oppenheimer Group and California Strawberry Commission
### Kiwi-Strawberry Chicken

This dish makes a stunning presentation.

2 cups halved California Strawberries

6 kiwifruit (green or gold), peeled and sliced*

2 cups cubed cantaloupe

2 teaspoons chopped fresh tarragon

1/4 cup olive oil

1/4 cup chopped shallots

1/4 cup raspberry vinegar

1/2 teaspoon ground black pepper

8 chicken breast halves

Combine all fruits and tarragon in a medium bowl. Refrigerate 2 hours. Heat oil in a saucepan. Sauté shallots until soft. Add vinegar and pepper and heat to boiling. Drizzle hot dressing over fruit and stir. Grill chicken. Spoon warm fruit compote over chicken. Makes 8 servings.

*Brands may vary by region; substitute a similar product.

**Candy suggests:**

- Pie (especially apple)
- Cake (especially carrot)
- Assorted hard cheeses (e.g., Cheddar)
- Pear or apple slices with assorted specialty chocolates

Costco Member
Candy Barnhart

## Candy's Pecan Delight

While pecans are not recognized as a northern product, we just couldn't resist sharing Candy's recipe, as it is one of her most popular desserts.

4 egg whites

1 cup sugar

1³/4 teaspoons baking powder

1/2 cup crushed soda crackers

1 cup chopped pecans

1/4 teaspoon pure vanilla extract

3¹/2 cups frozen whipped dessert topping, thawed

Preheat oven to 325°F. In a medium mixing bowl, beat egg whites until stiff. Gradually add sugar and baking powder, beating well to incorporate evenly. Fold in crushed crackers, 3/4 cup pecans and vanilla extract. Spread batter in a 9-inch square baking pan and bake 30 minutes. Cracks in the top of this after baking are to be expected. Cool in refrigerator, uncovered. Spread with whipped topping. Sprinkle with remaining pecans. Cut into small squares, as this is rather sweet. Best served cold or at least cool: set the pan on the table over a slightly larger pan filled with cracked ice (nestle the dessert pan in the ice pan so it doesn't slip around). Makes 16 servings.

**Costco suggests:**

### George Weston Bakeries Inc. Apple-Raisin Pandowdy

1/2 cup sugar, divided

1/2 teaspoon salt

1/2 teaspoon cinnamon

4 Thomas' Original English Muffins, split*

1/4 cup margarine or butter

2 large tart apples, peeled, cored and coarsely chopped

1/2 cup raisins

1/2 cup water

1/2 cup honey

Preheat oven to 375°F. Combine all but 2 tablespoons sugar, salt and cinnamon in large bowl. Spread muffin halves with margarine; cut into cubes and add to sugar mixture with apples and raisins; toss to coat. Combine water and honey; stir into muffin mixture. Spoon into greased 9-inch square baking dish. Cover with foil. Bake 20 minutes. Remove foil, stir and sprinkle with remaining sugar. Bake uncovered 30 minutes longer. Cool on wire rack 10 minutes. Serve with whipped cream dusted with cinnamon. Makes 6 servings.

*Brands may vary by region; substitute a similar product.*

## desserts

## Chocolate Chip Cookies with Pecans

1 pound margarine, softened

4 medium eggs

2 teaspoons vanilla extract

2 teaspoons baking soda

1 teaspoon salt

1 1/2 cups packed light brown sugar

1 1/2 cups granulated sugar

4 1/2 cups all-purpose flour

8 ounces large pecan pieces

36 ounces semisweet chocolate chips

**1.** Mix margarine, eggs, vanilla, baking soda, salt, brown sugar and granulated sugar together thoroughly, until creamed. Add flour—gently! You don't want a snowstorm in your kitchen.

**2.** Blend pecans thoroughly into batter.

**3.** Lastly, stir in the most important ingredient in chocolate chip cookies—the chocolate chips! Stir only until the chips are well integrated in the batter. Excessive mixing will cause batter to become too dark.

**4.** Put batter in airtight container and chill overnight.

**5.** Preheat oven to 375°F. Drop cookies by the heaping teaspoonful onto a lightly greased cookie sheet, about an inch apart. Baking time will vary depending on how cooked you desire your cookies. I'm a crunchy, you might be a softie. I don't know about you, but when I bake cookies at home, I never trust a kitchen timer—I watch over them to see when they're done to perfection! The cookies also like the attention. You might even want to talk to them. That's baking with love!

This recipe is larger than normal (it's Costco size) and will make approximately 250 bite-size cookies or a smaller quantity of larger cookies. Goes great with a nice chilled glass of homemade lemonade.

## Kimo's Hawaiian Lemonade

1/2 cup fresh lemon juice

3/4 cup sugar

1 1/2 quarts water

1 tablespoon pineapple juice

Lemonade, like everything else you touch, reflects your personality and attitude. So, add a generous helping of yourself to the recipe, mix thoroughly in a large pitcher, chill and serve with plenty of ice. Makes 12 servings.

### Wally Amos' Summer Delight

Wally Amos is an icon and his name is a household word. As founder of Famous Amos Cookies in 1975 and father of the gourmet chocolate chip cookie industry, he has used his fame to support educational causes.

His latest enterprise, Uncle Wally's Muffins, has been critically acclaimed by the media and consumers alike for its tasty, high-quality muffins.

"Two of life's great taste treats are chocolate chip cookies and homemade lemonade," he says. "The following recipes are guaranteed to satisfy your taste buds. Warning! Both can become habit-forming. Enjoy."

## Del Monte Gingersnap Peach Crisp

Del Monte Orchard Select premium peaches are hand-picked, sliced and packed in light syrup and provide 80 percent of the RDA (recommended daily allowance) of vitamin C.

*1 jar (26 oz.) Del Monte Orchard Select Sliced Cling Peaches*
*1¹/₂ cups coarsely crushed gingersnaps*
*¹/₄ cup butter or margarine, softened*
*¹/₃ cup sliced almonds or chopped walnuts*

**1.** Preheat oven to 350°F.

**2.** Drain fruit; arrange in a greased 8-by-8-inch baking dish.

**3.** Mix together cookie crumbs and butter. Stir in nuts. Sprinkle evenly over fruit.

**4.** Bake 15-20 minutes. Serve warm with vanilla ice cream, frozen yogurt or whipped cream, if desired.

Variation: Divide fruit and topping among 6 8-ounce baking cups. Bake 10 minutes.

Get Creative: For variety, substitute coarsely crushed oatmeal cookies for gingersnaps, or Del Monte Orchard Select Sliced Pears for peaches. Makes 6 servings.

## Primavera Cherry Pie

If ever there was a traditional all-American dessert, it's an old-fashioned cherry pie.

*³/₄ to 1¹/₄ cups sugar, depending on sweetness of cherries*
*¹/₃ cup flour*
*8 cups pitted Primavera Bing, Royal Ann or Tartarian cherries (about 3¹/₂ pounds)*
*Pastry dough for 9-inch 2-crust pie, chilled*
*¹/₄ teaspoon almond extract*
*2 tablespoons butter*

**1.** Preheat oven to 425°F.

**2.** In large mixing bowl, stir together sugar and flour. Mix well with cherries.

**3.** Line a pie pan with the pastry dough.

**4.** Add cherry mixture. Sprinkle with almond extract and dot with butter.

**5.** Moisten outer edge of crust with cold water. Cover pie with top crust, crimping edges and adding slits to allow steam to escape. Sprinkle with sugar.

**6.** Cover edges with foil to prevent excessive browning (remove for last 15 minutes of baking). Bake 35-45 minutes, or until crust is brown and juices are bubbly. Serve lukewarm. Makes 6-8 servings.

*Recipe provided by the California Cherry Advisory Board.*

# *Vendor Directory*

**AGRILINK FOODS INC.**
520 N. Broadway
Green Bay, WI 54307
920-435-5300
**www.agrilinkfoods.com**
*Nalleys, Birdseye, Bernsteins, Comstock, Vegall, Wilderness and Brooks foods*

**AIDELLS**
877-Aidells (243-3557)
**www.aidells.com**

**ALBERTO CULVER SPECIALTY PRODUCTS**
2525 Armitage Ave.
Melrose Park, IL 60160
708-450-3000
**www.albertoculver.com**
*Mrs. Dash seasoning and Molly McButter*

**ALPINE**
9383 N.W. 58th St., Suite 201
Miami, FL 33178
Phone 305-594-9117
Fax 305-594-8506
*Mangos, asparagus, raspberries, blueberries, blackberries, grape and heirloom tomatoes*

**ALSUM PRODUCE INC.**
N. 9083 Highway Ef, P.O. Box 188
Friesland, WI 53935
920-348-5127
**www.alsum.com**
*Potatoes and onions*

**AMERICAN POPCORN COMPANY**
4332 Grant St.
Sioux City, IA 51102
712-239-1232
**www.jollytime.com**
*Healthy Pop, Goldmine, Jollytime Blast-O-Butter and Kettle Mania*

**ANTHONY FARMS**
P.O. Box 4
Scandinavia, WI 54977
715-467-2212
*Potatoes*

**APIO, INC.**
P.O. Box 627
Guadalupe, CA 93434
800-626-2746
**www.apioinc.com**
*Broccoli florets, vegetable medley, garden vegetables and sugar snap peas*

**APPLE & EVE**
2 Seaview Blvd.
Port Washington, NY 11050
516-621-1122
**www.appleandeve.com**
*100% Juice boxes, 100% Juice blends and Ruby Red Grapefruit juice cocktail*

**ARIZONA BEVERAGE CONCEPTS LLC**
4283 S. Santa Rita
Tucson, AZ 85714
520-294-5112

**ARTHUR SCHUMAN INC. – CELLO PRODUCTS**
40 New Dutch Lane
Fairfield, NJ 07004
973-227-0030
**www.arthurschuman.com**
*Parmigiano-Reggiano, Grana Padano, Provolone, Reggianito, Pecorino Romano, Italian Fontina, Gouda, grated Pecorino Romano, grated Parmesan, shredded Parmesan and shredded imported 4-cheese*

**ATLANTIC VEAL & LAMB, INC.**
275 Morgan Ave.
Brooklyn, NY 11211
800-222-8325
*Veal*

**AUSTRALIAN LAMB COMPANY, INC.**
20 Westport Road, Suite 320
Wilton, CT 06897
203-529-9200
**www.auslamb.com**
*Southern Cross lamb, lamb chops, frenched racks and boneless legs*

**BABÉ FARMS**
1485 N. Blosser Road
Santa Maria, CA 93458
800-648-6772
**www.babyveggies.com**
*Gourmet salad blends*

**BARILLA AMERICA**
200 Tri-State International #200
Lincolnshire, IL 60069
847-405-7500
*Dry pasta, filled pasta and pasta sauce*

**BASIN GOLD**
2715 St. Andrews Loop, Suite C
Pasco, WA 99301
*Potatoes and onions*

**BC HOT HOUSE FOODS INC.**
5355 152nd St.
Surrey, B.C. Canada V3S5A5
800-663-1889
**www.bchothouse.com**
*Beefsteak tomatoes, tomatoes on the vine, sweet bell peppers and long English cucumbers*

**BEAR CREEK**
325 W. 600th South
Heber City, UT 84032
435-654-2660
**www.bearcreekfoods.com**
*Soups, pasta and cake mixes*

**BEE SWEET**
416 E. South Ave.
Fowler, CA 93625
**www.beesweetcitrus.com**
*Full line of citrus produce*

**BELGIOIOSO CHEESE INC.**
5810 County Road NN
Denmark, WI 54208
920-863-2123
**www.belgioioso.com**
*Provolone, Parmesan, Fresh Mozzarella, Mascarpone, Asiago and Peperoncino*

**BELL CARTER/LINDSAY OLIVE CO.**
3742 Mt. Diablo Blvd.
Lafayette, CA 94549
925-284-5433
**www.lindsayolives.com**
*Ripe, Spanish and specialty olive products*

**BOBOLI INTERNATIONAL**
3247 W. March Lane, Ste. 210
Stockton, CA 95219
209-473-3507
**www.boboli-intl.com**
*Cream puffs and eclairs frozen desserts*

**BOSKOVICH FARMS**
711 Diaz Ave.
Oxnard, CA 93032
805-487-7799
**www.boskovichfarms.com**
*Spinach and green onions*

**BROWN AND HALEY**
P.O. Box 1596
Tacoma, WA 98401
253-620-3000
**www.brown-haley.com**
*Almond Roca, Zingos and fine boxed chocolates*

**BUMBLE BEE SEAFOODS**
**www.bumblebee.com**

**CGI DESSERTS/CAMELOT**
#1 King Arthurs Ct.
Sugarland, TX 77478
877-240-1200
*Cakes and pies*

**CAL SALES/SUNNY COVE/ KIRSCHENMAN**
1122 N. Chinowth
Visalia, CA 93291
559-741-7030
**Ross@Calsales.Com**
*Citrus, potatoes, watermelon, tree fruit and grapes*

**CALAVO GROWERS, INC.**
2530 Red Hill Avenue
Santa Ana, CA 92705
949-223-1111
**www.calavo.com**
*Avocados and papaya*

**CALIFORNIA AVOCADO COMMISSION**
1251 E. Dyer Road, Suite 210
Santa Ana, CA 92705
714-558-6761
**www.avocado.org**
*Recipes and brochures*

**CALIFORNIA STRAWBERRY COMMISSION**
P.O. Box 269
Watsonville, CA 95077
831-724-1301
**www.calstrawberry.com**
*California strawberries*

**CAMPBELL SALES**
1 Campbell Place
Box 41A
Camden, NJ 08103
856-342-4800
**www.campbellskitchen.com**
**www.campbellseatsmart.com**
**www.campbellsoup.com**

**CARDILE BROS. MUSHROOM PKG. INC.**
8790 Gap Newport Pike
Avondale, PA 19311
610-268-2470
**cardilebro@aol.com**
*White, portobello and shitake mushrooms*

**CARTER THOMAS LLC.**
250 W. Main St., Suite 200
Woodland, CA 95695
530-662-8100
**www.barlettpear.com**
*Pears*

# Vendor Directory

**CERES FRESH FOODS
LLC./NEWSTAR**
900 Work St.
Salinas, CA 93901
www.newstarfresh.com
*Spinach, romaine hearts, green onions, iceberg lettuce and asparagus*

**CHEF AMERICA INC.**
20 Inverness Place E.
Englewood, CO 80112
303-790-0303
www.chefamerica.com
*Sandwiches and hand-held foods*

**CHICKEN OF THE SEA INT'L**
www.chickenofthesea.com

**CHRISTOPHER RANCH**
305 Bloomfield Ave.
Gilroy, CA 95020
408-847-1100
www.christopher-ranch.com

**CLEAR SPRINGS FOODS, INC.**
P.O. Box 712
Buhl, ID 83316
800-635-8211, 208-543-4316
www.clearsprings.com

**CLIFFSTAR CORPORATION**
One Cliffstar Ave.
Dunkirk, NY 14048
716-366-6100
*Kirkland Signature cranberry juice, various blends, and Kirkland Signature Newman's Own grape juice*

**CMI**
509-663-1955
www.cmiapples.com

**COCA-COLA**
One Coca-Cola Plaza
Atlanta, GA 30313
800-232-2652
www.coca-cola.com
*Coca-Cola, Diet Coke and Sprite*

**CONAGRA FOODS RETAIL
PRODUCTS CO.**
5 ConAgra Drive
Omaha, N.E. 60515
www.conagrafoods.com

**CONTESSA FOOD PRODUCTS**
P.O. Box 1950
San Pedro, CA 90733
310-832-8000
www.contessa.com

**CONTINENTAL MILLS**
18125 Andover Park West
Tukwila, WA 98188
800-426-0955
www.krusteaz.com
**Krusteaz Pancake, Muffin, Dessert and Bread machine mixes**

**COUNTRYSIDE BAKING CO. INC.**
1711 Kettering St.
Irvine, CA 92614
949-851-9654
*Rugala cookies and biscotti*

**D'ARRIGO BROS. CO.
OF CALIFORNIA**
383 W. Market St.
Salinas, CA 93901
831-753-5425
831-424-3136
www.andyboy.com
*Romaine hearts*

**D'ORAZIO FOODS INC.**
P.O. Box 243
Bellmawr, NJ 08099
888-328-7287
www.dorazio.com
*Stuffed shells, crepe manicotti and cheese ravioli*

**DFI GOLD RUSH LLC**
7638 N. Ingram Ave.
Fresno, CA 93711
559-446-2400
*Cantaloupe, honeydew melons and California cherries*

**DARE FOODS INC.**
5 Blossom St.
Marblehead, MA 01945
781-639-1808
www.15minutestofame.com
*Cookies and crackers*

**DEAN SPECIALTY FOODS GROUP**
P.O. Box 19057
Green Bay, WI 54303
920-497-8335
www.deanfoods.com
*Pickles, relishes, peppers, coffee creamers, sauces, olives, pudding and nutritional beverages*

**DEL MONTE FOODS**
P.O. Box 193575
San Francisco, CA 94119-3575
415-247-3333
www.delmonte.com
*Del Monte, S&W, Sun Fresh and Contadina*

**DELACRE-UNITED BISCUITS INC.**
6000 Midlantic Drive, Suite 1105
Mt. Laurel, NJ 08054
856-222-0065
www.delacre.com

**DELTA PRIDE CATFISH, INC.**
P.O. Box 850
Indianola, MS 38751
Phone 800-421-1045
Fax 662-887-5950
www.deltapride.com

**DIAMOND FRUIT GROWERS INC.**
P.O. Box 185
Odell, OR 97044
541-354-5300
www.diamondfruit.com
*Fresh pears and fresh cherries (all varieties)*

**DISCOVERY FOODS (LING LING)**
2395 American Ave.
Hayward, CA 94545
510-293-1838
www.ling-ling.com
*Potstickers*

**DNE WORLD FRUIT SALES**
1900 Old Dixie Highway
Ft. Pierce, FL 34951
772-465-1110
dne@dneworld.com
*Citrus produce*

**DOLE FOOD COMPANY**
P.O. Box 5132
Westlake Village, CA 91359
800-232-8888
www.dole.com

**DOMEX MARKETING**
151 Low Road
Yakima, WA 98908
509-966-1814
www.superapple.com

**DON MIGUEL
MEXICAN FOODS INC.**
2125 E. Orangewood
Anaheim, CA 92806
877-dmiguel (364-4835)
www.donmiguel.com
*Ultimate chicken & cheese chimichanga, shredded beef, cheese & green chili chimichanga, all white meat garlic chicken flautas, chicken chipotle flautas, shredded beef flautas, lean ole variety pack burritos, shredded beef tamale bowl, beef tamales, chicken and cheese tamales*

**DOUGLAS FRUIT COMPANY**
110 Taylor Flats Road
Pasco, WA 99301
509-547-2787
www.douglasfruit.com
*Red Delicious, Braeburn, Fuji, Granny Smith, Gala and Pink Lady apples, yellow and white flesh peaches and nectarines*

**DUNI DESTER CORPORATION**
225 Peachtree St., Suite 400
Atlanta, GA 30303
800-237-8270
www.duni.com
*Paper napkins, plates, table covers and cups*

**EARTHBOUND FARM**
1721 San Juan Highway
San Juan Bautista, CA 95045
800-690-3200
www.ebfarm.com

**EMMPAK,**
AN EXCEL FOOD SOLUTIONS CO.
1515 W. Canal St.
Milwaukee, WI 53233
800-558-4242
www.excelmeats.com
*Deli meats, fully cooked, and marinated beef, pork and poultry*

**ENACA INTERNATIONAL L.C.**
3900 N.W. 79th Ave., Suite 570
Miami, FL 33166
305-599-8877
sales@enacausa.com
*Shrimp and tilapia fish*

**EXCEL CORPORATION**
151 N. Main
Wichita, KS 67202
316-291-2500
www.excelmeats.com
*Beef and pork*

**FARMER JOHN/
CLOUGHERTY PACKING**
3049 E. Vernon Ave.
Los Angeles, CA 90058
323-583-4621
www.farmerjohn.com
*Fresh and processed pork products*

**FARMLAND FOODS INC.**
12200 Ambassador Drive
Kansas City, KS 64163
800-843-6603
www.farmland.com
*Kirkland Signature/Carando spiral sliced ham*

**FINLANDIA CHEESE, INC.**
1140 Parsippany Blvd.
Parsippany, NJ 07054
800-496-3822
*Regular and Jalapeno Muenster,*
*Imported regular and lite Swiss cheeses*

**FISH HOUSE FOODS INC.**
3285 Corporate View
Vista, CA 92083
800-238-3482
*Stuffed salmon fillets*

**FLETCHER'S FINE FOODS**
502 Boundary Blvd.
Algona, WA 98001
253-735-0800
*Bacon, ham and sausage*

**FORDEL INC.**
1000 Airport Blvd., P.O. Box 100
Mendota, CA 93640
559-655-3241
**www.fordelinc.com**
*All melons and sweet corn*

**FOSTER FARMS**
1000 Davis St.
Livingston, CA 95334
800-255-7227
**www.fosterfarms.com**

**FOUR STAR**
P.O. Box 1990
Delano, CA 93216
661-725-0186
**fourstarfruit@aol.com**

**FOWLER PACKING CO.**
8570 S. Cedar Ave.
Fresno, CA 93725
559-834-5911
**www.fowlerpacking.com**
*Peaches, plums, nectarines, grapes*
*and apricots*

**FRESH NETWORK LLC (IDAHO)**
1420 E. 17th St., Suite E
Idaho Falls, ID 83404
800-798-4571
**www.freshnetwork.com**

**FRITO-LAY, INC.**
7701 Legacy Drive
Plano, TX 75024-4099
800-352-4477
**www.fritolay.com**
*Tostitos, Lays, Ruffles, Doritos, Fritos,*
*Rold Gold, Cheetos and Sun Chips*

**G & D WALLACE INC.**
**"Samish River" Brand Potatoes from**
**the Skagit Valley**
P.O. Box 405
Burlington, WA 98233
360-757-0981
**www.wallacespuds.com**
*Red, white, yellow, and purple*
*potatoes, as well as organic red,*
*yellow and russet potatoes*

**GARDENBURGER**
c/o Linda Olson
800-459-7079

**GENERAL MILLS BAKERIES &**
**FOODSERVICE**
200 S. Sixth St.
Minneapolis, MN 55402
800-767-5404

**GENERAL MILLS, INC.**
One General Mills Blvd.
Minneapolis, MN 55426
800-328-1144

**GEORGE WESTON BAKERIES INC.**
55 Paradise Lane
Bay Shore, NY 11706
*Thomas' English muffins*

**GIORGIO FOODS**
P.O. Box 96
Temple, PA 19560
610-926-2139
**www.giorgiofoods.com**
*Mushrooms-canned, jars and fresh*
**GLOBAL FISHING INC.**
10500 N.E. 8th St., Suite 1925
Bellevue, WA 98004
425-455-2291
**www.globaltr.net**

**GRACE BAKING CO.**
3200 G Regatta Blvd.
Richmond, CA 94804
800-555-5755
**www.customerservice@gracebaking.com**
*Various breads*

**GREEN STRIPE INC.**
3525 S. Lawrence St.
Philadelphia, PA 19148-5605
215-468-2200
**E-mail: jorge@greenstripe.com**
**Fruits and vegetables**

**GRIMMWAY FARMS**
P.O. Box 81498
Bakersfield, CA 93380
661-845-5200
**www.grimmway.com**
*Carrots, baby carrots, citrus, potatoes*
*and organic vegetables*

**GROWER DIRECT**
**MARKETING LLC.**
2097 Beyer Lane
Stockton, CA 95215
209-931-7900
**www.growerdirect.net**
*Cherries, asparagus, blueberries*
*and apricots*

**H.J. HEINZ COMPANY**
**www.heinz.com**

**HANSEN BEVERAGE COMPANY**
1010 Railroad St.
Corona, CA 92882
909-739-6200
**www.hansens.com**
*All-natural beverages, natural sodas,*
*premium juice drinks, energy drinks,*
*soy smoothies and specialty food bars*

**HEBREW NATIONAL**
**KOSHER FOODS**
(516) 949-7500
**www.hebrewnational.com**
*Kosher meat products and condiments*

**HERITAGE SALMON LIMITED**
100-12051 Horseshoe Way
Richmond, B.C. V7A-4V4
604-277-3093
**www.heritagesalmon.com**

**HIGH LINER FOODS**
1 High Liner Ave.
Portsmouth, NH 03801
603-431-6865
**www.highlinerfoods.com**
*Premium frozen seafood*
**HOLTZINGER FRUIT CO.**
1312 N. Sixth Ave.
Yakima, WA 98901
509-457-5115
**www.royalpurpleapples.com**
*Apples, cherries and pears*

**HORMEL FOODS**
1 Hormel Place
Austin, MN 55912
507-437-9852
**www.hormel.com**

*Spam, Dinty Moore, Stagg Foods,*
*Chi-Chi's Foods, El Torito, Herdez,*
*Hormel Chili and Marrakesh Express*

**IBP INC.**
800 Stevens Port Drive
Dakota, SD 57049
800-416-0770
**www.ibpinc.com**
*Fresh beef and pork*

**INDEX FRESH, INC.**
18184 Slover Ave./P.O. Box 250
Bloomington, CA 92316
909-877-1577
**www.indexfresh.com**
*Avocados and Asian Pears*

**INTERNATIONAL**
**MULTIFOODS CORP.**
111 Cheshire Lane
Minnetonka, MN 55305
800-866-3300
*Dry and sweet bakery mixes*

**J & J SNACK FOODS INC.**
5353 Downey Road
Vernon, CA 90058
800-486-7622
**www.jjsnack.com**
*Fresh baked cookies*

**JELLY BELLY CANDY COMPANY**
One Jelly Belly Lane
Fairfield, CA 94533
**www.jellybelly.com**
*Jelly Belly jelly beans*

**KEEBLER**
One Hollow Tree Lane
Elmhurst, IL 60126
630-833-2900
**www.keebler.com**
*Keebler, Sunshine, Carr's, Famous Amos*
*and Austin cookies and crackers*
**KELLOGG'S COMPANY**
One Kellogg Square
Battle Creek, MI 49016
**www.kellogg.com**
*Cereals, Nutri-Grain bars, Rice Krispies*
*treats, Poptarts, Eggo waffles and*
*Morningstar Farms products*

**KEYSTONE FRUIT MARKETING**
11 N. Carlisle St.
Greencastle, PA 17225
717-597-2112
**www.keystonefruit.com**
*Year-round sweet onions and tree-ripe*
*southern peaches*

**KING PAK POTATO CO.**
P.O. Box 22A
Edison, CA 93220
661-366-3267
*Potatoes - whites, reds, Yukon golds
and russets*

**KINGSBURG APPLE SALES**
P.O. Box 38
Kingsburg, CA 93631
559-897-2986
*Asian pears, pluots and
saturn white peaches*

**KRAFT FOODS
NORTH AMERICA, INC.**
800-323-0768
**www.kraftfoods.com**

**L&M NORTHWEST**
304 S. First St., Suite A
Selah, WA 98942
866-541-0067
**www.lmcompanies.com**
*Apples, pears, melons, vegetables,
potatoes and onions*

**LA BREA BAKERY INC.**
15963 Strathern St.
Van Nuys, CA 91406
818-742-4242
**www.labreabakery.com**
*Artisan breads*

**LEE BRANDS LLC**
P.O. Box 971
Salinas, CA 93901
1-866-LEE4YOU
**www.leebrands.com**
*Asparagus and green onions*

**MANN PACKING COMPANY**
800-285-1002
**www.broccoli.com**
*Broccoli, vegetable medley, garden
vegetables and sugar snap peas*

**MAPLE LEAF FOODS INC.**
**www.mapleleaf.ca**
*Bacon*

**MARIANI PACKING COMPANY**
500 Crocker Drive
Vacaville, CA 95688
707-452-2800
**www.mariani.com**
*Dried plums, apricots, mixed fruit,
mango, cranberries, berries and cherries*

**MARINE HARVEST**
1600 S. Federal Highway, Suite 811
Pompano Beach, FL 33062
954-782-4015
**www.marineharvest.com**
**www.nutreco.com**

**MARTINELLIS**
227 E. Beach St.
Watsonville, CA 95076
800-662-1868
**www.martinellis.com**
*Sparkling Cider*

**MASTERFOODS USA/
UNCLE BEN'S INC.**
3250 E. 44th St.
Vernon, CA 90058
800-525-5273
**www.unclebens.com**
*Uncle Ben's Original Converted Brand
Rice and Uncle Ben's Long Grain &
Wild Rice*

**MASTRONARDI PRODUCE**
2100 Road 4 East
Kingsville, Ontario N9Y2E5
519-326-3218
sunset@winecom.net
*Greenhouse tomatoes, peppers,
cucumbers and eggplant*

**THE MAZZETTA COMPANY**
**www.mazzetta.com**

**MCCORMICK & COMPANY INC.**
Food Service Division
226 Schilling Circle
Hunt Valley, MD 21031
1-800-322-SPICE
**www.mccormick.com**
*Seasonings and flavorings*

**MCNEIL NUTRITIONALS**
7050 Camp Hill Road
Fort Washington, PA 19034
**www.splenda.com**
*Splenda sugar substitute*

**MERCER RANCH**
46 Sonova Road
Prosser, WA 99350 and
Holtville, CA 92250
509-894-4460
**www.mercerranch.com**
*Fresh carrots and sweet corn*

**MERIDIAN PRODUCTS /
DBA CON AGRA FOODS**
206-232-6709
**www.conagrafoods.com**

**MERISANT COMPANY**
10 S. Riverside, Suite 850
Chicago, IL 60606
312-840-6000
**www.equal.com**
*Equal sweetener*

**METZ FRESH LLC**
39405 Metz Road
King City, CA 93930
831-386-1015
**www.metzfresh.com**
*Spinach, celery, Brussels sprouts
and leeks*

**MEYER FOODS**
4611 West Adams St.
Lincoln, NE 68524
888-740-FOOD (3663)
**www.meyerbeef.com**
*MTC Gourmet Yakitori Beef, Korean
BBQ Beef Short Ribs*

**MICHAEL FOODS**
401 Carlson Parkway, Suite 300
Minatonka, MN 55305
877-727-3884
**www.michaelfoods.com**
*Better N' Eggs*

**MILTON'S BAKING**
3702 Via De La Valle, Suite 202
Del Mar, CA 92014
**www.miltonsbaking.com**

**THE MINUTE MAID COMPANY**
2000 Saint James Place
Houston, TX 77056
713-888-5000
**www.minutemaid.com**
*Orange juice*

**MISSION PRODUCE**
P.O. Box 5267
Oxnard, CA 93030
**www.missionpro.com**
*Avocados*

**MONTEREY MUSHROOMS INC.**
**www.montmush.com**
*Fresh, canned and marinated mushrooms*

**MONTEREY PASTA COMPANY**
1528 Moffett St.
Salinas, CA 93905
831-753-6262
**www.montereypasta.com**
*Pastas, sauces and calzones*

**MOTTS**
6 High Ridge Park
Stamford, CT 06905
203-968-7500
**www.motts.com**
*Apple juice, apple sauce, Hawaiian
Punch, Clamato and Yoo-hoo drinks*

**MOUNTAIN HIGH POTATO
AND ONION INC.**
P.O. Box 21627
Keizer, OR 97307
661-399-7060
*Onions, potatoes and watermelons*

**MOUNTAIN STREAM INC.**
6800 N.W. 36th Ave.
Miami, FL 33147
866-691-7997
**www.mountainstreamtilapia.com**
*Fresh tilapia fish*

**NABISCO BISCUIT AND
SNACKS DIVISION
KRAFT FOODS
NORTH AMERICA, INC.**
800-Nabisco (622-4726)
**www.nabiscoworld.com**

**NANCY'S SPECIALTY FOODS**
6500 Overlake Place
Newark, CA 94560
510-494-1100
**www.nancys.com**
*Quiche, appetizers, party spirals*

**NAUMES INC.**
#2 Barnett St.
Medford, OR 97501
541-779-9951
**www.naumes.com**
*Cherries, Asian pears, pears and apples*

**NESTLÉ USA**
800 N. Brand Blvd.
Glendale, CA 91203
800-289-7314
M-F 8 a.m.-8 p.m. EST
**www.verybestbaking.com**
**After Eight mints and Bacci
Italian chocolates**

**NESTLÉ WATERS
NORTH AMERICA**
777 W. Putnam Ave.
Greenwich, CT 06836
*Arrowhead, Calistoga, Ice Mountain,
Deer Park, Ozarka, Poland Spring,
Zephyrhills, Perrier and San
Pellegrino waters*

**NEW YORK STYLE SAUSAGE CO.**
1228 Reamwood Ave.
Sunnyvale, CA 94089
408-745-7675
*Hot Italian sausage, mild Italian sausage, sweet Italian sausage, breakfast link, L.A. hot link, garlic-Italian sausage, bulk fresh linguica, hot Italian griller, mild Italian griller, maple-breakfast sausage, chorizo, basil garlic Italian sausage, country-breakfast bulk sausage, mild turkey Italian sausage, hot turkey Italian sausage, mild bratwurst and hot bratwurst*

**NONNI'S FOOD COMPANY**
601 S. Boulder, #900
Tulsa, OK 74119
877-295-0289
**www.nonnis.com**
*Nonni's biscotti*

**NORCO RANCH INC.**
1811 Mountain Ave./P.O. Box 910
Norco, CA 92860
909-737-6735
*Eggs of all sorts*

**NORPAC**
**www.norpac.com**
*Asparagus stir-fry, stir-fry vegetables, ginger stir-fry, super sweet white cut corn, petite peas, petite extra fine green beans, broccoli normandy, triple berry blend, broccoli florets and creamy spinach*

**NORSELAND INC.**
1290 E. Main St.
Stamford, CT 06902
800-326-5620
**www.boursincheese.com**
*Boursin cheese, Jarlsberg cheese and Saga Brand cheeses*
**THE NUNES COMPANY/FOXY FOODS**
P.O. Box 80006
Salinas, CA 93901
**www.foxy.com**

**OCEAN SPRAY CRANBERRIES, INC.**
1-800-662-3263
M-F 9 a.m.-4 p.m. EST
**www.oceanspray.com**

**THE OPPENHEIMER GROUP**
2001 W. Garfield St./Box C-128
Seattle, WA 98119
206-284-1705
**www.oppyproduce.com**
*Apples and pears, citrus, hothouse tomatoes, grapes, kiwi fruit, mangoes, pineapple and stonefruit*

**ORCA BAY FOODS INC.**
P.O. Box C 389664
Seattle, WA 98138
425-204-9100
**www.orcabayfoods.com**
*All natural frozen seafood, shrimp and crab*

**OSO SWEET ONIONS/ SAVEN CORPORATION**
3901 Highland Road ,Suite G
Waterford, MI 48328
248-706-1445
**www.sweetonionsource.com**

**PACIFIC FRUIT INC. / BONITA BANANAS**
500 N. State College Blvd., Suite 560
Orange, CA 92868
714-939-9939
*Fresh bananas, pineapples and mangoes*

**PACIFIC SEAFOOD GROUP**
3220 S.W. First Ave.
Portland, OR 97201
503-226-2200
**www.pacseafood.com**
*Ahi Tuna, Clams, Cod, Dungeness Crab, Halibut, Mahi Mahi, Mussels, Oysters, Salmon, Sea Bass, Scallops, Shark, Shrimpmeat, Sole and Swordfish*

**PIERRE FOODS, INC.**
9990 Princeton Road
Cincinnati, OH 45246
513-874-8741
**www.pierrefoods.com**
*Fully cooked sandwiches, meat and bakery products*
**PREMIO FOODS, INC.**
50 Utter Ave.
Hawthorne, NJ 07506
973-427-1106
**www.premiofoods.com**

**PRIMAVERA MARKETING, INC.**
16461 E. Comstock Road
P.O. Box 419 (mail only)
Linden, CA 95236
209-931-9420
**www.primafrutta.com**
*Bing and Rainier cherries*

**PRIME TIME INTERNATIONAL**
86705 Ave. 54, Suite A
Coachella, CA 92236
760-399-4166
**www.primetimeproduce.com**

*Red, green, yellow and orange bell peppers, greenhouse tomatoes and seedless watermelon*

**QUAKER**
800-555-6278
**www.quakeroatmeal.com**

**RAIN FOREST AQUACULTURE PRODUCTS**
2501 S.W. 31st St.
Fort Lauderdale, FL 33312
954-792-8010
Sales 800-289-8452
**www.tilapia.com**
*Tilapia fillets and whole fish*

**READY PAC PRODUCE**
4401 Foxdale Ave.
Irwindale, CA 91706
800-800-7822
**www.readypacproduce.com**
*Spring mix (continental salad) and Grand Parisian salad*

**THE RED CHAMBER CO.**
1912 E. Vernon Ave.
Vernon, CA 90058
323-234-9000
**www.redchamber.com**
*Halibut steaks, black tiger shrimp, swordfish steaks, cooked black tiger shrimp, tuna steaks, marinated shrimp, salmon steaks, breaded shrimp, salmon fillets, batter shrimp, orange roughy fillets, raw peeled shrimp, mahi mahi fillets, scallops, king crab legs, snow crab legs and lobster tails*

**REYNOLDS CONSUMER PRODUCTS, A BUSINESS OF ALCOA CONSUMER PRODUCTS**
6603 W. Broad St.
Richmond, VA 23230
**www.reynoldskitchens.com**
*Reynolds aluminum wrap, Reynolds Steam Pans, Kirkland Signature*

**RICH-SEAPAK CORPORATION**
P.O. Box 20670
St. Simons Island, GA 31522
800-654-9731
*Mozzarella cheese sticks, French toast sticks (regular & cinnamon sprinkle), onion rings, full line of breaded shrimp, full line of appetizers, variety of marinated & grilled shrimp, crab cakes and clam strips*

**RUIZ FOOD PRODUCTS INC.**
501 South Alta Ave.
Dinuba, CA 93618
559-591-5510
**www.elmonterey.com**
*Authentic Mexican frozen foods*

**RUSSET POTATO EXCHANGE**
8550 Central Sands Road
Bancroft, WI 54921
715-335-8050
**www.rpespud.com**
*Potatoes and onions*

**SARA LEE COFFEE & TEA**
990 Supreme Drive
Bensenville, IL 60106
**www.superiorcoffeeshop.com**
*Kirkland Signature Columbian coffee, arabica decaf coffee, Hills Brothers regular and decaf, Superior Coffee cappuccino and McGarvey house blend coffee*

**SARA LEE FOODS**
10151 Carver Road
Cincinnati, OH 45242
800-351-7111

**SEA WATCH INTERNATIONAL**
8978 Globe Park Drive
Easton, MD 21601
410-820-7848
**www.seawatch.com**
*Chopped clams, clam strips and clam chowder*

**SHULTZ FOODS**
717-637-5931
*World-class pretzels*

**SKAGIT VALLEY'S BEST PRODUCE**
P.O. Box 2328
Mount Vernon, WA 98273
360-848-0777
**www.svbest.com**
*Red, White, Yellow and Purple Potatoes*

**SNAPPLE BEVERAGE GROUP**
709 Westchester Ave.
White Plains, NY 10604
Phone 914-397-9200 ext. 7515
Fax 303-706-9607
jmcneily@snapple.com

**SORRENTO LACTALIS INC.**
2376 S. Park Ave.
Buffalo, NY 14220
716-823-6262
**www.sorrentocheese.com**

**STARBUCKS COFFEE COMPANY**
888-447-5282
www.starbucks.com

**STAR FINE FOODS / BORGES USA**
postmaster@starfinefoods.com

**STAUFFER BISCUIT CO.**
Belmont and Sixth Avenue
York, PA 17405
www.stauffercookies.com
*Cookies and crackers*

**STEMILT GROWERS**
123 Ohme Garden Road
Wenatchee, WA 98801
509-662-9667
www.stemilt.com
*Apples, pears and cherries*

**SUN WORLD INTERNATIONAL**
P.O. Box 80298
Bakersfield, CA 93380
www.sun-world.com
info@sun-world.com
*California grapes (red, green and black-all seedless), California plums, sweet colored peppers, grapefruit, lemons and seedless watermelon*

**SUNKIST GROWERS**
14130 Riverside Drive
Sherman Oaks, CA 91423
818-986-4800
www.sunkist.com
*Navel oranges, Valencia oranges, moro oranges, lemons, grapefruit, pummelos, Fairchild tangerines, minneola tangerines and satsuma mandarins*

**SWIFT & COMPANY**
1770 Promontory Circle
Greeley, CO 80634
800-727-2333

**SWITZERLAND CHEESE MARKETING INC.**
704 Executive Blvd., Suite I
Valley Cottage, NY 10989
845-268-2460
www.switzerland-cheese.com
*Cheeses from Switzerland*

**TALKING RAIN**
30520 S.E. 84th St. / P.O. Box 549
Preston, WA 98050-0549
Phone 800-734-0748
425-222-4900
Fax 425-222-4901
e-mail: talk2rain
www.talkingrain.com

**TAM PRODUCE INC.**
330 S. Hale Ave.
Fullerton, CA 92831
714-992-5940
*Tomatoes and vegetables*

**TANIMURA AND ANTLE**
1 Harris Road
Salinas, CA 93908
831-455-3680
www.taproduce.com
*Romaine hearts, head lettuce, Caesar salad and salad mix*

**TARANTINO WHOLESALE FOODS**
2707 Boston Ave.
San Diego, CA 92113
800-4-MEAT, 800-9-GARLIC,
619-232-7585
*Products: Mild Italian Sausage, Hot Italian Sausage, breakfast, sausage, bratwurst, and garlic and ginger products*

**TILLAMOOK COUNTY CREAMERY ASSOCIATION**
P.O. Box 313
Tillamook, OR 97141
503-842-4481
www.tillamookcheese.com
*Cheese and ice cream*

**THE TOPPS COMPANY**
One Whitehall St.
New York, NY 10004
*Ring Pops, Push Pops, Baby Bottle Pop candy and Bazooka gum*

**TRAPPER'S CREEK INC.**
5650 B. St.
Anchorage, AK 99518
907-561-8088
www.trapperscreek.com
*Smoked kippered wild king salmon*

**TREE TOP INC.**
220 E. Second Ave.
Selah, WA 98942
509-697-7251
www.treetop.com
*Apple juice, frozen apple juice, applesauce, juice blends*

**TRIDENT SEAFOODS CORP.**
5303 Shilshole Ave. N.W.
Seattle, WA 98107
206-783-3474
www.tridentseafoods.com
*Seafood*

**TYSON FOODS INC.**
P.O. Box 2020
Springdale, AR 72765-2020
800-233-6332
M-F 8 a.m.-5 p.m. CST
www.tyson.com
*Seafood*

**UNILEVER BESTFOODS NORTH AMERICA**
800 Sylvan Ave.
Englewood Cliffs, NJ 07632
201-567-8000
www.unileverbestfoods.com

**VALCO ENTERPRISES**
3216 Kirkwood Hwy. Pmb 301
Wilmington, DE 19808-6130
877-654-8645
askmyquestion@ottaviofoods.com
*Ottavio Olive Oil*

**VALLEY FINE FOODS COMPANY, INC.**
3909 Park Road #H
Benicia, CA 94510
707-746-6888
www.valleyfinefoods.com
*Pasta Prima Spinach and Mozzarella Ravioli Entrée and Pasta Prima Ravioli Trio*

**VALLEY PRIDE SALES INC.**
15356 Produce Lane
Mount Vernon, WA 38273
360-428-2717
*Potatoes, berries, broccoli, cucumbers and pumpkins*

**VENTURA FOODS LLC**
14840 E. Don Julian Road
City of Industry, CA 91746
626-336-4527
www.venturafoods.com
*Oils/shortening, dressings, margarines, mayonnaise/sauces, soup bases, pan coatings and condiments*

**VIE DE FRANCE YAMAZAKI INC.**
2070 Chain Bridge Road, #500
Vienna, VA 22182
703-442-9205
*Bakery products and desserts*

**WALKERS SHORTBREAD INC.**
170 Commerce Drive
Hauppauge, NY 11788
631-273-0011
e-mail cs@walkersshortbread.com
www.walkersshortbread.com
*Scottish shortbread cookies*

**WASHINGTON APPLE GROWERS**
P.O. Box 18
Wenatchee, WA 98807-0018
509-663-9600
www.bestapples.com
*Apples*

**WEST PAK AVOCADO INC.**
42322 Avenida Avocado
Temecula, CA 92590
909-296-5757
*Avocados*

**WILCOX FARMS**
40400 Harts Lake Valley Road
Roy, WA 98580
360-458-7774
www.wilcoxfarms.com
*Milk and eggs*

**WILSON BATIZ LLC.**
2225 Avenida Costa Este
San Diego, CA 92154
619-661-5222
*Greenhouse tomatoes, peppers, cucumbers and grape tomatoes*

# Index

# Index

# Index

# Acknowledgments

There are many, many hardworking people at Costco and elsewhere who have contributed to this book. We thank them all. In particular we want to thank the following Costco employees: Joel Benoliel, Rossie Cruz, Susan Detlor, Pennie Clarke Ianiciello, Chris Eiche, Jodi Ellis, Sheri Flies, Dennis Knapp, Jim Klauer, Stephanie Gardner, Ginnie Roeglin, Ronda Miller, Tim Rose, Anita Thompson and Wendi Wamboldt. In response to a request in *The Costco Connection*, Costco's monthly magazine for members, we received more than 1,800 recipes and tips from members. We thank you all. Submissions were sorted into food categories and then 160 were selected for testing by a panel of Costco members. We want to thank the following testers who had the enviable but demanding task of narrowing the selections to the 48 recipes that received the "Tested and Approved" stamp to appear in the book: Janice Baroni, Glen and Jane Brookman, Heather Carey, Linda Carey, Maryjo Corrado, Lois Dalzell, Allison Doane, Dale Fine, Myra Hanover, Helen Kearny, Timiny Keegen, Pat Killingsworth, Jane Klein-Shucklin, Diane Larson, Hallie Larson, Jackie Majera, Jane Simpson, Steve Trump, Pat and Gary Volchok, Gale Wergeland, Chris and Walt Zabriskie. We want to especially thank these employees of the vendors and suppliers who took part in the creation of the book: at Iridio Photography, Seattle, photographers Darren Emmens, Devin Seferos and Chris McArthur, set stylist Michelle Keefler and food stylist assistant Christy Nordstrom, account coordinator Traci Joy; at PressReady Imaging, Seattle, Mike Tandy; at Dai Nippon Printing, Kosuke Tago; at AMS book distributors, Susan Latham, Adam Zoldan. We thank the following people for the loan of props used in our food photographs: Jan Block, Linda Carey, Myra Hanover, Helen Kearney, Jane Simpson, Chris Zabriskie. We also wish to thank Senior Rabbi James L. Mirel of Temple B'nai Torah, Bellevue, Washington, for advice on the Hanukkah chapter.

# Photo Credits

All photographs by Iridio Photography, with the following exceptions:

Photodisc, 10–13
Creatas, 14
Deborah Denker Photography, 18 b.r.
Tyson Foods, Inc., 19, 211 a.r., 242
Benjamin Benschneider/The Seattle Times, 20 a.r.
Marke Tuckett, Nestle USA, 21 a.l., a.r.
Getty Images, 22
Photodisc, 24 a.l., b.l.
Ed Young, 24 b.r.
Photodisc, 27 b.l.
Jelly Belly Candy Company, 27 a.c.
Corbis Stock Market, 28
Diamond Fruit Growers, Inc., 32 b.l.
Flavin Photography &
    Trapper's Creek Smoking Co. Inc., 32 a.c.
New Star/Ceres Fresh Foods, LLC, 33 a.l.
Corbis Stock Market, 36
Bertolli Pasta Sauces & Olive Oil,
    Sladchick Wheeler, 41 a.l.
John Sanderson, 43
Getty Images, 46
Tower Advertising, Stauffer Biscuit Co., 47 b.r.
Getty Images, 48
Getty Images, 54
Photodisc, 62–63
Photodisc, 64, 65 a.l., b.l.
Getty Images, 66
Robert Smith Photography, 68 a.r.
Christy Ball, 68 a.l.
Photodisc, 70 b.c.
Photodisc, 72 a.l.
Reid Photography, 72 a.r.
Corbis Stock Market, 76
Bob Hemmer, PIA Media, 77 a.r.
Getty Images, 80
Premio Foods, Inc., 85 a.
Washington State Potato Commission,
    Valley Pride Sales, Inc., 86 b.r.
Getty Images, 88
Aidells Sausage Company, 91
Finlandia Cheese, Inc., 92 a.r.
Boskovich Farms, Inc., 93 b.l.
Dole Food Company, Inc., 93 a.r., 94 b.r.
Photodisc, 95 background & a.r.
Angie Norwood Browne,
    Browne Photography, 95 b.l.
Corbis Stock Market, 96
Michael Toshio International, 98 b.l.
John Sanderson, 98 a.r.
Chris Shorten/OSO Sweet Onions, 99 a.l.
Frito Lay, Inc., 99 b.r.
Photodisc, 102 a.l.
Getty Images, 104
Photodisc, 106

Robert Pelletier, 107
Chuck Harris, 108 b.c.
James Scherzi, 108 a.l.
The Mazzetta Company, 109
Atlantic Veal & Lamb Inc., 110 a.l.
Christopher Conrad Studios, 111 a.l.
Nonni's Food Company, 111 b.r.
Getty Images, 112
Grant Haaker, Orca Bay Seafoods, 114 a.r.
The Nunes Company, Inc. 114 b.r.
Contessa Food Products, 115
Rick Mariani Photography, 116 a.r.
Getty Images, 118–119
Kellogg Company, 102 b., 103 a.
Getty Images, 120
Photodisc, 121 a.r.
Getty Images, 122
Borges USA, 124 b.r.
BelGioioso Cheese, Inc., 124 b.l.
Red Chamber Company 126 a.l., b.l., 127 b.l.
Australian Lamb Company Inc., 128 a.r. & 129 a.l.
Reprinted with permission of Sunkist
    Growers, Inc. All Rights Reserved, 131 b.r.
Photodisc, 134
Arizona Smoothie, 137 b.l.
The Merisant Company, 139 b.r., back cover
Corbis Stock Market, 144
Farmer John, 147 a.r.
American Egg Board, 149 b.r.
Jim Scherer, Dare Foods Inc., 149 b.l.
Getty Images, 152
France Freeman, Costco, 154 a.r., 190 a.r.
The Minute Maid Company, 155 b.l.
Sara Lee Foods-Jimmy Dean, 155 a.r.
California Avocado Commission, 156 b.l.
Corbis Stock Market, 160
Jim Wheeler, Sladcik Studios,
    Quaker Oats, 162 a.l.
Lindsay Olives, 163 b.r.
Corbis Stock Market, 168
General Mills, Inc., 171
Kelly Peterson, 174 b.r.
FoodPix, 176–177
Getty Images, 178, 179 b.r.
Getty Images, 180
Enaca International 185 b.c.
Rainforest Aquaculture, 185 a.l.
Getty Images, 187
Getty Images, 188
Lisa Kennan Photography,
    Foster Farms, 192 & 193
Photo and Recipe Courtesy of Nestlé USA, 195 b.l.
Corbis Stock Market, 196
Rich Villacres, Red Sky Photography, 198 a.l.
Tony Hurley Photography, 199
Hansen Beverage Company, 205 b.r.
Corbis Stock Market, 208
Elizabeth Watt, 210 a.r.
Sorrento/Precious, 210 b.l.

Richard Giachetto, Babé Farms, Inc., 210 b.r.
National Cattlemans Beef Association, 211 a.r.
Getty Images, 214
Jeff Hansen, Bear Creek Country Kitchens, 216 a.l.
Sea Watch International, 216 a.l.
Chicken of the Sea, 216 b.r.
Pierre Foods, Inc., 217 b.r.
Hormel Foods, 218 a.l.
Photodisc, 224
Photodisc, 226 background
Tom Owen, Owen Photography,
    Brown & Haley, 229 b.l.
McCormick & Co., Inc., 231 a.r., b.c.
Corbis Stock Market, 234
Studio 1501 Commercial Photography,
    235 a.r., 244 a.l. inset
Photodisc, 239 a.r.
Photodisc, 240 b.r., 241 b.l.
Recipe and photo courtesy of
    the Reynolds Kitchens, 241 b.r.
Delta Pride Catfish Inc., 241 a.l.
Photodisc, 242 a.l.
Photodisc, 244 a.r., 245 a.l.
Dana Edmund, 245 a.
Del Monte Foods, 246 a.l.
Page 20 b., 25 a.r, b.l., 33 b.c., 45 b.l., a.r., 59 b.r.,
    68 a.c., back cover, 69, 73 b.l., 83 b.r., b.l., 86 a.l.,
    108 a.r., 138 a.l., 140, 146 b.l., 147 b.l., 156 a.r.,
    162 a.r., 165 b.c., a.r., 183 a.r., 184, 204 a.r.,
    212 b.c a.r., 218 a.r., 219 a.r.

---

**Key for recipe on page 71**

## Nancy Stanton's Costco-Coded Supper Dish Translated

*12-15 small red-skinned potatoes*
*$1/3$ cup or more olive oil*
*1 tablespoon butter*
*2 large onions, chopped*
*1 each yellow, orange and red pepper,
    seeded and chopped*
*$1/4$ cup steak seasoning blend*
*Dash of cracked pure black pepper*
*1 large bag spinach*
*1 cup crumbled blue cheese, or to taste*
*$1/4$ cup pine nuts*

---

**1.** Place potatoes in boiling water and cook until just getting soft. Drain and return to burner until all water evaporates.
**2.** Heat a large skillet and add 3 tablespoons olive oil and butter. Add chopped onion and peppers to skillet and season with steak seasoning and pepper. Sauté, adding more olive oil if necessary. Cook 5-7 minutes.
**3.** Toss in 6 handfuls of spinach. Keep turning, adding a little more olive oil if sticking occurs.
**4.** Halve potatoes and add to the skillet—make room for them by sliding spinach mixture out of the way—so that potatoes touch the bottom of the pan and are seasoned with olive oil and bits from pan.
**5.** Now mix everything together in the pan. Add blue cheese to your liking. Leave on stove, covered, and the cheese will just melt into the mixture.
**6.** To serve, top with pine nuts.